FIGHT TOWN

FIGHT TOWN

LAS VEGAS — THE BOXING CAPITAL OF THE WORLD

TIM DAHLBERG

Project Manager: Jim Laurie
Designer: Ched Whitney
Editors: Darrell Christian, Monica Micelli

Library of Congress Cataloging-in-Publication Data
Dahlberg, Tim
Fight Town: Las Vegas—the boxing capital of the world/Tim Dahlberg.
—Las Vegas, Nev.: Stephens Press, 2004, 2007.
p.; cm.
ISBN 10: 1-932173-66-8
ISBN 13: 978-1-932173-666
1. Boxing–Nevada–Las Vegas. 2. Boxing–United States–History. 3. Las Vegas (Nev.)–Description and travel. I. Title. II. Las Vegas—the boxing capital of the world.
GV1125.D34 2004
796.83/09793/135—dc22 2007922949

Post Office Box 1600
Las Vegas, Nevada 89125-1600
702-387-5260 / 702-387-2997 FAX

Printed in Hong Kong.

ACKNOWLEDGEMENTS

To my Dad, who would be proud. And to Donna, Brian and Eric, who mean everything to me.

Thanks to the following for their insights and help: Ron Amos, Bill Caplan, Debbie Munch, Pat Putnam and Ed Schuyler Jr.

Special thanks to Jeff Scheid, whose photo help was invaluable, and Marc Ratner for graciously providing his ticket and poster collections. Also to Sherman Frederick, who had the vision for this project.

EXIT

FIGHT TOWN

FOREWORD BY GEORGE FOREMAN 8
1 ON THE VERGE OF SOMETHING BIG 28
2 ALL IN THE BEGINNING 40
3 SONNY, ONCE SO TRUE 56
4 THE GREATEST 68
5 SUGAR RAY AND THE HITMAN 94
6 A PLACE TO FIGHT 118
7 THE VEGAS TOP 10 134
8 ONLY IN VEGAS 160
9 A FIGHTER'S KIND OF TOWN 172
10 IRON MIKE 184
11 THE FAB FOUR OF THE STRIP 204
FIGHT POSTERS 218

FOREWORD

Las Vegas: A Fighter's Kind of Town >> By George Foreman

Boxing and Las Vegas just seem to go together. I've fought around the world, even in the jungle of Africa, but my best memories are of the times I was in Las Vegas. I sparred with Sonny Liston and got free tickets to the Silver Slipper buffet when I first came to Las Vegas. All the lights, the food, the celebrities were really something. It was all so exciting to me.

I became the oldest heavyweight champion ever when I knocked out Michael Moorer in 1994 at the MGM Grand Hotel to win the title. The impossible dream came true for me on the Yellow Brick Road in the Emerald City. But I remember coming to Las Vegas as an amateur when no one paid any attention to me, and knowing that one day I would make it big there. When you went to New York City, Madison Square Garden was king of them all, but Las Vegas was on its way to becoming the king of boxing.

After I won the gold medal in the 1968 Olympics and turned pro, one of my early fights was in Las Vegas. It was on the undercard of the Sonny Liston-Leotis Martin fight in the showroom at the International Hotel, which is now the Las Vegas Hilton. It was on *Wide World of Sports*, and Howard Cosell was there. I think I knocked my guy out in the first round.

I got a chance to see the stars and celebrities go by. The play *Hair* was in the showroom, and all the music people were there, and they were all kind of odd. James Brown was making his first appearance there and I got a chance to meet him and get my picture taken with him. I was star struck. And I didn't have to leave my hotel room to get a sandwich. This was the happening of my life at the time. I kept writing postcards home telling people what a great place it was.

Sonny Liston and I were stablemates, so I would spar with him. I went to Sonny's home and I'd never seen a home with a big closet like that and a pool. The best kept secret in the world was Las Vegas.

I came to Las Vegas after that, but it wasn't until after I lost the title that I fought there again. I stayed at Caesars Palace, and I'll never forget training everyday and seeing the stars walk by.

I was fighting Ron Lyle in the first fight in the Caesars pavillion and a few nights before the match we went and saw Frank Sinatra perform. I was sitting in the audience and he said, "I'd like you to say hello to a friend of mine," and had me stand up. Later, we went backstage and Frank's mom was there and she was so nice.

I've got all the photos of when I was there, pictures of my name on the marquee. So many people kid me and say Joe Louis was the host at Caesars Palace, but whenever I go to hotels there I act like I'm a host. I stand near doorways and walk around rooms, and the security people ask if people are bothering me. I'm always nice to people because if you come to Las Vegas, you deserve to see a Joe Louis or a George Foreman and have your picture taken with them.

I lost my title in Africa and it was dreary. If I had lost it in Las Vegas, I probably wouldn't have been half as bitter as I was. All the buffets, people patting you on the shoulder. . . .

When I came back to fight again after my retirement, I stayed away from Las Vegas at first. I wanted to prove myself before I fought there. You gotta be right in Vegas. You gotta be in shape. No one gives you an easy fight there.

What a wonderful moment it was for me to win the title in Las Vegas. It was great not only because it happened, but because it happened in a city of dreams for boxers.

I still come to Las Vegas all the time, and about the only time I'm happy traveling is when I have a chance to go there. Whenever someone in my family or a friend does me a favor, the first thing I give them is a trip to Las Vegas. For boxers, it's like heaven. The best thing that ever happens to an athlete is being invited to Las Vegas to box. That's what Las Vegas is, and that's why it is so great for boxing. It truly is the Fight Town.

Before Las Vegas ever thought of laying claim to the title "Fight Town," there was a fighter who could steal the show on the Las Vegas Strip—even when he wasn't fighting. His name was Cassius Clay, and he was a 21-year-old contender with a big mouth when he jumped into the ring July 22, 1963, moments after Sonny Liston knocked out Floyd Patterson to keep his heavyweight title at the Las Vegas Convention Center rotunda. Under a solitary spotlight, Clay yelled and screamed at Liston, promising he would knock him out in eight rounds. Las Vegas police seem more amused

VERLAST
GERRY

Later, there would be those who would become king and one who became king. A pensive Gerry Cooney is captured with his trainer, Victor Valle, as dusk turns to darkness just moments before he met Larry Holmes in the biggest heavyweight fight of the decade June 11, 1982, at Caesars Palace. Cooney and Holmes engaged in an epic battle before the challenger was finally stopped in the 13th round. A youthful Mike Tyson was all fun and games as he donned the crown and jewels at the Las Vegas Hilton, where he and Don King were promoting an upcoming fight with James "Bonecrusher" Smith in 1987.

The year before, Tyson stood dramatically as his hand was raised in triumph and he became the youngest heavyweight champion ever with his November 22, 1986, second round knockout of Trevor Berbick at the Las Vegas Hilton.

EVERLAST
bon
EVERLAST
bon

Fighters had their own way of celebrating and they did it in arenas, ballrooms, pavilions and stadiums up and down the Las Vegas Strip. Larry Holmes jumped in the Caesars Palace swimming pool after beating Ken Norton to win the heavyweight title for the first time, and here Michael Dokes jumps for joy after stopping Lynn Ball in the first round in 1982 to win the vacant NABF heavyweight title at Caesars Palace.

ITT
CAESARS

Sometimes others joined in, like the witch doctor Yory Boy Campas brought along for good luck in his 1998 light middleweight title defense against Larry Barnes. At other times, it was good to be alone, even among 15,000 screaming fans who had just seen George Foreman become the oldest heavyweight champion ever when he knocked out Michael Moorer with one big right hand in the 10th round of their November 5, 1994, title fight.

Winning wasn't the only thing to make a fighter happy. Just the knowledge that he's on his way to Las Vegas for a big fight can be enough. Here, Oscar De La Hoya enjoys a light moment while training in his Big Bear, California, camp for his February 1999 fight against Ike Quartey at the Thomas and Mack Center. De La Hoya had reason to be happy; he would come off the canvas in the sixth round to win a split decision over Quartey.

JEFF SCHEID—LAS VEGAS REVIEW-JOURNAL

If there was nothing like a major fight in Las Vegas, there was nothing at all like a major heavyweight fight. If it involved Mike Tyson, it was even bigger. The MGM Grand Garden was packed the night of August 19, 1995 when Tyson made his return to the ring after being released from prison for rape. Tyson would knock Peter McNeeley down twice before his corner through in the towel, touching off a turbulent scene in the ring as McNeeley wanted to go back after Iron

ROCK

Over the years, Las Vegas grew dramatically and so did its reputation as the only place for a big fight. Whether in the old outdoor arena at Caesars Palace or in the state-of-the-art arenas at MGM Grand and Mandalay Bay, a Vegas fight was like no other.

With that, we bid you welcome to *Fight Town*, a celebration of a city and the fights and fighters who helped put it on the map.

1 >> ON THE VERGE OF SOMETHING BIG

The date was May 27, 1960, and Las Vegas didn't know it yet, but it was on the brink of something big. Something really big. Out on the growing Strip, Frank Sinatra and the Rat Pack were making the city their personal playground. They filmed the movie Oceans 11 during the day, played the Sands' Copa Room in the evening and then partied through the night.

Downtown drew cowboys to drink and throw the dice, and gawkers to see the lights. Teenagers cruised Fremont Street in hot rods, and the town of about 60,000 was still mostly just desert and dreams.

East of the Strip, off dusty Paradise Road, sat the city's brand new convention center, built a year earlier with a unique rotunda that seated about 7,000. Naysayers called it a white elephant and predicted it would never be filled.

Casino operators, though, knew better. They were in search of the kind of dice-rolling, card-playing, Sinatra-loving gamblers the city so

The ticket wasn't fancy, but the new digs were. The first title fight in the city's history was held in the spanking new rotunda of the Las Vegas Convention Center, where 4,805 showed up to see Benny Paret take the welterweight title from Don Jordan.

In the days before tigers and lions roamed the Strip, before pirates battled outside hotels, fighters in training were the stars.

coveted. These were just the kinds of players who might like a good fight. And now, the city finally had a place to put one on.

That's what they got the night of May 27 when Benny "Kid" Paret beat Don Jordan in a unanimous 15-round decision for the welterweight championship at the Convention Center.

It was the first title fight in the city's history, and drew a crowd of 4,805. The fans didn't pay much to get in, with a gross gate of only $30,410. But there were bigger payouts for the city itself.

Around the country, millions watched on television as NBC broadcast the bout on its *Friday Night Fights*. Most had heard about the gambling city in the desert, but for many it was the first time they had actually seen something from Las Vegas.

In the audience was 15-year-old Marc Ratner, who would go on to become the executive director of the Nevada Athletic Commission.

"I knew Don Jordan was supposed to be the longtime champion and I had seen Paret on Friday Night Fights," Ratner said. "I had just started going to fights and I just liked the atmosphere."

At the time, most of the big fights were controlled by Madison Square Garden, which served as both promoter and the site for top title bouts.

Garden matchmaker Teddy Brenner, though, was a childhood friend of Thunderbird casino executive Ash Resnick, who convinced Brenner that Las Vegas could hold a title fight in its new Convention Center. As an added bonus, NBC wouldn't have to black out the lucrative New York television market.

Jordan was guaranteed $85,000 from the sponsor, Gillette Razor Blade Co., while the challenger was to get 20 percent of the gross gate after taxes. Paret ended up with only $4,000, but the son of a Cuban sugar cane cutter had his first title shot.

An early poll of sports writers favored Jordan by a 4-1 margin, but the wise guys knew better. At the old Derby book downtown, Paret was a 2-1 favorite.

The 20-year-old Paret soon stripped Jordan of his title by beating him to the punch through most of the 15 rounds and piling up his winning advantage through the middle five rounds. Neither man came close to a knockout, but the crowd seemed as happy as the new champion over the city's first title fight.

"I've always wanted to be a champion," Paret told reporters.

It went so well that the new champion's manager, Manuel Alfaro, said he wanted to return to Las Vegas to defend the title.

"Everybody treated us so nice here," Alfaro said.

Paret would return to Vegas a year later, but this time he would be knocked out by Gene Fullmer after moving up in weight and trying for the middleweight title. In his next fight in New York City, Paret was stopped by Emile Griffith in the 12th round and fell into a coma, dying 10 days later.

By then, Las Vegas was already on its way to bigger and better things.

A young fighter named Cassius Clay came to town in 1961 to fight a Hawaiian giant named Duke Sabedong, and the city was looking forward to more top title fights.

"They saw with Paret-Jordan that it worked," said Ron Amos, who covered the fight for the Las Vegas Sun. "There was no looking back after that."

Over the next seven years, 13 world title fights would be held at the Las Vegas Convention Center. Sonny Liston fought Floyd Patterson, Muhammad Ali fought Patterson, and Griffith defended his welterweight title three times.

Las Vegas not only got some valuable television exposure, but the newspaper coverage was intense in the weeks leading up to a fight. At the time there were nine daily papers in New York City, and most would send writers a month in advance to carry training dispatches from the gambling city.

It was a big shot of publicity for a desert town served only by a few daily airline flights and linked to Southern California by the old two-lane Los Angeles highway.

It would be years before casinos started hosting fights themselves. But they bought tickets for their high-rolling gamblers—and plenty of them.

By the time Paret challenged Fullmer for the middleweight title on December 9, 1961, a near-capacity crowd of 6,169 paid $65,130 to see the fight, and promoters were touting the Convention Center Rotunda as the finest boxing facility in the United States.

Along the Strip, gamblers would take breaks from the dice tables to watch fighters train in hotel showrooms.

In the day before tigers and lions roamed the Strip, before pirates battled outside hotels, fighters in training were the stars during the day. High-rollers would stand elbow-to-elbow with gangsters to watch the workouts, trying to figure out an edge so they could get a winning bet on the fight.

"The gamblers showed up and so did the mob," Amos said. "The exposure for Las Vegas was humongous. It made Las Vegas what it is today."

Bobby Goodman was a fight publicist helping his father, Murray, when he came to Las Vegas in the early days. He later went to work for Don King as a matchmaker and was involved in putting on some of the city's classic fights.

Like most Las Vegas visitors he had an East Coast mentality. New York was still the boxing mecca, and, he figured, would always be.

There was something special about the odd confluence of gambling, boxing and partying that was beginning to take place on a regular basis in a town just starting to flex its muscles. Still, no one could foresee what Fight Town would eventually be.

"We never thought it would grow like this," said long-time judge and boxing official Art Lurie, who moved to Las Vegas in 1953, just in time to witness the explosion of boxing. "The

From a bird's eye view at the top of the Convention Center rotunda, fans watch the welterweight title fight between Benny Paret and Don Jordan on May 27, 1960. The fight was telecast across the country on Gillette's Friday Night Fights.

LAS VEGAS NEWS BUREAU

town was 30,000 people and you knew everybody. Now there's 2 million people and you don't know anybody. It used to be more fun when it was less people."

More people meant more fights, though, and soon Las Vegas was hosting some of the biggest fights in the world. The small desert town was beginning to boom with new hotels on the Strip, and big fights became a special attraction.

New York used to get the big fights, but now Las Vegas had the money to get whatever it wanted. About the only time the city failed was when Caesars Palace tried to get the Los Angeles Olympic Organizing Committee to farm out the 1984 Olympic boxing matches to the hotel. Olympic officials declined, but Caesars did manage to land the Olympic boxing trials, where a young fighter named Mike Tyson stormed out in tears after failing to make the team.

"All of those fights were some of the greatest fights in the history of our sport," Goodman said. "Who would have thought it would become the place where you do the biggest fights in the world?"

LAS VEGAS REVIEW-JOURNAL

Dick Tiger stumbles out of the way after knocking Roger Rouse down in the 12th round, then celebrates his second successful light heavyweight title defense in the November 17, 1967 fight at the Convention Center. A month later, Tiger would take a commission in the rebel army of Biafra in his native Nigeria, returning to the ring in May 1968 only to lose his title on a fourth round knockout to Bob Foster at Madison Square Garden.

Gene Fullmer gets some help holding the heavy bag as he trains at the old Thunderbird Hotel for his February 23, 1963, fight with Dick Tiger. Fullmer had lost his middleweight title to Tiger four months earlier at Candlestick Park in San Francisco, and his career was winding down. He and Tiger fought to a 15-round draw at the Convention Center, and six months later Fullmer quit on the stool after the seventh round of their third fight in Tiger's native Nigeria. It was the last fight for Fullmer, who earlier had beaten Sugar Ray Robinson and Benny Paret in title defenses in Las Vegas.

LAS VEGAS REVIEW-JOURNAL

SCORING THE GLOVES

Carlos Ortiz had just beaten Joe Brown in a lightweight title fight on April 21, 1962, and a pair of teenagers enamored with the excitement of the fight had somehow followed the press into Ortiz's locker room at the Las Vegas Convention Center. Just being in the room was thrilling enough for Marc Ratner and Sig Rogich. Looking around, something else caught their attentions.

The gloves Ortiz had just used had been cut off and were setting on a nearby table. The teens didn't think twice. Each grabbed a glove and quickly got out of there. "For years, Sig and I each had a Carlos Ortiz world championship glove," Ratner said with a laugh.

Rogich would go on to become a confidant of presidents, run a lucrative ad agency, and be the chairman of the Nevada Athletic Commission. Ratner eventually became the commission's executive director, and one of the most respected figures in the sport.

In those days, the two would go to fights and buy tickets in the top row of the Las Vegas Convention Center. There, they would look down at ringside and try to spot the stars. Ratner and Rogich would make bets on who could see the most famous people. They thought they saw Frank Sinatra or Tony Curtis, but were so far up in the rotunda that they couldn't be sure.

We never dreamed back in 1960 that either one of us would go far into that sport," Ratner said. "It's amazing how our fates were intertwined with boxing. From the highest row, I've come full circle and have my fingers on the canvas now."

A night of boxing in the rotunda was always a special event. Writers came in from around the country to watch from ringside, where teletype machines were set up to speed the copy to the next morning's papers. On this night, June 12, 1964, Emile Griffith and Luis Rodriguez met for the third time, with the world welterweight title at stake. A year before, Rodriguez beat Griffith at Dodger Stadium, then lost a split decision rematch at Madison Square Garden. The third fight was just as close, and it was controversial. Griffith won a 15-round split decision, and the two warriors embraced, perhaps grateful they would never have to do it again.

LAS VEGAS REVIEW-JOURNAL

Jose Torres is interviewed while Eddie Cotton gets his hand raised in victory by his corner following their August 15, 1966, light heavyweight title fight at the Convention Center. The two went after each other for 15 brutal rounds before Torres emerged with a split decision. The fight was so full of action that *Ring Magazine* named it the 1966 Fight of the Year.

LAS VEGAS REVIEW-JOURNAL

Sugar Ray Robinson had announced his retirement from boxing when he visited Las Vegas on February 4, 1953, to put on a clinic. The new Sahara Hotel put up a makeshift ring by the pool and Robinson offered some instruction to local amateur fighters. Here, he gives final instructions to a pair of diaper dandies who were doing their best just to keep their gloves up. Ironically, Robinson couldn't even stay at the hotel at the time since the Strip was segregated. He came back from retirement and fought in Las Vegas for the first time on March 4, 1961, when he lost a decision to Gene Fullmer in a middleweight title fight at the Convention Center.

LAS VEGAS NEWS BUREAU

PLAY IT TO THE BONE

Ferd Hernandez was a pretty good fighter, and an even better bartender. There were some nights that he made more money tending bar in darkened places like the old Flame on the Strip than he got for facing the legendary Sugar Ray Robinson. But it wasn't money that lured Hernandez into the ring against Robinson on July 12, 1965. He was the Nevada middleweight champion, for all that was worth, and he had a chance to fight one of the biggest boxing names of all time.

Hernandez was strong and awkward, while Robinson was old and tired. Sugar Ray loved Las Vegas, but it was only the second time he had ever fought in the city, and at age 44 it would be his last. Still, he needed the money badly and the Robinson mystique lured 1,100 fans into the tiny showroom at the Hacienda Hotel and Casino, where the Mandalay Bay Resort and Casino now stands, to watch Hernandez challenge the great former champion.

Ferd's younger brother, Art, had fought a draw against Robinson two years earlier, and Hernandez thought his hard head would give him a good chance. "Doctors say my skull is twice as thick as most people. It will really take a blow to knock me out," he said a few days before the fight.

Among those in the showroom was cab driver Benjamin Franklin, who had driven Robinson and a woman in from the airport two months earlier in search of a wedding license. Franklin knew them only as Walker Smith and Mildred Bruce, and he served as their best man at the ceremony at the Silver Bell Chapel. Until he got a call from Robinson a few days before the fight, Franklin had no idea that Walker Smith was actually the great Sugar Ray Robinson.

"I almost fell over when he told me he wanted me to come to the fight," Franklin said.

Robinson had already had 190 fights in his career, and he was playing out the string. He would fight only a few more months before finally hanging up his gloves.

In his prime, Robinson would have had no trouble with the light-hitting Hernandez, who would get about $500 for the fight. But Robinson's legs were shot, and his reflexes weren't much better. Robinson staggered Hernandez with a left hook in the first round, prompting Hernandez to run for three rounds while the Sugar Man pursued him as best he could on his aging legs. Finally, Hernandez slowed Robinson down, buried his head under his chin, and pushed and punched for the next seven rounds.

It wasn't pretty, but when it was over, Hernandez had won a split decision. "I just remember how old Sugar Ray looked," said Marc Ratner, who was at the fight.

Hernandez would lose his next two fights and finally quit in 1968 with a record of 33-9-4, and only seven knockouts. His win over Robinson was his big claim to fame, but he never made more of it than what it was. "I beat a guy named Sugar Ray Robinson," he would tell bar patrons for years. "I didn't beat the real Sugar Ray Robinson."

The same night, but almost unnoticed in the local newspapers, was an eight-round semi-main event that had the crowd on its feet. Pulgo Serrano and Leopoldo Corona were middleweights from Mexico who lived in Los Angeles and trained in the same gym. When Robinson's sparring partner, Milo Calhoun, cut his eye while driving a go-kart on the track outside the Hacienda and his bout with Al "Tiger" Williams was called off, promoter Bill Miller had to find a replacement fight, and quick.

He called Serrano and Corona in Los Angeles, told them they had to be at the Hacienda Hotel and Casino by 6 p.m., and they got into a car and drove to Las Vegas together.

That night they tried to beat each other's brains out. "It was like Arturo Gatti and Mickey Ward," said fight publicist Bill Caplan. "These two guys just kept going after it."

Serrano won a split decision over his friend and sparring partner. Later that night, Caplan walked into the casino and saw the two fighters shooting craps together. "They were cut, bruised, bandaged. It looked like they had been in a war," he said. "And there they were, side by side shooting craps like they were best friends, which they were."

Years later, Caplan would mention the fight and the circumstances to filmmaker Ron Shelton, who vowed to turn it into a movie. *Play it to the Bone* starred Antonio Banderas and Woody Harrelson as two friends who drove to Las Vegas at the last minute to fight on the undercard of a fictitious Mike Tyson-Alexi Rustinov fight at Mandalay Bay Resort and Casion. Unlike the real thing, though, it wasn't a box office smash.

Banderas, left, and Harrelson as friends-turned-ring-combatants in *Play it to the Bone*.

The real thing: An aging Sugar Ray Robinson takes a right to the head from bartender-fighter Ferd Hernandez in their July 12, 1965, fight at the Hacienda Hotel. Hernandez would win a split decision over the ring legend.

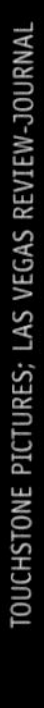
TOUCHSTONE PICTURES; LAS VEGAS REVIEW-JOURNAL

19

2 >> ALL IN THE BEGINNING

The early Las Vegas fight promoters were a lot like their modern day counterparts—either incurable optimists or downright liars. When light heavyweight champion Archie Moore moved up to the heavyweight division to fight Cuba's Nino Valdes in the first big-name fight in the city's history on May 2, 1955, promoter Jack "Doc" Kearns claimed more than 14,000 people would watch outdoors at old Cashman Field, home of the city's semipro baseball team. Kearns went around to local hotels to line up money for a fight he told everyone would bring in $250,000.

Newspaper skeptics thought it was more likely the actual crowd would be half that size, and even they were a bit optimistic. In the end, about 6,000 people paid a reported—and questionable—$102,316 to watch Moore try for a win that would put him into a fight for the heavyweight title at age 41 against Rocky Marciano.

The fight was big and the crowd wasn't that bad, considering the town was little more than a few clusters of casinos and an Air Force base at the time.

But it wasn't the biggest thing in town. Over the weekend, Sam Snead and others were at the young Desert Inn golf course playing for a wheelbarrow of silver dollars in the Tournament of Champions. Many writers who came for the golf tournament—the second richest in the world with a total purse of $37,500—would stay over another day to cover the fight.

About 70 miles north of Las Vegas, thousands of Army troops were camped out in the barren desert awaiting Operation Cue, the latest in a series of atomic bomb explosions set off above the Nevada Test Site. When the bomb detonated, their job was to storm ground zero in tanks and armored vehicles to test their readiness for atomic warfare.

Compared to that, boxing was a breeze.

The bomb attached to a 500-foot tower at Yucca Flat was to have been exploded six days before the fight, but rain and winds kept postponing it. The town's hotels and motels, meanwhile, were full with an odd collection of bomb observers, military men, newsmen, fight fans and golfers.

Kearns had gone up and down the two-lane Strip to find backers for his fight, and proudly reported he had lined up an astounding $100,000 in guarantees from casino operators.

"The hotels and Las Vegas businessmen are going right down the line with us," Kearns told the *Las Vegas Review-Journal* at the time.

Las Vegas Sun publisher Hank Greenspun wrote that the fight "is probably the greatest event for the town since the government started using the area for atom bomb tests."

The 15-rounder was an elimination fight with the winner getting a date with Marciano for the heavyweight title. Ringside tickets were $30, and you could sit in the bleachers for $5. Even better, the daily workouts in the weeks before the fight were free and several hundred people gathered every afternoon at the Silver Slipper and Moulin Rouge to watch.

Moore had been favored since he got off an airplane at the city's tiny airport a month earlier. The two boxers had met in St. Louis two years earlier and Moore won a unanimous decision, but Valdes was the bigger fighter at 209 pounds

Las Vegas was a cowboy town in 1955, and this group of cowboys sat on the top of their folding wooden chairs to get a good view of the action when Archie Moore and Nino Valdes met in the first big-name fight in the city's history. Optimistic promoters hoped to get 14,000 people to the old Cashman Field north of downtown, but were happy when about 6,000 showed up in the late afternoon on May 2, 1955, to watch the 41-year-old Moore win a disputed decision over Valdes and earn the right to fight Rocky Maricano for the heavyweight title. The fight had to compete with a few other big events in the burgeoning city — a big golf tournament at the Desert Inn and an atomic explosion at the nearby Nevada Test Site.

LAS VEGAS NEWS BUREAU

to 196 for the light heavyweight champion.

There were rumors the 41-year-old Moore was suffering from a heart problem, though several doctors had cleared him to fight. Retired *Review-Journal* sports editor John Cahlan wrote an op-ed piece on April 10 advising Kearns to take the fight elsewhere.

That brought a heated response from Greenspun, who was only to happy to fuel the city's increasingly bitter newspaper war with some vitriol of his own.

"If Mr. Cahlan's head was half as sound as Moore's heart he wouldn't be filling his lying newspaper with that sort of drivel," Greenspun wrote.

Three years earlier, Kearns had come to town to promote a fight between Moore and Joey Maxim for the light heavyweight title, but couldn't get local backers to put up the $150,000 guarantee and eventually moved the fight to St. Louis.

Now, Kearns warned, "this is Las Vegas' first, last and only chance to become the sports capital of the world."

Las Vegas bought into the hype—though there were probably as many empty seats as paying customers when the fight began about 6 p.m. on a damp spring day.

A brilliant sun was setting behind the baseball backstop at Cashman Field, and the wily Moore quickly maneuvered Valdes toward the center field portion of the ring.

As Valdes squinted into the setting sun, Moore hit him with three quick rights to the head that he never saw.

Moore, in the 170th fight of his career, landed heavy lefts to the head of Valdes, but Moore was bleeding from the nose and mouth and his right eye was swollen from the Cuban's jab. Valdes was in even worse shape, half blinded and desperately trying to hang on in the late rounds.

Moore came on strong in the final rounds, winning the last three on the scorecard of referee Jim Braddock, the former heavyweight champion, to take the fight by an 8-5-2 margin.

"Valdes died in the last three rounds," Moore said.

It wasn't long before Las Vegas had its first boxing controversy.

Valdes staggered around the ropes in his corner and fell, dazed, when the decision was announced. He rose, grabbed a microphone and blurted in Spanish, "They don't want me to fight Rocky Marciano. I'm not good enough. I won the fight, but I can't fight Marciano."

Valdes then began crying, great sobs wracking his body. He reached his arms out to the crowd, as if imploring them to do something.

Valdes fired "a salvo of Spanish," the *Review-Journal* reported.

A few fans hurled cushions, though mostly because a Las Vegas city policeman jumped into the ring and yelled, "Don't throw cushions."

New York comedian Al Schrenk, who was doing his bombastic best as the ring announcer, implored the crowd to stop throwing the cushions "lest you injure someone seriously."

Moore went on to fight Marciano for the heavyweight title four months later at Yankee Stadium. Moore knocked Marciano down, but was dropped five times himself before finally being stopped in the ninth round.

The Moore fight was the last big chance for Valdes, though he would be knocked out by Sonny Liston four years later.

Out on Yucca Flat, the bomb was finally detonated three days after the Moore-Valdes fight.

And it wasn't until 1969, when Kirk Kerkorian's new International Hotel hosted a fight in the showroom between Liston and Leotis Martin, that big-time boxing was held at a hotel. On the undercard was a young heavyweight named George Foreman, who demolished his opponent in the first round.

The mushroom cloud rose high over the desert and could be seen from the very ballpark where Moore and Valdes had brought big-time boxing to town.

The explosion was called a success by scientists and military officials.

So was the fight, though it would be five years before big-time boxing would return to Las Vegas—this time indoors, in the rotunda of the new Convention Center.

The new arena would feature the likes of Liston, Muhammad Ali and others over the next few years, though it would be nearly two decades before the city began getting notice as the nation's new fight capital.

The fights received national television exposure, and they brought both attention and gamblers to town.

Bobby Goodman remembered traveling from New York City with his father, Murray, a top publicist of his time.

"People would go to Las Vegas, but it was nothing really steady in the early days," Goodman said. "It wasn't a big tourist attraction then where you could sustain a regular program of big events."

The early fights were scattered over months, all at the Convention Center and most aired on network television as the fight of the week.

Middleweight champion Gene Fullmer was a regular, fighting three times in the Convention Center between 1961 and 1963. Fullmer, from Utah, was a popular attraction, and he won his first two fights before getting a draw against Dick Tiger in the third.

After Fullmer knocked out Benny Paret in the 10th round of their December 9, 1961, fight, Paret came up with one of the earliest—and most unusual—excuses for his loss.

"He never hurt me with any punches. It was his pushes and holding that caused me to be knocked out," Paret said.

Emile Griffith defended his welterweight title three times at the Convention Center in the early 1960s, and an up-and-coming young Olympic champion known as Cassius Clay made his Las Vegas debut in a 10-round main event in 1961.

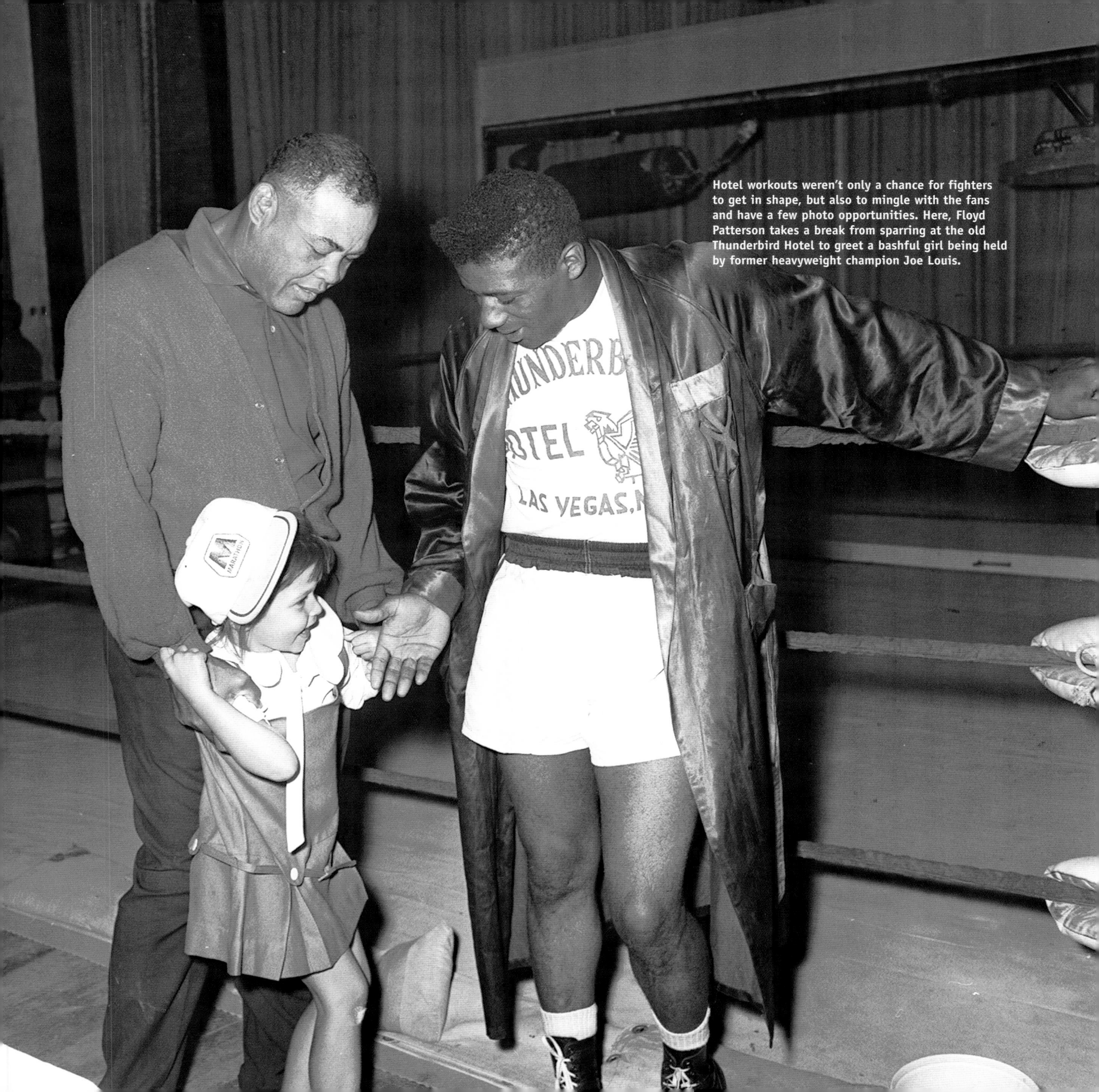

Hotel workouts weren't only a chance for fighters to get in shape, but also to mingle with the fans and have a few photo opportunities. Here, Floyd Patterson takes a break from sparring at the old Thunderbird Hotel to greet a bashful girl being held by former heavyweight champion Joe Louis.

UNLV SPECIAL COLLECTIONS

THE MANASSA MAULER

The eight-page *Las Vegas Evening Review* carried news both comforting and exciting to residents of the dusty desert town the afternoon of June 19, 1929.

The big headline atop the front page heralded the beginning of something big — "Dam Contracts Sure," it read. For a town struggling to survive, it was big news indeed. The Boulder Dam project that would give work to thousands and give birth to neighboring Boulder City was closer to reality than ever.

Just beneath the headline was a story many found far more interesting. Former heavyweight champion Jack Dempsey was in town for a brief visit that would last only two and a half hours, but would set the town abuzz.

Dempsey came in on a Western Air Express trimotor, on his way from Southern California to Salt Lake City to visit his mother. It was big enough news that a plane would land in those days, much less one with the former champion and his manager, Gene Normile.

The reporter who went to greet the plane noted Dempsey was "bronzed and apparently in fighting shape," but the former champ would not comment on whether he would return to the ring again.

"Yes I'm still working out and maybe I'll fight again," Dempsey said. "But not this fall."

The Manassa Mauler had just turned 34 and hadn't fought since losing the title to Gene Tunney in the infamous "Long Count" fight in September 1927. He announced his retirement in April 1928, saying he was having trouble with a left eye muscle, and was keeping busy doing vaudeville on the road.

During his brief stopover, Dempsey posed for pictures with locals and fondly recalled fighting in 1915 in Goldfield and Tonopah when he fought a pair of draws with Johnny Sudenberg. In one of those fights, Dempsey was floored nine times in the first round.

It would be 34 years before Las Vegas would host a heavyweight title fight of its own, but Dempsey raised hopes as he climbed aboard his plane to continue his trip to Salt Lake.

"I'll be back," he said.

F-TEN

UNLV SPECIAL COLLECTIONS

But it wasn't until July 22, 1963, that Las Vegas got its first world heavyweight title fight when Liston and Floyd Patterson met in a rematch of Liston's first-round knockout the year before.

And it wasn't until 1969, when Kirk Kerkorian's new International Hotel hosted a fight in the showroom between Liston and Leotis Martin, that big-time boxing was held at a hotel. On the undercard was a young heavyweight named George Foreman, who demolished his opponent in the first round.

Modest beginnings, for sure, but it would get better. While the big fights were sporadic in the 1960s, there were also weekly and monthly boxing cards promoted by Bill Miller and Mel Greb.

Las Vegas was on to something, even if the young city wasn't quite sure what to do with it.

The big problem was finding a place to put a big boxing match. The Convention Center saw 13 world title fights in the 1960s and a number of other cards, but it always took a promoter to go up and down the Strip selling tickets to all the hotels to bring it off.

"I was intrigued with the fact the Convention Center could be a big venue for fights," said promoter Bob Arum. "But it really puttered along in the late '60s and '70s when there weren't that many big fights in Vegas compared to those at the Garden and other venues."

Still, Fight Town USA was being born.

If it had mayors, they were visionaries like Barron Hilton and Caesars' Cliff Perlman, who recognized the benefits of keeping gamblers at hotels for the fights and building arenas to host them.

It also took people like Caesars publicist and event director Ron Amos, casino and fight

Middleweight Ace Hudkins puts on an exhibition in Las Vegas in 1929. Hudkins, whose nickname was "The Wildcat" twice fought for the middleweight title and was a favorite in California, though he never fought in Las Vegas. In fact, there is only one listed fight in Las Vegas in 1929, on March 10 when Bert Colima knocked out Eddie Mackey in the second round. The other fighter with Hudkins is not identified.

Promoters would do anything to sell tickets to a fight, and the fighters dutifully went along for the ride. That's why Archie Moore and Nino Valdes dressed up in cowboy duds, donned some Stetsons and posed together in front of Happy Vic's bar downtown. Once the fight was underway, the wily Moore quickly lured Valdes to where he was facing the setting sun, then hit him with a series of punches he couldn't see.

LAS VEGAS REVIEW-JOURNAL

host Ash Resnick, Mel Greb and Jim Deskin to dream up the fights and make them happen.

By the time the Las Vegas Hilton built a pavilion to hold the Muhammad Ali-Leon Spinks heavyweight title fight on February 15, 1978, the city was becoming a major player in the boxing world.

And if Fight Town USA had a town hall, it was Caesars Palace, where huge arenas were built, and Ali-Larry Holmes in 1980 ushered in an era of megafights that still happen on a regular basis nearly a quarter-century later.

"The biggest night in Las Vegas has always been New Year's Eve," said Ali confidante Gene Kilroy. "The big fights created New Year's Eve in June and August. Forget about getting a room in town. You couldn't get a call into a hotel."

Joe Louis hung out as a casino host at Caesars, and Ali would come to town long after he stopped fighting. Boxers moved to town to train at Johnny Tocco's rundown gym on East Charleston, and Arum moved from the East Coast to base his empire in the new fight center.

Fight nights became events bigger than the biggest stars in the showrooms. Gamblers lured in by the prospect of a good fight dropped millions of dollars, and celebrities were always eager to be seen at ringside.

In the days leading up to a big fight, Ali might hold court in a coffee shop, signing autographs for all. And there was always a buzz in the sports books and casinos.

Casinos began to depend on fights so much that Steve Wynn flew Buster Douglas around in his private jet and offered him $20 million to fight at the Mirage after he beat Mike Tyson. Tyson and promoter Don King were given $27 million in MGM Grand stock in 1995

A disconsolate Valdes is interviewed after losing a decision to Moore. "They don't want me to fight Rocky Marciano. I'm not good enough," Valdes said, breaking down in huge sobs. "I won the fight, but I can't fight Marciano."

to sign a six-fight deal with the hotel.

The outdoor arenas erected first at Caesars and later at the Riviera, Dunes and Hilton eventually gave way to arenas built with big fights in mind. The MGM Grand can put 16,000 people in its arena, while Mandalay Bay's 12,000-seat building became home to fighters like Oscar De La Hoya and Lennox Lewis.

The faces of fight fans have changed since Moore and Valdes got together in the infield of a semipro ballpark nearly a half-century ago. So has boxing itself in so many ways.

The headquarters for that first fight was a dumpy room off a downtown side street. At the weigh-in, promoters had to borrow a local grocery store's scale normally used to weigh vegetables.

Still, even in 1955 they were thinking—and talking—big.

It wasn't enough that promoter Kearns billed the fight as, the "real" heavyweight championship, when it was nothing of the kind. He also claimed a crowd of 10,800 and a gate of $102,316.

Newspapermen of the time were as skeptical as their present day counterparts.

"They couldn't have cleared a hundred grand if they had put the entire take on a craps table and doubled it," reported Jerry Boyd in *The (San Bernardino, California) Sun*.

Boyd also had some fun with comedian-turned-ring announcer Schrenk, who spent the night giving lengthy introductions of anyone sitting near ringside who he deemed worthy enough to introduce. After one long-winded string of platitudes for a British boxing promoter, Boyd wrote:

"I was disappointed when promoter Jack Solomons and not Winston Churchill stood up."

One thing rang true after the city's first big fight card, though. Las Vegas liked the fights, and liked being the center of attention. Over the years, it took some heavyweights both inside the ring and out to stake the city's claim as the fight capital of the world. Now, though, they're not about to let it go.

"It's the heart of boxing," veteran trainer Emanuel Steward said. "New York is a big city, but Las Vegas is the big city of boxing."

SEEING LAS VEGAS

It took Emanuel Steward and his team of fighters four days to drive from Detroit for the 1964 AAU national championships in Las Vegas. He brought a small camera along and took pictures, certain he'd never see the city again. "I remember it was a small little town, but it had all these lights," Steward said.

Steward's team won the title, and as a reward they got to go see Louis Armstrong and Robert Goulet at one of the Strip hotels. Even better, they got to go on stage and take a bow. "I got home and was telling my mama I saw Louis Armstrong in person and they had us all onstage," Steward Said. "All of those lights and stuff. Just to be up on that stage—it was like we went to heaven."

The city Steward thought he would never see again eventually became his second home. He came back as a amateur coach for the Olympic trials in 1972, then returned on May 29, 1979, when a young welterweight prospect named Thomas Hearns fought Harold Weston at the Dunes Hotel and Casino. "I remember looking up at the top of the Dunes and seeing the sign Thomas Hearns vs. Harold West." Steward recalled. "I said, let's enjoys this 'cause this will probably be the last time we're here."

Hearns of course, would go on to fight in some of the more memorable Vegas fights of the 80s. In all, the Hit Man would fight seventeen times in Las Vegas, with Steward in his corner every time. Steward would return as the trainer for others, including Evander Holyfield, and Lennox Lewis. The city became more than just a second home for him.

"It really became a big part of my life. When I train my boxers today, my whole mindset is about holding him up when we hit Las Vegas, and he's set to fight at Mandalay Bay, Caesar's Palace, or the MGM Grand," he said. "I don't even get excited about guys winning a fight until they get to Vegas. My goal for every fighter is to prepare him to hit Las Vegas and have his name up there."

And if Fight Town USA had a tow
ushered in an era of megafights

Thirty years after Moore and Valdes met, Las Vegas was skilled at holding big outdoor fights. Early in the evening at Caesars Palace was a magical time, where thousands gathered for huge fights as the sun set behind the western mountains. On this night, June 11, 1982, Caesars pulled out all the stops for its biggest fight ever, when Larry Holmes beat Gerry Cooney to retain his heavyweight title.

ll, it was at Caesars Palace, where huge arenas were built and Ali-Holmes in 1980 still happen on a regular basis nearly a quarter-century later.

Las Vegas couldn't pass up the opportunity to promote itself as well as its fights. Here, middleweight champion Dick Tiger is greeted as he arrives at the old McCarran Field for his February 23, 1963, fight with Gene Fullmer by a welcoming committee there to present him a stuffed tiger in front of an ad display listing all the current Las Vegas headliners of the time. Giving Tiger the tiger is Ash Resnick, a casino host who was a force behind many of the fights and fighters of the '60s.

LAS VEGAS REVIEW-JOURNAL

Sonny Liston throws a right uppercut in the first round of his July 22, 1963, heavyweight title fight with Floyd Patterson. Liston was an overwhelming favorite to defend his title against Patterson in the first heavyweight title fight in Las Vegas, and he didn't disappoint, knocking Patterson out at 2:10 of the first round. After the fight, an up-and-coming heavyweight named Cassius Clay got into the ring to taunt Liston into giving him a fight.

3 >> SONNY, ONCE SO TRUE

When Sonny Liston stared, people got nervous. Long before Mike Tyson was even born, Liston was the most feared fighter on the planet, a brooding ex-con who made his living before boxing as a street enforcer and was just as good at that job as he was in enforcing his will in a boxing ring.

Liston and Las Vegas were made for each other, and not only because both had deep connections to underworld elements. Sonny was so taken with the women, the gambling, and the excitement of the town that he, like Tyson, he ended up moving to Sin City late in his career.

A fearsome heavyweight who would stare his opponents down before the bell and then usually pummel them into submission, Liston could be just as intimidating outside the ring.

A gambler at the old Thunderbird Hotel found out the hard way one day in 1964.

Liston was training for his first fight with Muhammad Ali, and he would hit the heavy bag, jump rope and spar every day in a ring set up in the hotel's showroom. The workouts were open to the public, and they drew crowds curious to see the heavyweight champion. Liston had knocked out Floyd Patterson in the first round the year before at the Las Vegas Convention Center and he was a big favorite for his fight in Miami against the untested young heavyweight known then as Cassius Clay.

Ron Amos, sports editor of the *Las Vegas Review-Journal*, was doing double duty as Liston's press guy for the fight. He set up headquarters for Liston in the hotel's coffee shop, where the first booth was roped off with a sign that read "Sonny Liston, heavyweight champion of the world. No one sits here."

No one did.

They wouldn't dare mess with Sonny. At 6-foot-1, 215 pounds, he was a big heavyweight for his day, and the darkness he carried with him was scary enough for everyone around him.

Even Amos was a bit worried about his new client. Before taking the job, he insisted the hotel bring in a boyhood friend of Liston who might be able to get the champ to behave.

"He scared the hell out of me," Amos recalled. "Sonny was surly unless he knew you. But I found out later he was a pretty good guy."

A planeload of gamblers flew into town on a casino junket a few weeks before the fight, and Liston's daily workouts became part of their day. One short, chunky gambler from New York in particular would sit in the front row of Liston's workouts every afternoon and heckle the champion.

LAS VEGAS REVIEW-JOURNAL

Liston liked to party and have fun in his adopted town, but he was all business in getting ready for a fight. He trained on the stage of the old Thunderbird Hotel for Patterson, where crowds gathered daily to watch him hit the heavy and speed bags and maybe spar a bit. After the workouts, Liston liked to hold court in the hotel's coffee shop, where he had a special booth reserved just for him.

LAS VEGAS REVIEW-JOURNAL

The gambler would laugh when Liston hit the speed bag, and make fun of him when he jumped rope. Sonny pretended not to notice, even when the gambler got personal.

"You're going to fall on your ass," he would yell at Liston while he jumped rope.

On his last day of training before breaking camp, Liston was in his customary spot in the booth at the coffee shop when Amos spotted the heckler shooting craps in the casino.

"Hey, champ, want to have some fun?" Amos said.

"Let's go," Liston replied.

The casino was packed with gamblers when Liston walked out from the coffee shop. Suddenly, a hush came over the room as the heavyweight champion walked to the craps table, where the gambler, his back to Liston, was throwing dice.

Liston stood behind the man, who finally sensed he was there. The gambler finally turned around and looked up at Liston, who gave him The Stare.

"The blood drained from this guy's face and he just passed out cold," Amos said. "They had to haul him out on a stretcher. The whole casino was going crazy laughing."

Liston laughed himself, then put his arm around Amos.

"You're my friend for life," he said.

Liston would fight only three times in Las Vegas, with two of those fights coming in the final months of his career. But he was a fixture on the Strip from his 1963 fight with Floyd Patterson until he died seven years later.

Liston was in his 30s, or so he said, during the 60s. His date of birth was always in dispute, and most people around him figured he was at least a decade older.

Always dressed to kill, he would tool around town in his pink Cadillac, often with a woman other than his wife, Geraldine, at his side. Liston loved to play blackjack and was up late at night in the casinos even when he was in training.

Liston was basically illiterate and had trouble signing his name. He had a stack of mimeographed sheets of paper with his signature on them to hand out to fans seeking autographs.

Some who might have been watching Liston train for his first fight with Ali might have picked up on some clues that he was not taking the brash challenger too seriously. Behind the old Thunderbird at the time was a horse track called the Joe Brown Race Track, and Liston would go out there in the morning with a younger boy from Florida whom people in his camp called his mascot.

"The track was a half-mile and they'd run it twice. It was only a mile, but Sonny wasn't training too hard," said gambler Lem Banker, a longtime friend of Liston. "He thought he was unbeatable."

Thunderbird casino host Ash Resnick went with Liston to Miami for the fight, along with Joe Louis and Sammy Davis Jr. The day before, Ali carried on so much at the weigh-in that many thought he was terrified of Liston.

Liston was a heavy favorite in the sports books, and Resnick was so confident of his chances that he called Banker after the weigh-in and wanted him to bet $50,000 that the fight would not go past the fourth round.

Liston would fight only three times in Las Vegas, with two of those fights coming in the final months of his career. But he was a fixture around town. At the time, Liston was in his 30s, or so he said. His date of birth was always in dispute, and most people around him figured he was at least a decade older.

Banker didn't have that kind of money then, but he bet $5,000 and kept another $5,000 himself. Then he went to the Convention Center rotunda, where he sat with Sheriff Ralph Lamb and watched the fight on closed circuit.

The fight went seven rounds before Liston quit, complaining of a shoulder injury. Ali was the new champion, and Liston would be stopped even quicker by a phantom punch in the first round when they met the next year in Lewiston, Maine.

Liston lost his title, and his friends lost their bankrolls.

"I never asked Sonny what happened," Banker said. "It was a lot of money in those days, but I never said a word to him about it."

Ali may have gotten to Liston long before they met in Miami. The two had several altercations during the previous year, when Liston was training to defend his heavyweight title July 22, 1963, at the Convention Center.

It was the first heavyweight title fight ever held in Las Vegas, and the town was abuzz, even though most expected Liston to decapitate the smaller Patterson.

He had nearly done so 10 months earlier when he stopped Patterson in the first round at Comiskey Park in Chicago, and there was little doubt the outcome would be the same in the rematch.

After Liston knocked him out in Chicago, Patterson was so embarrassed he donned a fake beard and glasses for the drive home to New York so no one would recognize him.

After flying into Las Vegas for the rematch, he admitted to reporters that he had brought the disguise with him.

It wasn't a good sign for Patterson.

"I'd get my disguise and go back to New York," Liston said, when asked about it. "I wouldn't fight me."

The fight was so big that some 500 sportswriters flooded the Strip looking for angles. Many were predictable, with Patterson being cast in the role of the good Negro, while Liston was por-

trayed as something far more threatening.

Liston, though, understood his role in the selling of the fight.

"A boxing match is like a cowboy movie. There's got to be good guys and there's got to be bad guys," Liston said. "That's what people pay for—to see the bad guy get beat. So I'm the bad guy. But I change things. I don't get beat."

Ali, looking to goad Liston into giving him a shot at the heavyweight title, was more than happy to give the writers a new angle for their stories.

The fight was on a Monday night, and the Thursday before, the 21-year-old Ali and his entourage strolled nonchalantly into Liston's public workout at the Thunderbird and began berating the champion.

"I told you this day would come, Sonny Boy,"

Fed up with Clay's antics before and after Liston's fight with Patterson, Liston's handlers were ready to grab some headlines for him. After Liston knocked out Patterson they were ready with a special edition proclaiming his greatness. Liston was illiterate, and unfortunately his handlers weren't very good spellers, either, misspelling Clay's name in the headline.

LAS VEGAS REVIEW-JOURNAL

Ali yelled. "I'll show you I'm not just mouth, just all action, man."

Liston tried to ignore Ali as he began to shadow box in front of a crowd of his supporters.

"Why, you're too ugly to be champion. The champion should be good lookin' . . . like me," Ali taunted.

Ali tried to climb into the ring but was stopped by Liston's handlers. He then went to a back booth in the showroom before standing up and reciting one of his earliest poems to the crowd.

"If you like to lose your money,
"Be a fool and bet on Sonny.
"But if you want a good day,
"Put a bundle on Clay."

Liston had put up with enough by the time Ali yelled "Pop" loudly every time one of Liston's punches hit the heavy bag.

"That's exactly how your bones are going to sound when I start punching you," Liston yelled at his young tormentor.

Liston was more than just irritated. He was downright mad.

The workout was over when he saw Ali in the hotel's casino. Liston walked up to Ali and slapped him on the cheek.

"I was just trying to take some steam out of him," Liston said.

Asked how hard he hit Ali, Liston replied:

"I didn't have no gauge on it."

Ali was bombastic as ever when asked about the exchange.

"I didn't know whether he was mad or playing, but it took two special policemen to hold me off him," Ali said.

Liston may have been irritated by Ali, but he was still ready to take care of business against Patterson. The first heavyweight championship fight in Las Vegas had generated plenty of excitement, but Liston was an overwhelming favorite to dispose of Patterson and keep his title.

"When I heard the crowd booing me, I said to myself, 'I'll fix them,'" Liston said.

Las Vegas Sun publisher Hank Greenspun put $300 on Patterson at odds of 6 ½–1.

"I couldn't pass up those odds," Greenspun explained.

Patterson had good reason to bring his disguise. If the memory of the first fight wasn't enough to bother him, he would be outweighed by 21 pounds in the rematch. For sure,

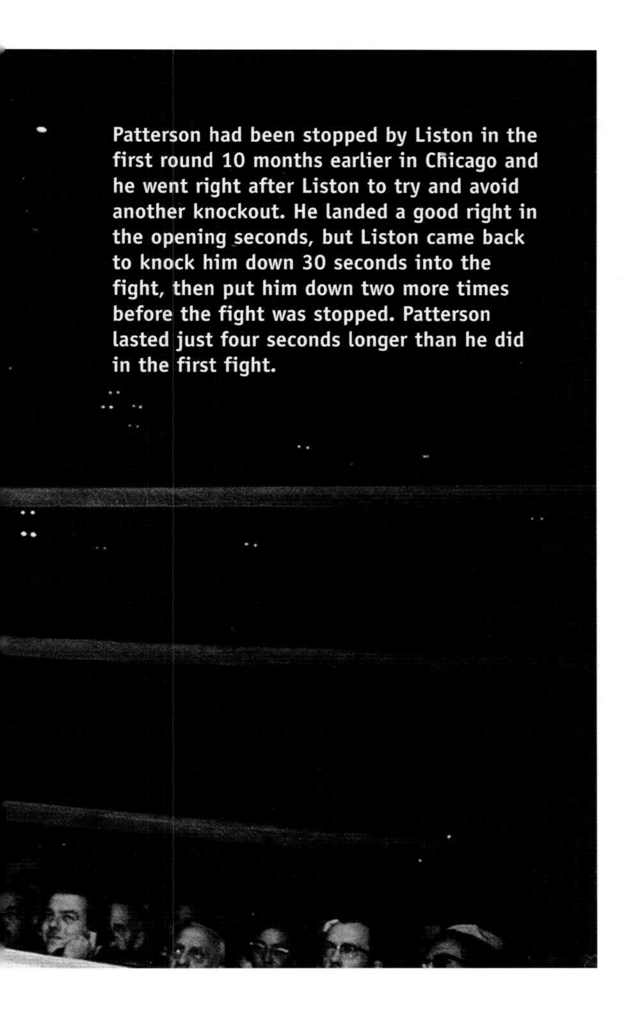

Patterson had been stopped by Liston in the first round 10 months earlier in Chicago and he went right after Liston to try and avoid another knockout. He landed a good right in the opening seconds, but Liston came back to knock him down 30 seconds into the fight, then put him down two more times before the fight was stopped. Patterson lasted just four seconds longer than he did in the first fight.

Patterson wasn't brimming with confidence.

Asked if Liston, who hadn't lost in nine years, could be knocked out, Patterson said he thought someone might be able to do it.

"I'm not saying I'm the man who will do it, but he's human just like everybody else."

The apparent mismatch didn't stop a near capacity crowd of 7,816 from coming out on a hot summer night. Tickets were priced from $10 to $100 at ringside, and the fight was televised on closed circuit to 143 outlets around the country.

They didn't get much for their money. The only fight on the undercard ended at 2:23 of the first round. The main event was even shorter.

Most of those watching were rooting for Patterson. The glowering Liston was so unpopular he was booed as he entered the ring.

Liston came out and was all over Patterson, landing his big left hook and thudding rights to the challenger's head. The crowd was urging Patterson on, but it was obvious from the beginning it was going to be a short night.

Patterson landed a solid right and a left hook in the opening seconds, but Liston dropped Patterson with a left hook and a right 30 seconds into the fight. Patterson got up, but went down from another right. The end finally came when the Big Bear put Patterson on his back with a crushing left hook and he was counted out at 2:10 of the first round.

Patterson had lasted just four seconds longer than he did 10 months earlier.

"Let me get one thing straight," Patterson told reporters afterward. "I was not afraid of Liston. I was not tense. Perhaps I was a little nervous, but not tense."

Liston didn't even have time to celebrate before Ali jumped into the ring to steal his thunder.

A SHORT NIGHT

Floyd Patterson had so little confidence in his chances of beating the fearsome Sonny Liston in the first heavyweight title fight in Las Vegas that he brought along a disguise so people wouldn't recognize him afterward. Not many others gave him a chance, either.

Comedian Shecky Green was working at the Riviera Hotel and Casino and wanted to get to the fight at the nearby convention center between shows. He took a cab and sped over so he could catch the big event.

"Keep the meter running, I'll be right out," Green told the driver. Inside the arena, vendors were hawking their wares before the first bell sounded. "Peanuts, popcorn. Last round coming up," a few shouted. It turned out they were right.

Liston demolished Patterson, knocking him down three times before the fight was stopped at 2:10 of the first round.

LAS VEGAS REVIEW-JOURNAL

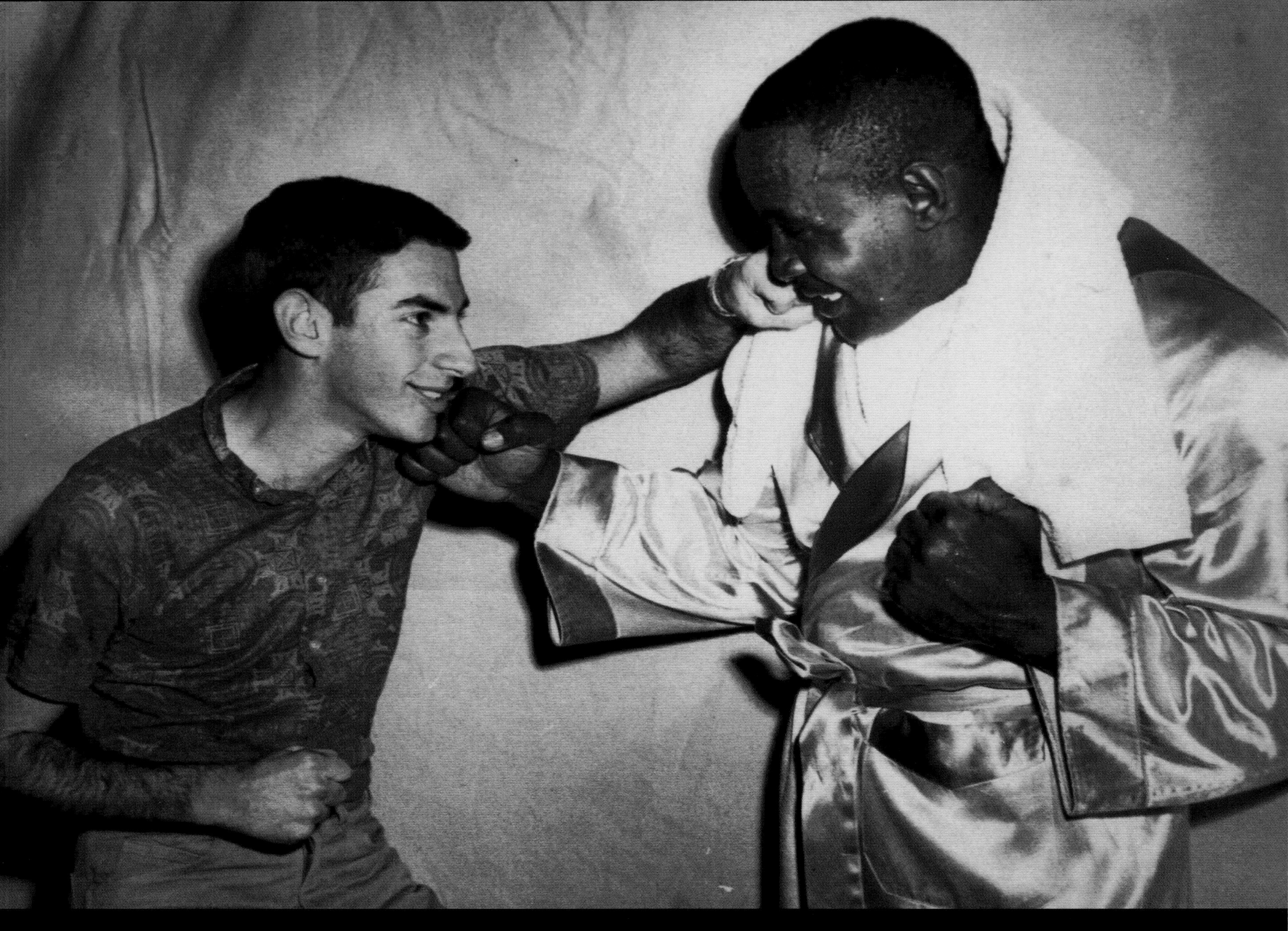

COURTESY MARC RATNER

FIRST IN LINE

Marc Ratner wasn't going to be left out of the first heavyweight title fight in Las Vegas. The 18-year-old who would go on to become the leading regulator in boxing set his alarm early and raced down to the Las Vegas Convention Center the first day tickets went on sale for Sonny Liston's title defense against Floyd Patterson.

He got to the box office at 7 a.m. expecting a line. It turned out he was the line.

Ratner, now executive director of the Nevada Athletic Commission, bought four $10 tickets in the top row of the convention center. Today, they're proudly displayed in a large folder of tickets from fights Ratner attended or worked. The $10 tickets were for Section 24, row Q, seats 1, 2, 3, and 4.

"They were the first four tickets sold," Ratner recalled. "I knew I wasn't going to miss that fight."

"I'm the real champion and I'm going to prove it," Ali yelled to the crowd, which greeted him with boos.

Liston himself was irate.

"When I heard the crowd booing me, I said to myself, 'I'll fix them,'" Liston said.

Years later, another heavyweight champion understood.

"He wanted people to love and respect him," Mike Tyson said. "But you are who you are."

Liston would not fight again in Las Vegas for six years. After Ali beat him twice, he fought in Sweden his next four fights and didn't return to fight in his adopted city until May 19, 1969, when he stopped George "Scrap Iron" Johnson in the seventh round at the Convention Center.

Liston was a fearsome presence, with an intimidating scowl that scared people. But he could be a soft touch, too. At left, he playfully taps the chin of a teen-age Marc Ratner, who would go on to become one of boxing's most respected figures as executive director of the Nevada Athletic Commission. Above, he shares a joke with a Stardust Hotel security guard.

Five months later he fought for the last time in Las Vegas, taking on former sparring partner Leotis Martin in a fight from the showroom at the International Hotel televised by ABC's *Wide World of Sports*.

On the undercard was the young heavyweight gold medalist from the 1968 Olympics, George Foreman. The aging Liston and Martin were supposed to go 10 rounds, but it didn't look like it would last that long as Liston was putting a beating on Martin.

Liston, though, had hardly trained, and he was old beyond his years, whatever they were. He was ahead on all cards when he simply ran out of gas and Martin stopped him in the ninth round.

"He never should have taken that fight," Banker said. "He was in Tucson doing a bit for the television show 'Love American Style' and ABC called him with an opening. He wasn't in shape and he was probably 10 years older than his birth certificate. Martin hit him with a left hook and that was that."

LAS VEGAS REVIEW-JOURNAL

At Liston's funeral, the Checkmates sang "Sonny" and mourners from the boxing world gathered to pay their respects. Among them was former heavyweight champion Joe Louis, who was one of the pallbearers. Some flowers and the short saying "A Man" mark his gravesite.

Liston fought only once more, then retired to the Las Vegas home he shared with Geraldine. He still loved the glitz and glamour of the city, but most of his money had been squandered or taken from him by his mob-connected handlers.

Still, Liston had a new Cadillac and was enjoying the life of a man about town. But he was getting too deep into some things he didn't understand.

One day in late 1970, then-Sheriff Lamb called Banker and warned him that Liston needed to clean up his act.

"He said they were going to make a drug bust on the West Side and he knew Sonny was hanging around with drug dealers," Banker recalled. "He knew Sonny was a friend of mine and wanted him to stay out of the way."

Liston did, and later he stopped by Banker's house with his adopted child. He had cut a record and was trying to get in the singing business.

The holidays were coming, and they exchanged gifts.

A few days later, Liston's housekeeper, Mildred, phoned. Sonny had been found dead in his bed.

The former champion's body was bloated by the time he was found, but it didn't take authorities long to find needle marks on his arms and heroin in the bedroom. Banker said Liston was afraid of needles, though, and over the years there were rumors Liston had crossed the line with drug dealers and been forced to take an overdose at gunpoint.

The official ruling was death by natural causes.

"They said he was doped up and shot up, but I was close with the sheriff at the time and I had them make it look like it was a heart attack," Banker said. "I didn't want his name to be defaced and I had respect for his wife and mother."

At Liston's funeral, the Checkmates sang "Sonny." Banker and Joe Louis were pallbearers as the body was taken from the chapel to the cemetery. On the way into the cemetery, a guard saluted.

"Sonny would get a kick out of that," Louis told Banker. "Imagine that, a cop saluting him."

Liston was buried just a few hundred yards from where jets touch down at McCarran International Airport.

There, a simple headstone reads: "Charles 'Sonny' Liston 1932-1970. A man."

LAS VEGAS REVIEW-JOURNAL

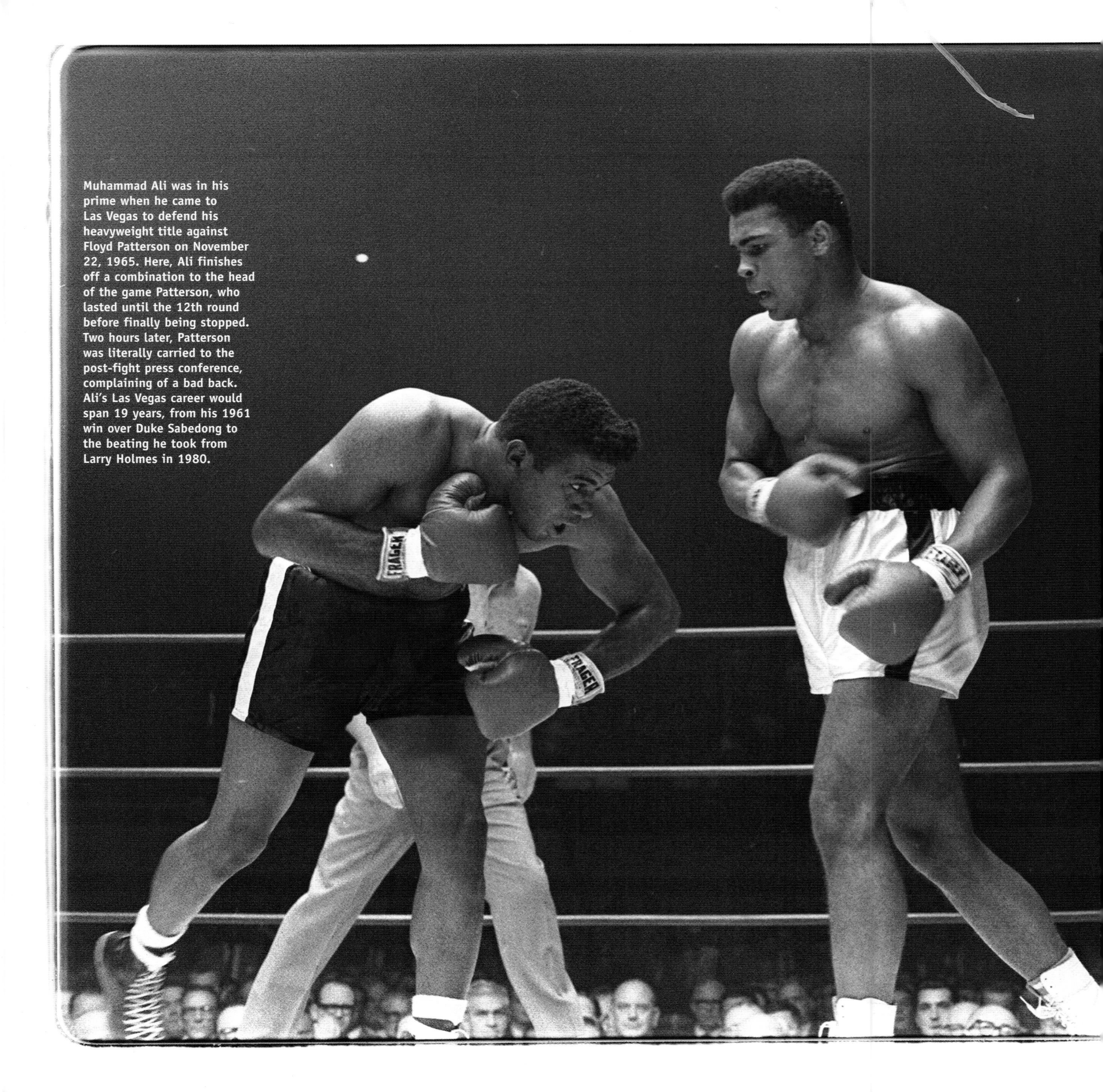

Muhammad Ali was in his prime when he came to Las Vegas to defend his heavyweight title against Floyd Patterson on November 22, 1965. Here, Ali finishes off a combination to the head of the game Patterson, who lasted until the 12th round before finally being stopped. Two hours later, Patterson was literally carried to the post-fight press conference, complaining of a bad back. Ali's Las Vegas career would span 19 years, from his 1961 win over Duke Sabedong to the beating he took from Larry Holmes in 1980.

4 >> THE GREATEST

Even in a town filled with legends, he was The Greatest. Muhammad Ali wasn't just a star on fight night in Las Vegas. For weeks his training sessions at the Stardust or Caesars Palace were the hottest tickets in a town where stars like Frank Sinatra, Dean Martin and Sammy Davis Jr. roamed the Strip.

As a 19-year-old Cassius Clay in 1961, he fought a Hawaiian giant named Duke Sabedong at the Convention Center, then proclaimed that he would indeed be The Greatest.

Two years later, he showed an early flair for the dramatic, heckling at ringside as Sonny Liston knocked out Floyd Patterson in the first round of the first heavyweight title fight in the city.

Liston was the feared champion, but Ali stole the show as he taunted Liston, then jumped into the ring afterwards to pretend he was going after him.

"Liston will fall in eight," Ali yelled out, holding up eight fingers. "I am the real champion."

The act was real enough, but not everyone was convinced he could stand a chance against Liston.

"It appears Clay is the next up to be knocked out," a *Review-Journal* columnist wrote. "The fiasco, they say, will be held in Philadelphia on September 30."

Ali, of course, would go on to upset Liston in the seventh round in Miami Beach the next year, and boxing would never be the same.

Ali fought eight times over a 19-year span in Las Vegas, an era that began with his youthful exuberance against Sabedong and ended on a sad note when Larry Holmes tormented the aging former champion for 10 rounds before the fight was finally stopped in the first outdoor arena at Caesars Palace.

But Ali made his mark in brighter days in a town that frowned on black people staying at Strip hotels when he first arrived.

It was in Las Vegas where he mastered the art of self-promotion, picking up some tips the night before his fight with Sabedong when he went to a wrestling event at the Convention Center featuring Gorgeous George and later mimicking his style.

It was in Las Vegas where he beat Floyd Patterson, then later took on the likes of Jerry Quarry, Ron Lyle and Joe Bugner at the Convention Center. And it was in Las Vegas where he lost his heavyweight title in one of boxing's biggest upsets to gap-toothed Leon Spinks.

Before he even became Muhammad Ali, though, he was exciting crowds in a town where he was becoming king.

He was an Olympic gold medalist known as Cassius Clay when he brought a 6-0 record and a lot of press clippings to a fight with Sabedong that drew a crowd of 2,500 to the Convention Center on June 26, 1961.

But it was Sabedong who did most of the clowning, faking as if he was going to hit Ali after each bell and making faces whenever Ali hit him.

Ali's lightning-fast hands and quick moves were way too much for the 6-foot-6 Hawaiian, though, who lost every round on two of the three ringside cards.

"You fight pretty good for a bum," Sabedong whispered in Ali's ear during clinches.

Trainer Angelo Dundee quickly proclaimed the fight a learning experience for Ali, who had never gone 10 rounds in his previous six pro fights.

"We wanted two big answers from this fight and we got them—the kid can go 10 rounds and he can take a punch on the chin and in the midsection," Dundee said.

Sabedong wasn't as impressed.

"He's an average fighter," Sabedong said, obviously not realizing his place in history. "He just doesn't hit like a heavyweight."

Ali wouldn't fight again in Las Vegas for another four years, returning on November 22,

LAS VEGAS REVIEW-JOURNAL

1965, to defend his heavyweight title against Patterson. In between, though, he would come to harangue Liston, and tell anyone who would listen that he was indeed going to be The Greatest.

At the time, fight fans and sportswriters didn't know what to think about the brash young Kentuckian who spoke in rhymes and boasted with a bravado never seen before.

The crowd booed Liston when he entered the ring to knock out Patterson. But they booed even louder when Ali pranced about at ringside and then got into the ring to issue a challenge to Liston.

By the time Ali returned to Las Vegas two years later to fight Patterson, he was no longer Cassius Clay, though the newspapers insisted on still referring to him as that.

Ali had a new name and was now a Muslim. The week before the fight, he jetted to Phoenix to get some "spiritual advice" from Elijah Muhammad, then leader of the Black Muslims.

He would need no advice on how to fight Patterson, whose last fight at the Convention Center didn't even last a round before Liston knocked him out. Ali wanted to punish Patterson, who refused to call him by his new name and questioned his ties to the Black Muslims.

"I don't dislike Clay at all," Patterson said. "'He is young and downgrades everybody. He doesn't believe what I do, and I don't believe what he does."

"I don't dislike Clay at all," Patterson said. "'He is young and downgrades everybody. He doesn't believe what I do and I don't believe what he does."

For a dollar, fans could go to the Stardust and watch Ali train, and they packed the hotel's ballroom to see him. Patterson trained more quietly down the street at the Thunderbird Hotel.

A crowd of 8,106 filled the Convention Center on a rainy night expecting to see Ali at his best. For the first round, though, Ali merely circled and looked at Patterson, who landed a few punches and won the round.

It was the last round the challenger would win. Ali danced and jabbed at will, toying with

Patterson, after the Ali fight.

WHAT'S MY NAME?

The easiest way to get to Muhammad Ali in his prime was to call him by his given name, Cassius Clay. Floyd Patterson insisted on doing just that before his November 22, 1965, title fight with Ali at the Convention Center — and he paid the price.

Ali knocked Patterson down in the sixth round and gave him a beating before the fight was finally stopped in the 12th round. During the fight he taunted Patterson, hitting him and saying "What's my name?"

"I said I would punish him and I did," Ali yelled out from the ring, drawing boos from the crowd.

Before the fight, Patterson insisted he didn't dislike Ali but said he wanted to "win back the heavyweight championship for America."

The local newspapers weren't quite sure what to call Ali, either. In almost all stories he was called Cassius Clay, with an explanation inside the story that would read "Muhammad Ali, as Clay refers to himself."

Ali called his given name his "slave name" and refused to answer to it.

The presence of Black Muslims around the fight caused some worry about town. It seemed only a matter of time before there was an incident, and it came the night of the fight.

Four Black Muslims were arrested after they exchanged punches with sheriff's deputies who moved in when they marched down into the $100 seats at ringside during the second round and refused to move.

The *Las Vegas Review-Journal* reported that the four "emitted the Muslim call for help" and others came to aid in the fight.

"All of a sudden I found myself surrounded by swinging, screaming, fighting Negroes and police," said a photographer who was knocked down in the scuffle.

The men were later released from the Clark County jail after posting $25 bond, and the newspaper quoted sports writers as praising police for keeping the peace.

As for Patterson, it would be years before he could bring himself to call Ali by his new name.

It was 1986 and Patterson was in Las Vegas to watch Mike Tyson win the heavyweight title from Trevor Berbick. Ali's confidante, Gene Kilroy, was having dinner with Patterson when the old champ asked, "Is Clay here?"

"I said, 'Floyd, when Mary Smith marries Tom Brown, you call her Mary Brown. When John Kennedy became president his brother, Robert, called him Mr. President. Muhammad deserves the same respect anyone else would want,'" Kilroy recalled.

The next night, Kilroy and Ali were having dinner at the Dunes and Patterson walked up to the table.

"Hello, Muhammad Ali," he said.

Ali stood up and hugged Patterson. Suddenly, with three words, all was forgiven.

ALI'S BUS

Muhammad Ali didn't like to fly much. But he loved to drive a bus. Before Ali fought Floyd Patterson at the Convention Center in 1965, he posed for photographers at the wheel of a bus. He had a thing about buses, and some day he would have his own.

It was a Bluebird Wanderlust, and Ali and Gene Kilroy found it loaded with a bed, toilet, stereo and all the modern conveniences at a Pennsylvania distributorship.

What better way to break it in, Ali figured, than to drive it to Las Vegas for his fight with Joe Bugner.

Ali, Kilroy and Ali's brother, Rahaman, set out with sparring partner Alonzo Johnson, who doubled as a driver, and soon they were making good time across country.

"He thought it was heaven," Kilroy said. "He loved to drive it himself."

Outside of St. Louis, they ran into a big snowstorm and stopped to help a motorist who had slid off the road and was stuck in a ditch.

Ali got out and began helping push the man's car, much to the man's astonishment.

"He couldn't believe it was Ali," Kilroy said.

"Where are you going?" the motorist asked.

"I'm going to Las Vegas to beat up Joe Bugner," Ali replied.

The bus rolled into town in the early morning hours and pulled up to the front door of Caesars Palace. Tired from the road and hungry, Ali and his small entourage headed for the coffee shop.

In the casino you could have heard a pin drop. Gamblers stopped shooting dice to watch the champion walk in their midst.

The Greatest behind the wheel in 1965.

LAS VEGAS REVIEW-JOURNAL

Ali was 23-years-old and a marvelous physical specimen when he came to town to fight Floyd Patterson. With him, as always, was trainer Angelo Dundee, who helped the champ with some gloves during training at the Stardust.

LAS VEGAS REVIEW-JOURNAL

With supreme confidence, Ali pushes out a left hand to the face of his sparring partner during a training session at the Stardust. Ali's workouts would draw hundreds of fans who packed the room to get a glimpse of the brash, young heavyweight champion who even then was larger than life.

LAS VEGAS REVIEW-JOURNAL

Patterson throughout and dropping him in the sixth round.

In the late rounds, Ali was so in control that he leaned over and had a chat with ringside photographers between punches.

"Am I giving you enough action?" he asked.

Patterson had no chance, though he gamely kept on until the fight was finally stopped in the 12th round. Two hours later, he was literally carried to the press conference complaining of a bad back.

It would be seven years before Ali returned to fight in Las Vegas. He stopped Quarry in the seventh round, then beat Bob Foster later in the year at the Convention Center and followed with a win a few months later against Bugner.

Ali returned as heavyweight champion on May 16, 1975, just seven months removed from his big upset of George Foreman in the Rumble in the Jungle in Zaire. He was fighting Ron Lyle, a tough ex-con who could hit like a mule.

Ali gave away rounds early and was getting beaten to the punch by Lyle. After the 10th round, Lyle was ahead on points and in Ali's corner there was plenty of reason to worry.

"You're losing it. You're losing it, Champ," his brother, Rahaman, told Ali between rounds.

Ali went out in the next round and landed a jab and a right to the jaw that hurt Lyle. He followed with 33 unanswered punches until referee and local bartender Ferd Hernandez stopped the fight.

Three years later, Ali wouldn't be as fortunate.

The setting was the Las Vegas Hilton, hosting its first big fight in an indoor pavilion that seated only a few thousand people. Ron Amos, who had brought boxing to Caesars Palace, was now at the Hilton and had landed the heavyweight championship that would be broadcast on CBS.

Ali was getting $3 million to fight Spinks, the Olympic champion who had a 6-0-1 record and, many thought, no reason to be in the ring with the greatest fighter of all time.

"Ali will win any time he wants to," the great boxing writer Barney Nagler predicted.

The sellout crowd of 5,000 watched in disbelief as the fight unfolded and Spinks pounded away on Ali's aging body and head. Ali gave away rounds early and couldn't solve the unorthodox challenger's style late. He ended up a split decision loser.

"I should be sad, but I'm not," Ali said as he was consoled by the jubilant new champion.

There would be plenty of sadness two years later, in Ali's last fight in Las Vegas and, at age

LAS VEGAS REVIEW-JOURNAL

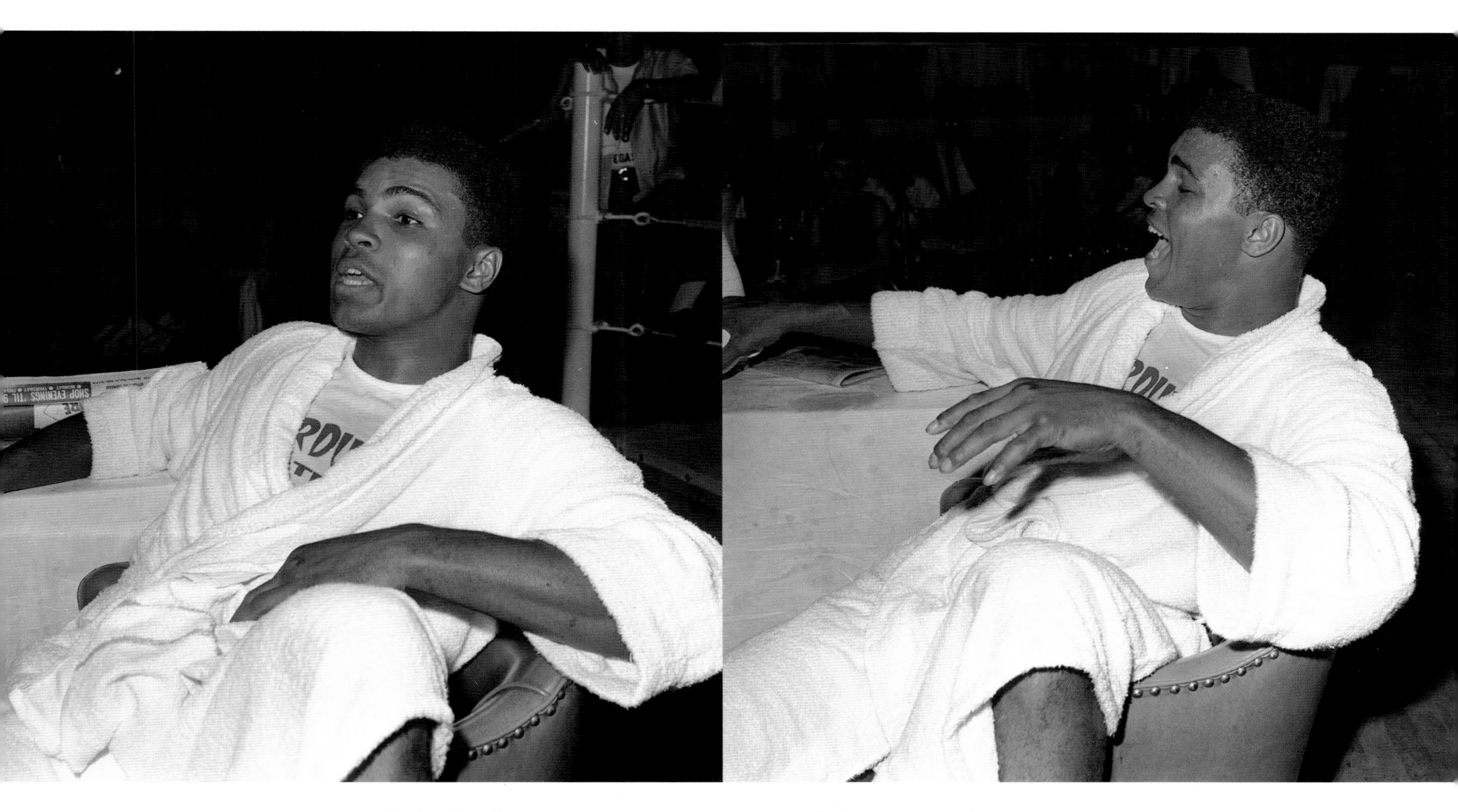

38, his last fight for a heavyweight title.

Frank Sinatra was playing the showroom at Caesars Palace that night and opened the show with a song before stopping.

It was time for one legend to pay tribute to another.

An hour or so earlier, Holmes had beaten up Ali in the hotel's parking lot, exposing his aging reflexes and diminishing skills. Afterward, Holmes cried, and Sinatra seemed like he was on the verge of tears, too.

"Ali had a tremendous way of being able to make believers out of people and people wanted to be believers," said matchmaker Bobby Goodman.

"When I was growing up, I loved Joe Louis. He was my idol," Sinatra said. "There's a fellow in the hotel tonight lying down in his room. He has nothing to be ashamed of. He's a blessing to boxing and a blessing to the world."

The crowd rose in a standing ovation, and Ali adviser Gene Kilroy went up to Ali's room to tell him what had happened.

Ali was asleep, trying to recover from the beating he had just taken. He woke to hear what Kilroy had to say.

"Isn't that nice," Ali said. "As long as they don't pity you, it's fine. I never want to be pitied."

Earlier, Kilroy was in Ali's room where he cried over the loss.

Ali was subdued and ready to go to bed.

"I saw his head and couldn't throw the punch," Ali said. "I was tired even coming down from the dressing room."

The fight was the first big outdoor fight on the Las Vegas Strip, drawing a sellout crowd of 24,570 to the temporary arena hastily constructed on a parking lot behind Caesars Palace.

Caesars sports director Bob Halloran was a friend of Ali's from his days in Miami as a sportscaster and convinced his boss, Cliff Perlman, to bid for the match.

If there was one thing Ali loved better than fighting, it was talking. Here, he holds court wth sportswriters after a workout at the Stardust.

LAS VEGAS REVIEW-JOURNAL

Before he became Muhammad Ali, a young Cassius Clay visited Las Vegas in June 1961. Clay was 19 and the Olympic light heavyweight gold medalist, and was fighting for only the seventh time as a pro. He weighed 194 ½ pounds for the fight against Duke Sabedong, who outweighed him by 30 pounds. Sabedong took Clay 10 rounds for the first time at the Las Vegas Convention Center, losing the decision but telling reporters afterward that he thought the 19-year-old was nothing special. Here, Clay takes a break from training to pose with promoter Mel Greb and trainer Angelo Dundee. At far right is KO Phil Delmont, whose big claim to fame was he knocked out Mickey Walker, who would later become middleweight champion, in his first fight in 1919.

COURTESY STEVE DELMONT

THE FIGHT THAT WASN'T

It was billed as "The Fight of the Century," and it lived up to the hype. When Muhammad Ali and Joe Frazier met for the heavyweight title March 8, 1971, at Madison Square Garden the atmosphere was as electric as the full length fur coats the men were wearing at ringside.

What no one knew was how close the fight had come to being in Las Vegas nearly two years earlier. It was 1969, and Ali was banned by most states from fighting while he appealed a conviction for refusing to be drafted. Frazier was undefeated and about to take the heavyweight title that Ali had to give up.

Promoter Bob Arum had signed contracts from both fighters to meet. All he had to do was find a place to stage the fight, and he figured Las Vegas might take a gamble.

Arum was in New York, but across the country gambler Jimmy "The Greek" Snyder was in Las Vegas trying to get the Nevada State Athletic Commission to rescind its ban on Ali and let him fight there.

The Greek convinced the commission and the governor at the time, Paul Laxalt, to allow the fight. He linked up with promoter Harold Conrad, who called Arum and urged him to come to Las Vegas to go before the commission for final approval. Arum flew out and checked into the Desert Inn, which was owned by the reclusive billionaire and top-floor resident Howard Hughes.

Hughes had bought the hotel from reputed mobster Moe Dalitz, who was still involved in running the casino. The next morning, Dalitz saw Arum and Conrad having breakfast in the hotel's coffee shop and came over to see what they were doing. "I said we were going to go before the commission that day and get Ali licensed," Arum recalled. "Dalitz went crazy. He said: `That no-good, draft-dodging SOB shouldn't be allowed to fight in this town.'"

Arum tried to calm Dalitz down, and he and Conrad left to go to the Algiers Motel, where the commission was meeting. Once there, they met with Snynder and saw Laxalt inside. "He came in and said he was happy to do this and that." Arum said. "Just as I'm talking to him the phone rings at the front desk, and they called Jimmy over. He went white as a ghost."

On the phone was Bob Maheu, Hughes's right-hand man. He told Snyder that Hughes didn't want Ali and Frazier fighting in Las Vegas. Arum knew what it meant. Hughes owned five hotels in Las Vegas and wielded enormous power.

"I told the governor I didn't want any trouble and was withdrawing the application," Arum said. "The commission was stunned, but I knew in those days if Hughes was against it I had no chance."

Arum's choice of hotels had cost Las Vegas its biggest fight."If we had stayed at any other place other than the Desert Inn, it would have been approved," he said. "But we had to stay there and have breakfast in that coffee shop. That ruined the whole thing."

JIM LAURIE/LAS VEGAS REVIEW-JOURNAL

Above, Ali gestures to Sonny Liston after Liston's 1963 knockout of Floyd Patterson in this rare photo. Ali heckled Liston into giving him a title shot the next year, which Ali won to become heavyweight champion for the first time.

"How much will I lose?" Perlman asked Halloran.

"You won't lose anything," Halloran replied.

"Then do it," Perlman said.

Halloran was walking away when Perlman remembered something.

"Isn't Ali shot?" he asked.

"Yes," said Halloran, " but by the time the fight starts he'll have everyone convinced he will win."

Ali did just that, working his magic and seemingly getting into shape for one last great show while dismissing the abilities of his former sparring partner.

"I taught Larry Holmes everything he knows," Ali said. "But I didn't teach him everything I know."

Ali came into camp weighing 252 pounds and by the time he left for Las Vegas two weeks before the fight he was 30 pounds lighter. He ran four miles each morning at the Dunes Hotel golf course, and seemed to have reached back for a final performance to thrill boxing fans.

Don King was promoting the fight, and even he was buying into Ali's mystique. "He grew a mustache during that time, put on sunglasses and called himself 'Dark Gable.' That was amazing," King said. "He could feed into the public imagination like no one in history. He had convinced me he could win and was going to do it again, and I knew Holmes was one of the most underestimated fighters there was."

Ali was popping pills before the fight, though, some for a misdiagnosed thyroid condition, others to lose weight.

"A week before the fight someone suggested he take steroids and he did," Kilroy said.

Nevada boxing authorities had Ali take three days worth of medical tests at the Mayo Clinic to show he was still physically able to fight at the age of 38. An anonymous British neurologist who had studied Ali's tapes for several years and who had now noticed an increased slurring of his words said Ali could have brain damage. Nevada ringside physician Dr. Donald Romeo, though, said the Mayo Clinic brain scan showed no problems and called the brain-damage charge "a bunch of bunk."

On the night of the fight, people stood on top of fences outside the outdoor arena, while others stopped their cars on a freeway overpass to watch Ali make history once again.

"Ali had a tremendous way of being able to make believers out of people and people wanted to be believers," said matchmaker Bobby Goodman. "He got himself in great condition, or at least the best condition he could. The weight thing was very important to him that he got

LAS VEGAS REVIEW-JOURNAL

down to the same weight he was earlier in his career."

At the weigh-in the day before, Ali tipped the scales at 217 pounds and he looked debonair with a new mustache and his graying hair dyed black. It seemed like he had miraculously wiped away 10 years.

Now people believed, though Goodman wasn't one of them. He had been with Ali in Zaire when he upset Foreman, but this was different.

"People thought this was the daddy who was going to spank his child," Goodman said. "I didn't think he had a chance. I was with him so many years and at a certain point you see the great skills and great reflexes start to diminish somewhat."

Those around Ali weren't too sure he had anything left, either. His cornermen worried the reflexes were gone, and they saw what was happening when he sparred during training. Outside the ring, it was much the same, with Ali giving up on running one day at the Dunes Hotel golf course. He blamed it on Allah's will, saying "I ran two miles and couldn't go on because of something inside."

"He's just a shell," said veteran trainer Billy Prezant, after watching Ali work out days before the fight. "A beautiful shell, but there's nothing inside. The legs are gone. I got to make Holmes a thousand to one."

Holmes agreed.

"I do not believe in miracles," Holmes told a

The greatest greets the Brown Bomber in this 1965 photo taken at McCarran Airport. Ali has one arm around Joe Louis's shoulder and is shaking his hand as the two great heavyweights get together. On the left is casino host Ash Resnick.

LAS VEGAS REVIEW-JOURNAL

crowd that came for one of his pre-fight sparring session. "And I'm sure that on October 2, none is going to happen that night. It's true that Ali performed miracles in his day. But this is 1980, ladies and gentlemen, this is my day."

Still, Ali had his believers. How could you not believe the man, given the amazing things he had done in the ring the previous two decades? He had beaten George Foreman in Zaire when no one gave him a chance, and he promised he

LAS VEGAS REVIEW-JOURNAL

would work miracles again against Holmes.

"They forget who I am," Ali said. "I'm Muhammad Ali."

The fighter who entered the ring that October night had Ali's name on his back, but it was soon clear this was no Ali. He entered the ring trying to intimidate Holmes, running after him several times as if he were looking for a fight. But it was Holmes who would do the fighting, not Ali.

From the opening bell, Holmes played with Ali, hitting him at will with his stinging left jab and rocking him with right hands. Ali landed almost nothing, and didn't win a round on any of the scorecards of the three ringside judges. Any other fighter would have gone down, but Ali's legendary chin and courage kept him upright.

"All I could think of after the first round was, 'Oh, God, I still have 14 rounds to go,'" Ali said. "I had nothing. Nothing. I knew it was hopeless."

Ali's once menacing jab was little more than a push. His reflexes were shot and he just tried to hang on as Holmes pounded him round after round. The crowd that was so hopeful grew quieter as the rounds went on in monotonous fashion.

Finally, after the 10th round, trainer Angelo Dundee stopped it with Ali sitting on his stool. At the same time, ring doctor Donald Romeo was coming toward the corner to see if Ali could take anymore.

Holmes came over, embraced his former sparring partner and kissed him on his cheek.

"I love you," Holmes said.

Ali was all business as he weighed in at the Las Vegas Convention Center for his November 1965 title fight with Floyd Patterson. Ali weighed 210 pounds, light for today's heavyweights, but still much bigger than the 196 that Patterson weighed. After the weigh-in, Ali went outside to do some proselytizing about the religion he had converted to a year earlier, though his claims to be a religious convert were still mocked by many in the press. Ali would go on to stop Patterson in the 12th round of the scheduled 15-round heavyweight title bout.

THE ASSOCIATED PRESS

Elvis strikes an almost comical pose against the Champ.

IS PRESLEY ESTATE

ALI AND THE KING

The celebrity planets were all in alignment the night Ali met the King. It was early 1973 and Elvis was playing the Las Vegas Hilton showroom. Ali was in town for a Valentine's Day fight with Joe Bugner and made a date with adviser Gene Kilroy to see the show.

Ali and Kilroy watched as the music from *2001: A Space Odyssey* played, lights flashed and the curtains opened to Elvis breaking into "CC Rider."

Fans screamed in delight as the King opened his show.

"He's cool," Ali said to Kilroy.

From the stage, Elvis acknowledged Ali's presence

"There's a man in the audience I admire," he told the crowd. "He said he's the greatest and, Muhammad, you are the greatest."

The stage lights flashed to Ali, nervous for once in his life.

"No, Elvelis," he said, mispronouncing his name. "You're the greatest."

That night, Elvis sang a birthday song to his daughter, Lisa Marie, who turned five that day and was in the audience. Later, he chatted with Ali backstage, where Ali implored him to get out in public more.

A few nights later, Elvis invited Ali to his suite, where he had a gift waiting. It was a boxing robe, weighed down with sequins and studs with the inscription "The People's Champion" written in

rhinestones on the back..

Ali gave Elvis some boxing gloves with an inscription, and Elvis showed Ali some of his karate moves.

A picture of the moment shows Elvis in a comical karate pose facing Ali, who is wearing the robe.

"Elvis, you're too pretty," Ali said. "You do the singing, I'll do the fighting."

Ali would wear the robe to his fights with Joe Bugner and Ken Norton. After Norton broke his jaw and beat him, the robe was never seen again.

Ali recalled the times long after he quit boxing.

"I was the Elvis of boxing," he said.

Then again, maybe Elvis was the Ali of singing.

Muhammad Ali's arrival in town was always a big event, certain to draw a crowd of admirers. Here, Ali walks from a Western Airlines plane at McCarran Airport shortly after landing in Las Vegas for his November 1965 heavyweight title defense against Floyd Patterson. With Ali is singer Eddie Fisher, who was playing the Strip at the time and would sing the national anthem at the fight. Behind Fisher in the suit is Ali's brother, Rahaman.

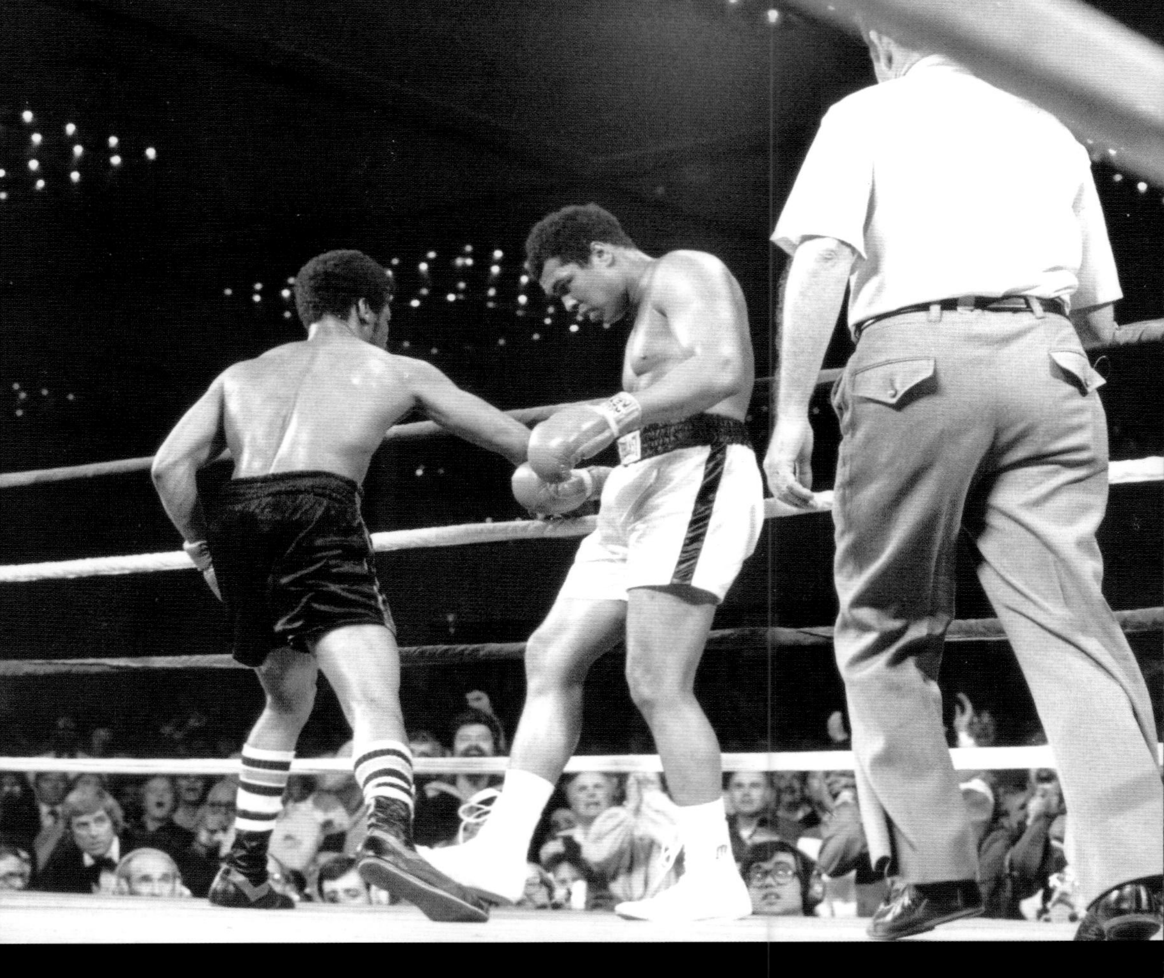

ALI'S BIG LOSS

Muhammad Ali was coming out of the elevator at the Las Vegas Hilton on a cold February morning, on his way to the Dunes Hotel golf course to do roadwork for his title defense against Leon Spinks.

He took only a few steps before spotting Spinks, coming in for the night with a big grin on his toothless face and a woman on each arm.

"Hey, Ali," Spinks said. "How's the champ?"

The champ was irritable, mostly because he didn't

enjoy getting up at 4:30 in the morning to run.

Seeing Spinks coming in from a night of partying only made him feel worse.

It was hard enough for Ali to force his aging body to train when he didn't think much about the abilities of a challenger who had only seven pro fights. Ali had trained in Miami instead of his usual camp in the Poconos because his wife wanted to be somewhere warm with their newborn daughter, Laila.

But now Ali was wondering why he was bothering trying to get in shape at all.

"What am I doing here?" He asked confidante Gene Kilroy.

While Spinks headed upstairs for who knows what, Ali decided he wasn't going to run that day. He sat in the Hilton coffee shop and told Kilroy he wasn't sure he was going to run many more days, either.

"I'm a three-time AAU champ, a three-time Golden Gloves champ and a two-time heavyweight champion," Ali said. "How's this amateur fighter going to beat me?"

Ali was nearing the end of his illustrious career, but there weren't many others who thought Spinks could beat him, either.

Ali had approved Spinks as an opponent only after watching him fight and figuring he would be an easy $3 million payday. Spinks was so lightly regarded that promoter Bob Arum had to get him a match with Italian Alfio Righetti a few months earlier to get a WBA ranking and sanctioning for the Ali fight.

Spinks had won the gold medal as a light heavyweight in the 1976 Olympics, but he was only 6-0-1 when he got the chance to fight Ali February 15, 1978, in the pavilion of the Hilton.

"Everybody castigated me when I made the fight because they didn't figure Spinks had a chance," Arum said.

It was the first heavyweight title fight in Las Vegas held at a hotel, and 5,298 people crammed into the Hilton pavilion to get a glimpse of Ali performing his magic.

The pavilion was on the other end of the huge hotel from the suite where Ali stayed in the days leading up to the fight. He walked with his small entourage through the hotel and to the arena, finally sitting on a bench in his dressing room.

"I'm tired. That was a long walk," Ali said.

It was a Wednesday night and the fight was being televised by CBS in prime time. Network executives knew the appeal of Ali, but they were concerned the scheduled 15-rounder wouldn't go long enough to allow them to sell all the advertising they needed to unload.

"Some CBS people came into the dressing room and told Ali, `We need this to go a few rounds at least, just play with him for a few rounds,'" Kilroy recalled.

Ali did just that, fighting halfheartedly against his young opponent for a few rounds. But as the rounds started to pile up, Ali was getting more tired and Spinks was getting stronger.

At the end of the 12th round, Ali was ahead on one scorecard and even on another. But for one fight Spinks had trained just as hard as he partied and he was the fresher fighter. He would not be denied, while Ali's age began to show.

"I didn't worry about just having seven pro fights. I just worried about getting in there and getting out," Spinks said. "And Ali talks to you all the time, so that just made me try harder."

In the 13th round, Spinks landed some good hooks and a strong right to the jaw before closing the round with a smashing left to the jaw. He hurt Ali with a hook to the head in the next round and won that one, too.

Ali sat in his corner before the 15th round, his left eye swollen and his title on the line. He came out determined to win the final round and the two fighters went back and forth, hurting each other with head shots as the crowd stood and roared its approval.

"I had studied Ali a lot and I knew what it took to overpower him," Spinks said. "My combinations and my will to keep going made the difference. He was still a good fighter, but I had a lot of will and a lot of strength."

It was a split decision, though not many argued with the result. Judge Art Lurie had Ali winning 143-142, while Harold Buck had Spinks ahead 144-141 and Lou Tabat had him winning 145-140.

"Spinks proved you guys wrong," Ali told the press later.

The world had a new champion, though Spinks would have the shortest heavyweight title reign ever before losing a rematch to Ali in New Orleans seven months later.

Everyone loved Spinks and his toothless smile, but his party habits were legendary and his career was never the same.

"He was the nicest guy in the world but totally nuts," Arum said. "He wouldn't harm a flea outside the ring. He was just a goofball."

For one night, though, Spinks had accomplished the unbelievable.

"I didn't find out until afterwards that Spinks was crazy," Arum said. "He would be out 'til four in the morning training for fights and be drunk the night before. For this fight he actually trained and it paid."

AP WIDE WORLD

A short time later, Holmes went up to Ali's room.

"Are you OK, Champ?" he asked. "I didn't want to hurt you."

"Then why did you?" Ali asked, laughing.

Holmes said later he, too, cried after the fight.

"It was hard to win the fight but lose at the same time," he said. "He was a friend, a legend, and he gave me an opportunity. I was always in a no-win situation."

Holmes was King's fighter, but even the hardened promoter didn't like what he saw. Ali had given him his first big chance, allowing him to promote the Rumble in the Jungle with George Foreman, and watching him take a beating was hard even as he was counting his profits.

"It really broke my heart," King said. "Even I had to shed a few tears at the end of that fight."

Sinatra, meanwhile, was downstairs in the showroom giving his fans a show, as Ali rested in the darkness of his room.

"Well, they've got no picture of me down on my back," he told Kilroy, pride intact until the end.

There was nothing better than a Muhammad Ali road show, even when he was well past his prime. Hundreds came daily just to see Ali work out for his 1980 fight with heavyweight champion Larry Holmes at Caesars Palace, and the two fighters seemed to enjoy the fun as much as the crowd. Much to the crowd's delight, Ali is taunting Holmes, who motions as if the former champion were crazy.

JOHN GURZINSKI—LAS VEGAS REVIEW-JOURNAL

In his later years, Ali had to share the stage with his daughter, Laila. At left, father and daughter Laila sit together under a giant painting of the Greatest in his prime at the opening of Absoloot Boxing and Fitness.

Above, Laila lands a right to the face of Valerie Mahfood during their Women's Super Middleweight unification bout on November 8, 2002, at the Stratosphere Hotel and Casino. Ali won when referee Joe Cortez stopped the fight 1:14 into the eighth round.

AMY BETH BENNETT—LAS VEGAS REVIEW-JOURNAL

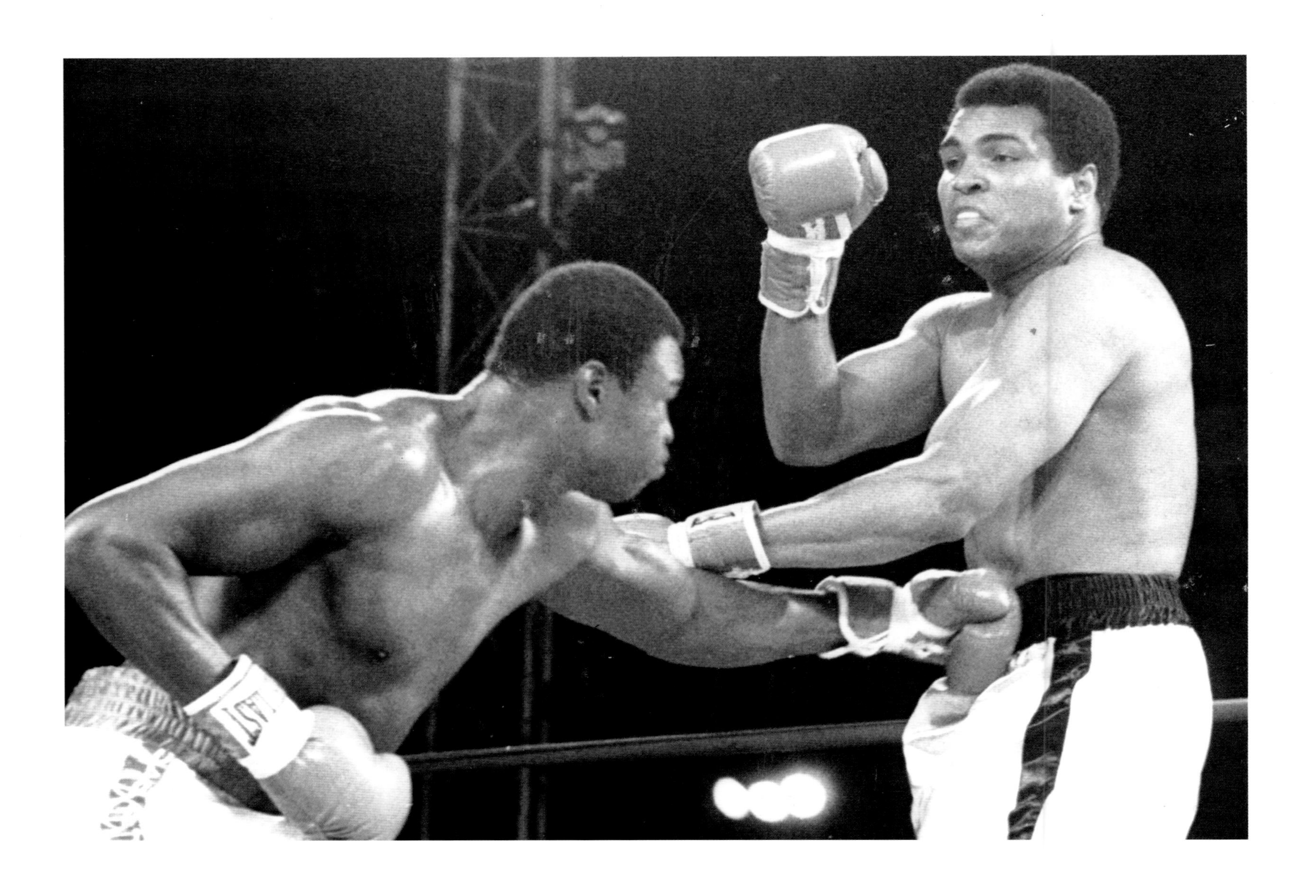

LAS VEGAS REVIEW-JOURNAL

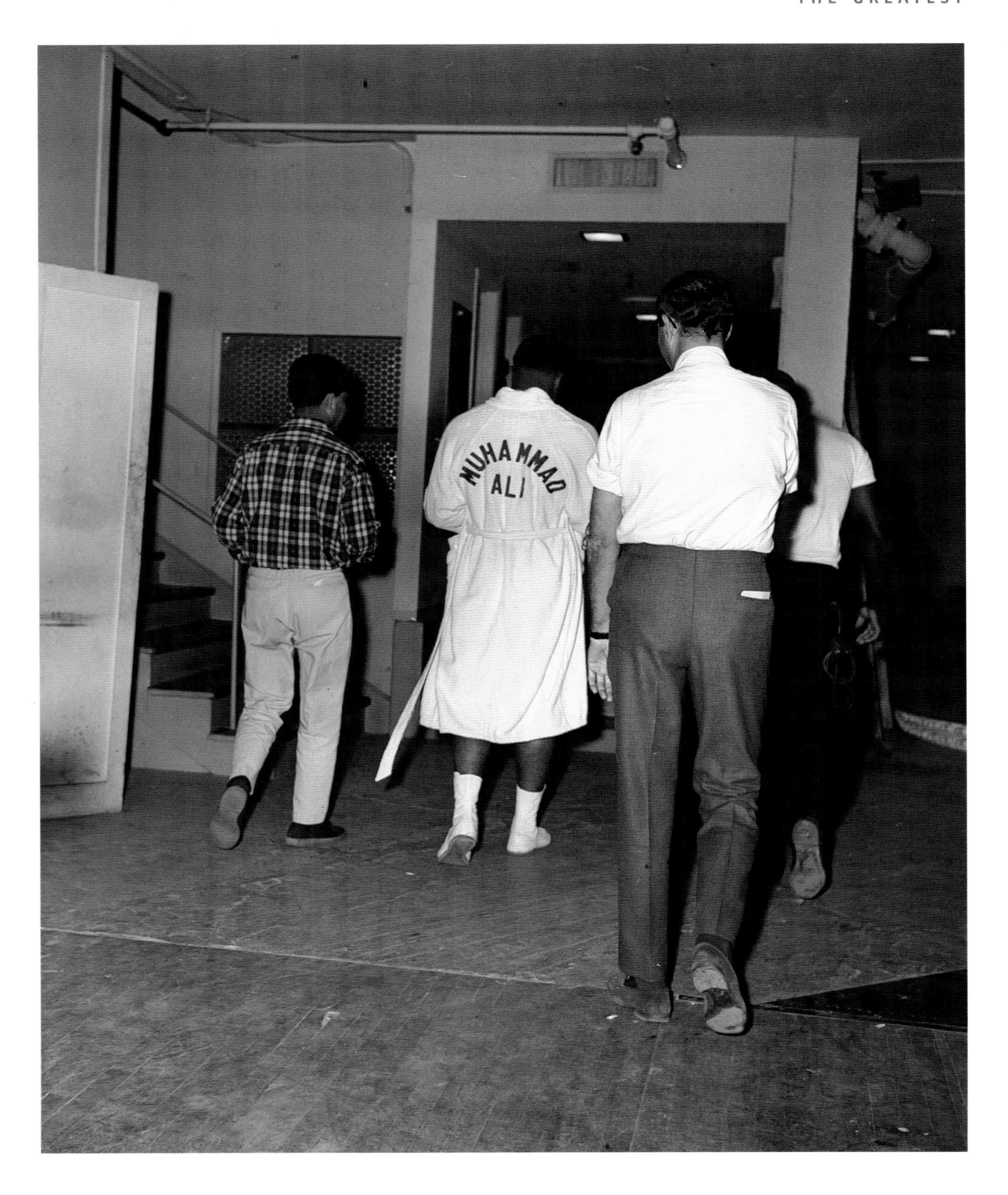

LAS VEGAS REVIEW-JOURNAL

Ali heads out the door after a training session at the Stardust Hotel. Ali's training sessions were headline events on the Las Vegas Strip, drawing curious tourists, locals and top entertainers such as Bill Cosby to see the champ.

INTER-CONTINENTAL PROMOTIONS
ROBERT A. NILON, President

Assisted By MEL GREB
JACK DOYLE

15 ROUNDS

WORLD'S HEAVYWEIGHT CHAMPIONSHIP

LAS VEGAS CONVENTION CENTER

MON., NOV. 22 7:00 P.M.

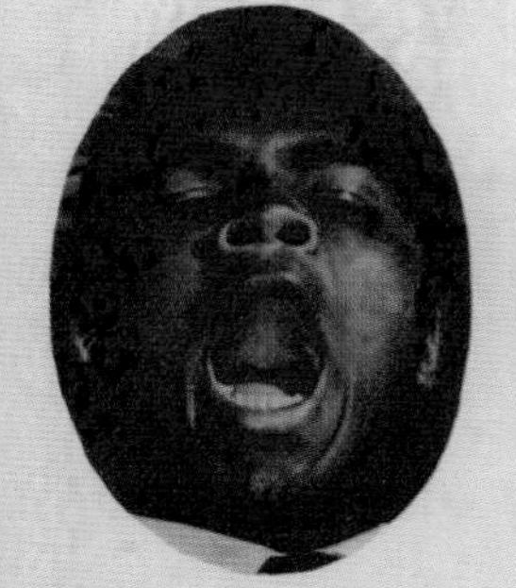

CHAMPION

CASSIUS
CLAY
(Muhammad Ali)

FLOYD
PATTERSON

No. 1 CONTENDER

ADDED ATTRACTION

THAD
SPENCER
No. 5 HEAVYWEIGHT CONTENDER

- VS -
10 ROUNDS

AMOS
LINCOLN
No. 10 HEAVYWEIGHT CONTENDER

NO TELEVISION

Ringside & Loge $100.00 — Club Circle & Arena $50.00 — Balcony $20.00 — Upper Balcony $10.00

TICKETS ON SALE LAS VEGAS CONVENTION CENTER – Phone Reservations 734-1101

DESERT INN, Casino Cashier
EL CORTEZ, Casino Cashier
STARDUST, Casino Cashier
DUNES, Casino Cashier
SAHARA, Casino Cashier
THUNDERBIRD, Casino Cashier
BLUE ONION RESTAURANT
DAVEY'S LOCKER

Bonanza Printers

Muhammad Ali had changed his name but still couldn't get promoters to make the change when he defended his heavyweight title against Floyd Patterson in November 1965 at the Las Vegas Convention Center. It was the first of four title fights in Las Vegas for Ali, who won two of them and lost the other two. The end of an era came outdoors at a hotel that had not even been built when Ali beat Patterson. There, on October 2, 1980, Ali fought in the last title fight of his illustrious career against Larry Holmes in a specially constructed outdoor stadium at Caesars Palace. Sadly, Ali was only a shell of the fighter he once was, and Holmes dominated him completely before the fight was finally stopped at the end of the tenth round.

DON KING, IN ASSOCIATION WITH CAESARS PALACE, PRESENTS

HOLMES VS ALI

UNDEFEATED CHAMPION · VS · THREE-TIME CHAMPION

WORLD HEAVYWEIGHT CHAMPIONSHIP

October 2, 1980

5 >> SUGAR RAY AND THE HIT MAN

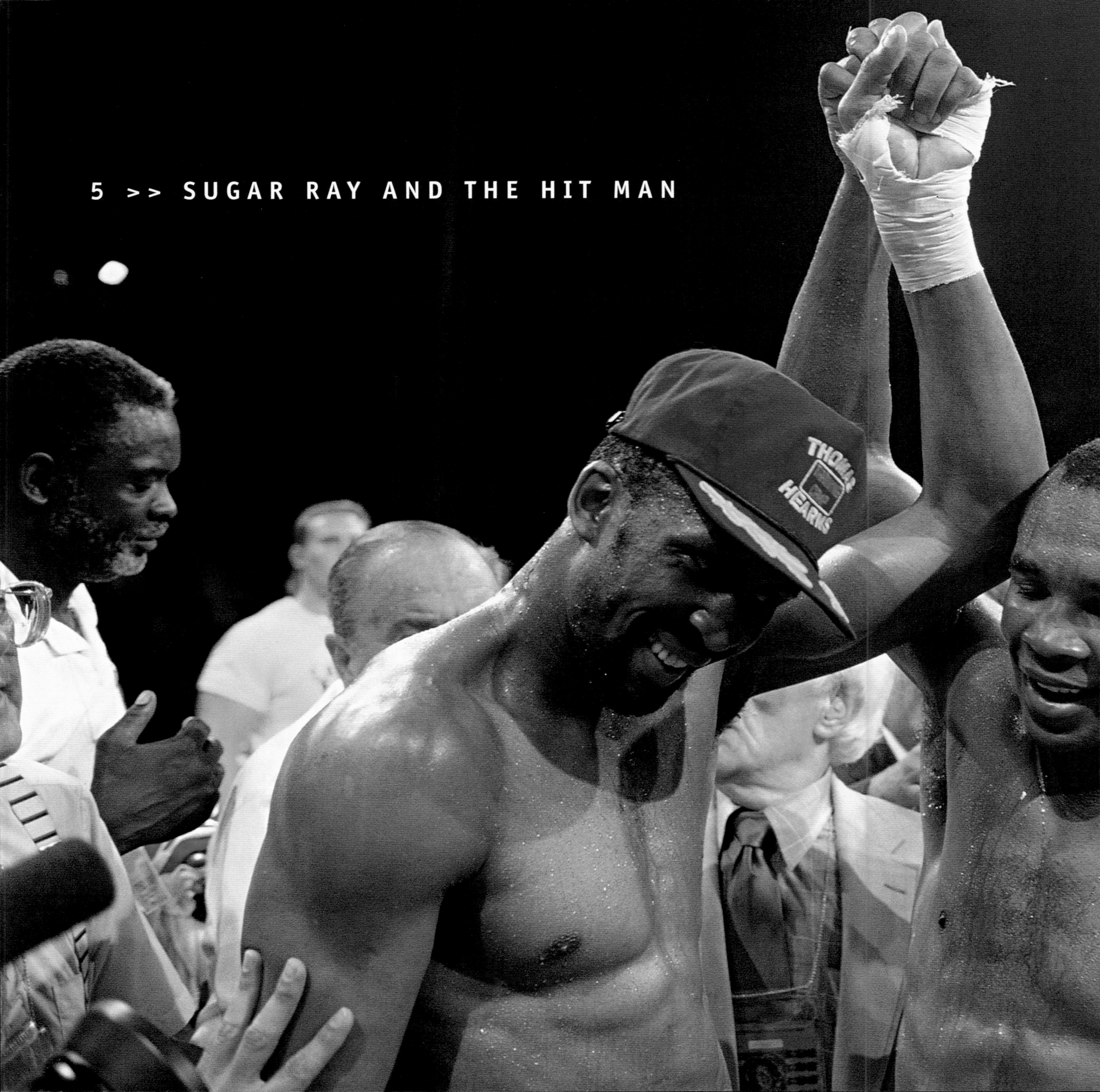

It was the '80s, a time when welterweights and middleweights reigned and Las Vegas firmly staked its claim to being the boxing capital of the world.

It was a great time to be a fighter, and a magical time to be a fan. Sugar Ray Leonard was in his prime, and so was the Hit Man, Tommy Hearns. Marvelous Marvin Hagler kept knocking people out, and Roberto Duran was eager to fight them all. It was the '80s, a time when welterweights and middleweights reigned and Las Vegas firmly staked its claim to being the boxing capital of the world.

At the center of it all was Caesars Palace, where fight nights always built in anticipation as the sun gradually went behind the mountains and the outdoor arena behind the hotel filled with celebrities, fight fans, gamblers and journalists.

Draped down the hotel's high rise was a giant American flag, which served as a backdrop as some of the greatest fighters in the world took the long walk from their dressing rooms through the crowd and into the ring.

Thomas Hearns and Sugar Ray Leonard share a moment together after their second fight, on June 12, 1989 at Caesars Palace. The two were well past their primes but that didn't stop a crowd of 12,064 from coming to see two fighters trying for one last chance at glory. Hearns knocked Leonard down twice, but Leonard came back strong in the 12th round to get a disputed draw.

It was there on September 16, 1981, when Leonard and Hearns stepped into the ring for the welterweight title in the most anticipated fight of the time. They didn't know it then, but their memorable bout would kick off a decade of big fights that didn't really end until Leonard and Hearns met a second time eight years later.

Hearns and Leonard had both fought in the hotel's tiny pavilion early in their careers. But the stage needed to be much bigger for the megafight between WBA welterweight champion Hearns and WBC titleholder Leonard.

In an outdoor stadium built atop the tennis courts at Caesars, they fought a brilliant duel that thrilled fans from the opening bell through the 14th round. The buildup to the fight had a bit of everything, and the fight turned out every bit as good, if not better.

Leonard was America's fighter, the 1976 Olympic champion with the bright smile, quick wit and 7-Up commercials. He had lost only once, to Duran, a defeat he later came back to avenge in the infamous "No Mas" fight.

Hearns was the lanky welterweight with bird-like legs who packed a wallop in his right hand like no 147-pounder ever before. He was undefeated in 32 fights, had knocked out 30

JEFF SCHEID—LAS VEGAS REVIEW-JOURNAL

SUGAR'S STRATEGY

It was a week or so before his megafight with Marvelous Marvin Hagler, and Sugar Ray Leonard had the perfect plan to win. Or so he thought.

Hagler expected Leonard to come into the ring and throw jabs and quick combinations, dance a bit and quickly move away. Leonard was going to fool the hard-punching middleweight champion. He was going to go right after Hagler, turn the fight into a slugging match and beat him at his own game. It was the same strategy Hearns employed with disastrous results two years earlier. But Leonard was nothing if not a thinking man's fighter, and he had thought this one out.

"I was going to surprise Hagler and go right at him," Leonard recalled. "He had a tendency to cut so I thought I would try and hurt him and cut him early and win the fight that way."

Leonard hadn't fought in three years, since his second retirement, and his decision to get back into the ring against Hagler of all people both surprised and alarmed boxing fans. There were concerns about how his once-detached retina would stand up to being punched. Others wondered how he could be sharp after such a long layoff. And now he was planning to slug it out with a puncher who was both bigger and stronger than he was. "My plan was to fight Hagler toe-to-toe. I figured that plus a big prayer was my only shot," Leonard said.

Luckily for Leonard, that plan changed, and he can thank a sparring partner for it. Five days before the fight Leonard sparred in a gym across the freeway from Caesars Palace before dozens of reporters who were already in town for the fight. It was his last chance to impress and sell the fight with reports on how good he looked.

Leonard was getting in some rounds when sparring partner Quincy Taylor unloaded a right hand. The gloves may have been padded and he was wearing headgear, but the punch landed true. Leonard was wobbled, and then he began to think some more. "Quincy Taylor hit me with a right hand and I was on queer street," Leonard said. "I thought if this guy can hurt me, Hagler will kill me. Thank God Quincy hit me because I changed the plan."

In the van riding back to his rented home in Spanish Trail after the workout, no one said a word. Leonard heard the whispers, though, from his own camp. They didn't think he could win. They wondered if the fight would go past the first round.

"I'm looking around and thinking these sons of bitches think I'm gonna lose," Leonard said. "I called (adviser) Mike Trainer and told him that. Then I said I had a bad day in the gym, but I guarantee you Hagler won't touch me."

Instead of slugging with Hagler, Leonard decided he would outbox him. It turned out to be a special night for a charmed fighter. And he had Quincy Taylor to thank for it.

Sugar Ray Leonard liked to look good when he fought. After a workout, he brushes his hair, careful to retain the look that America saw when he won a gold medal and later took on the best fighters of his era.

Marvelous Marvin Hagler lands a left hand in the first round of his epic 1985 fight with Thomas Hearns at Caesars Palace. Both fighters went at it from the opening bell in what many boxing historians say was the greatest first round of any big fight.

In the early rounds of their first fight, Thomas Hearns dominated Sugar Ray Leonard. The fight was a classic see-saw affair finally won by Leonard in the 14th round. It was the first Las Vegas megafight to live up to its hype, and firmly established Caesars Palace as the mecca of boxing.

opponents and seemed invincible.

The intensity built in the days leading up to the fight, and the boxing community was split. Could Leonard overcome the size differential and outbox Hearns or would the Hit Man catch the Sugar Man with a right hand that would end it all?

A crowd of 23,306 filled the outdoor arena, buzzing in anticipation of what was to come. Muhammad Ali was at ringside, along with Larry Holmes, Joe Frazier and Jake LaMotta. So was comedian George Carlin, Jack Nicholson, Bill Cosby and the Rev. Jesse Jackson. This was an event, and Hollywood and the boxing fraternity were there to see and be seen.

They didn't have long to wait to find out they were in for a real show.

Leonard was cautious early, wary of Hearns' right hand. But it was the left jab from the 6-foot-1 Hearns that caused most of the damage as he won the early rounds by flicking it in Leonard's face.

Hearns was building up points, but the fight suddenly turned in the sixth round when Leonard became the big puncher. He landed a double left hook that staggered Hearns and in the next round he battered Hearns around the ring. Hearns was in so much trouble that his trainer, Emanuel Steward, briefly thought about stopping the fight. But he let it go on and now Hearns got on his bicycle, turning boxer and skipping around the ring peppering Leonard with left jabs and causing a big swelling under his left eye.

Hearns was winning the fight by outboxing Leonard instead of outpunching him. And it seemed there was little Leonard could do about it.

Leonard's eye was nearly swollen shut and Hearns was boxing circles around him. Leonard had his moments, but if Hearns could hold for a few final rounds the big showdown between two undefeated welterweight champions would go the Hit Man's way.

In the corner after the 12th round, trainer Angelo Dundee let his fighter know where he stood.

"You're blowing it, son. You're blowing it," he yelled at Leonard.

Across the ring, Steward was even more worried. His fighter was winning, but it had taken a toll.

"I was talking to Tommy and all of a sudden his head slumped down," Steward recalled. "He was out of gas. I knew right then it was over."

Hearns had overtrained and lost too much weight for the fight.

By now he had nothing left, and Leonard was digging deep into his reserve.

Leonard came on to turn the tide in the 13th round, then finished Hearns off with a flurry of punches on the ropes in the 14th that forced referee Davey Pearl to stop the fight.

Before an arena filled with overdressed high rollers, celebrities, hookers and their pimps and thousands of avid fans, Leonard and Hearns had put on a show for the ages. They fought an epic ebb-and-flow fight that ended as it did only because Leonard had something left when Hearns had expended his all.

It was magnificent, yet it was only the beginning of much more to come.

"There was so much drama and excitement there that it was hard to imagine," Steward said. "I still haven't found anything to compare with it."

Later that night, Caesars executive Bob Halloran went up to Leonard's suite to see the winner, who he figured would be basking in his victory. Leonard's wife let him in, and he walked toward the bathroom where Leonard

Referee Richard Steele gives instructions as Thomas Hearns and Marvelous Marvin Hagler meet in the center of the ring before their fight. Both had vowed not to back down, and neither did.

was standing in front of a mirror examining his swollen, bloodied eye.

Leonard was known for his vanity, and he didn't like what he saw staring back at him.

"Bob," he said, "I don't know if this shit is worth it."

Leonard and Hearns would meet again in 1989 to close a decade of boxing unlike any the city had ever seen. In between, there would be fights with Hagler and Duran as the welterweights and middleweights took center stage over a fading heavyweight division.

A new era in boxing had dawned, and Leonard and Hearns brought it in with style.

"Back then it was an event, a major event," Leonard said. "People saved their week's earnings to buy an outfit to come to Las Vegas. It was bigger than the Oscars. It was just huge. People had the opportunity to get involved in a moment of history and they were thrilled to be there."

Leonard first fought in Las Vegas in November 1977 when he had his fifth pro fight against Augustin Estrada, a 3-10 fighter who was brought in just to fatten up the Olympic gold medalist's record. The fight was in the Caesars Pavillion, and Leonard didn't disappoint, stopping Estrada in the fifth round.

It would be two more years before Leonard returned to Las Vegas, and then it was at the Dunes Hotel, where he won a 10-round decision over Adolfo Viruet to run his record to 21-0. By then, Halloran had joined Caesars and knew that there was something special in the fighter with the big smile and even bigger punch.

Halloran called Leonard's trainer, Angelo Dundee and asked him about the fighter's manager, a Maryland attorney named Mike Trainer. Dundee filled him in on Trainer's negotiating ability and his love for golf. That was all that Halloran, himself a scratch golfer, needed to know.

Halloran called Trainer, arranged a golf date in Maryland and flew down to meet him. He rented a car at the airport, drove to Trainer's house and found the fight manager practicing his swing on the front lawn.

"By the ninth hole that day, we had made a deal," Halloran said.

Soon, Leonard was fighting almost exclusively at Caesars, and finally on Nov. 30, 1979 he met Wilfredo Benitez for the WBC welterweight title in the pavilion. More than 4,500 people packed into the tiny arena to watch, and Caesars took in a million-dollar gate.

Both fighters were undefeated, but the expectations were so high for Leonard that he was a 3-1 favorite. He came into the ring in a gleaming white robe with red tassles on his shoes while his theme song "Sugar Ray" blared out. He was the overwhelming crowd favorite, but he was going up against a gritty fighter known for his defensive abilities and he knew it wasn't going to be an easy night.

Sill, Leonard won all but four rounds, and finally stopped Benitez with six seconds left in the 15th round after knocking him down for the second time in the fight. Three years after he turned pro he finally had his first real title—not to mention a $1.5 million purse.

"Everybody keeps saying Sugar Ray Leonard isn't nothing but Hollywood," he said, "but I showed them tonight I'm determined to be a great fighter."

Overshadowed by the flashy Olympian's win was another fight on the card involving a fighter Leonard would soon become to know well. Marvelous Marvin Hagler finally got his long-awaited shot at the middleweight title, and he and Vito Antoufermo went at it for 15 bloody rounds.

Hagler stood in disbelief as he heard the scores announced. He won 145-141 on one scorecard, and another judge had it 143-143. The third judge had Antoufermo winning 144-142, meaning he would keep his WBA and WBC 160-pound titles with a draw.

Sitting at ringside was Tip O'Neill, the powerful Massachusetts congressman who was upset that Hagler was 46-2-1 but was just getting his first title shots.

"You can tell the promoters if Hagler doesn't get some more big fights there will be an investigation," O'Neill told Halloran.

Leonard may have been the flashy star, but Hearns was the blue collar workhorse whose very presence in a Las Vegas fight in the '80s made it a big event.

Leonard would retire with a detached retina

"I was having fun using psychological warfare," Leonard said. "I never said anything to piss him off or make him dislike me. Fighters like Hagler and Duran must create aggression to get motivated and train hard. If I never activated that, he couldn't feed off of it."

Sugar Ray Leonard misses with a right hand as Roberto Duran moves out of the way December 8, 1989. The fight was the third between the two boxers, but by then both were more curiousities than they were factors in their divisions. Still, they drew a full house to an outdoor arena behind the Mirage Hotel, which Steve Wynn had opened that week. Wynn would later get disillusioned with the fight business, but he wanted a big event for his new hotel to make a splash.

before coming back to beat Hagler in a huge upset and fight Hearns for a second time. But Hearns fought an average of once a year in Fight Town during the '80s, and his legend grew even in defeat.

At times it seemed the whole city of Detroit was in Las Vegas to cheer Hearns on in one big fight or another. They would come to bet big money, scream for their fighter and bet even bigger on the casino tables.

One day, Hearns was training in the Caesars Pavillion for his fight with Hagler and an enormous crowd followed him from the hotel into the pavilion to watch. Many wore the gold and red shirts of Hearns's Kronk Gym, and they all swarmed together trying to get closer to their fighter.

Watching it all was wisecracking Associated Press boxing writer Ed Schuyler Jr.

"The streets of Detroit are a whole lot safer tonight," Schuyler said.

Hearns would knock out Duran in two rounds at Caesars Palace and get off the canvas to stop Juan Roldan to win his fourth championship title at the Las Vegas Hilton. He made tens of millions of dollars mostly because there was something you could always be sure of when the Hit Man entered the ring—there would be plenty of action.

That was what fans were anticipating on April 15, 1985, when Hearns, undefeated since losing to Leonard, challenged Hagler for the middleweight title at Caesars Palace.

They got even more, in a slugfest that produced arguably the most thrilling first round ever in a major title fight.

Hearns had come back from his loss to Leonard to win eight straight fights. The year earlier, he had flattened Duran with a savage right hand in the second round.

MAKING THE FIGHT

One of the biggest fights in history was negotiated in 12 minutes in an airport coffee shop in Syracuse, N.Y. Thomas Hearns and Sugar Ray Leonard were both welterweight champions and on a collision course. Before they could do so, though, the all-important matter of just how much each fighter would make had to be settled. Leonard was fighting Larry Bonds at the Carrier Dome in Syracuse, so Hearns' manager, Emanuel Steward flew in to meet with Leonard's adviser, Mike Trainer.

Reporters in town for the fight heard rumors of the meeting and went to the hotel to stake it out. Instead, Steward and Trainer met at the airport.

Steward said Trainer wanted to offer Hearns $500,000, which was promptly rejected.

"I said, 'Hold it. I did some research here and here are my figures," Steward recalled. "I wanted $5 million for Tommy." Steward was asked what Leonard deserved, and he said $8 million.

"They were shocked because they thought I wanted parity," Steward said. "I gave credit to Leonard for his exposure, the Olympic gold medal. He deserved more. The two sides quickly agreed to another $1 million for promotional expenses and $3 million for the promoter, which was to be a relatively unknown New Jersey company called Main Events.

"I took the same flight back I flew over on," Steward said. "By Tuesday we had signed contracts."

Iran Barkley found Thomas Hearns' weakness — his jaw. Hearns was a 4-1 favorite in the fight at the Hilton Hotel and dominated the first two rounds. But Barkley hit him with a crushing right hand in the third round and soon he was the new WBC middleweight champion.

"Now I know how my opponents feel when I hit them," Hearns said.

Many thought he would do the same thing to Hagler. But Hagler simply refused to lose.

Hagler knew the only way he could beat Hearns was to trade bombs with him and hope that Hearns tired. He came out at the opening bell and attacked with a vengeance, only to get rocked by a Hearns right hand that seemed to split his face open. The two threw shots back and forth to the head nonstop and toward the end of the round it was Hagler who nearly had Hearns out on his feet.

Mercifully, the three minutes of fury finally came to an end when the bell sounded amid the din of a packed arena on its feet, screaming in glee.

"They came out like two animals," Steward said. "It was one of the most vicious and intense rounds in the history of boxing."

It didn't seem humanly possible to follow the brutality of the first round with a second. But the two fighters went at it again, winging shots to the head with little regard for defense.

What no one outside Hearns's corner knew at the time was he had broken his right hand on Hagler's bald head in the first round. In the corner between rounds, he told Steward his hand was hurting.

By the third round, Hagler was bleeding from cuts over both eyes. Referee Richard Steele briefly stopped the fight to have the ring doctor take a look at him, then allowed it to continue. Steele knew Hagler had hurt Hearns late in the second round with several left hooks. He told the champion this was his chance to fight.

Knowing he might not get another, Hagler unleashed a series of crushing right hands that finally put Hearns on the canvas. Steele counted to nine before waving the fight over as Hearns somehow struggled to his feet.

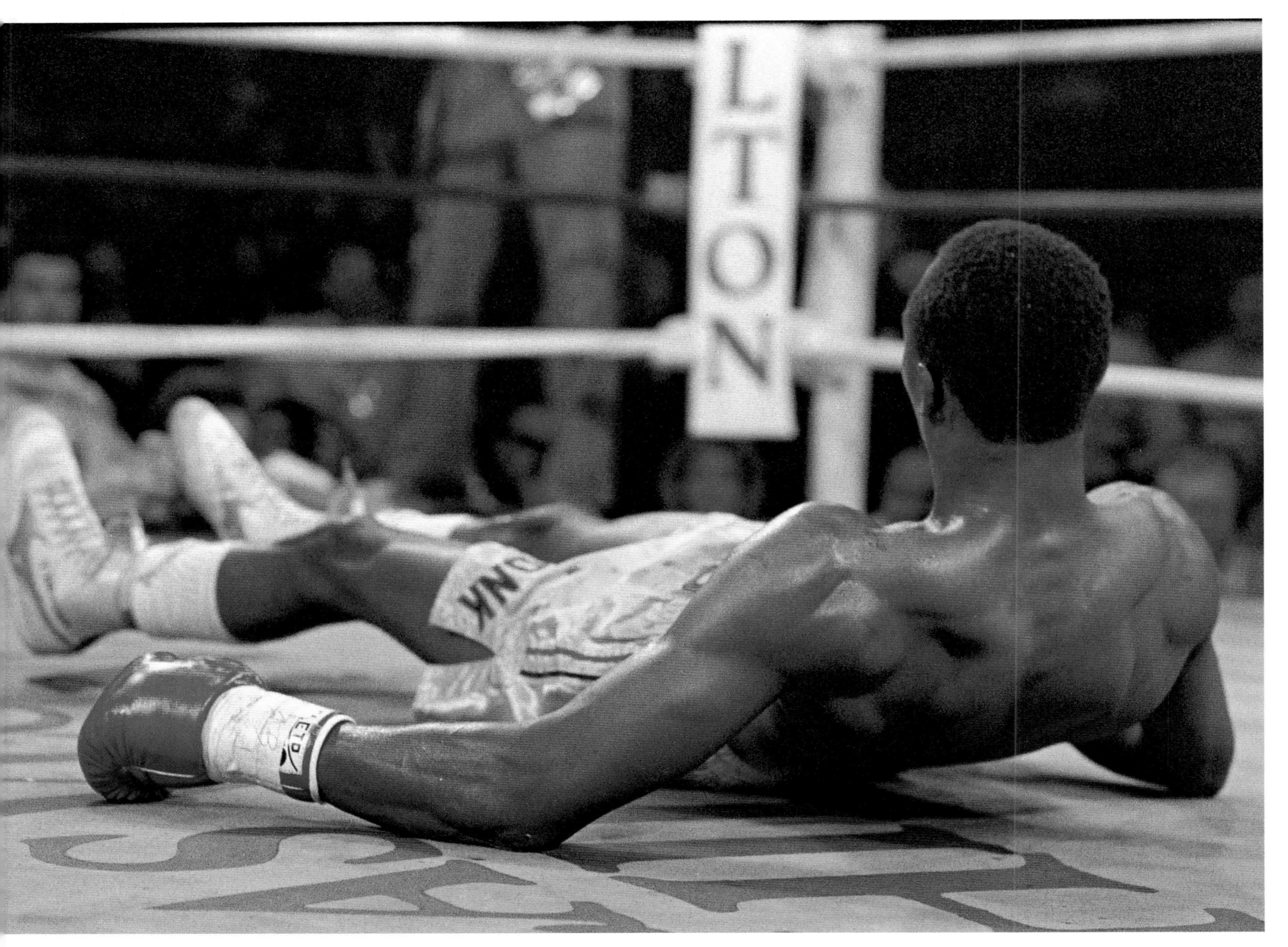

Hearns tried to lift himself from the canvas, then rolled over to try and push himself up ...

ILTON
RONK

Hearns fell again, and he had to be carried back to his corner like a rag doll, the loser of one of the most thrilling eight minutes and one second in boxing history.

"I haven't seen that much action in three rounds ever," Steele said.

Hearns was taken to his room to recover before meeting the press. He was disheartened, but wanted to know something.

"Was it a good fight?" he asked Steward. "Did the fans get their money's worth?"

Steward assured Hearns they did, then told him not to say anything about his broken hand. A few days later he returned to Detroit and had it put in a cast.

"That's why Tommy Hearns could lose a fight and go back two months later and outsell guys who won fights," Steward said. "He gave the fans their money's worth and didn't make excuses."

Hagler had made the best of a chance he had been waiting years for. He was the middleweight champion but had always felt unappreciated and complained after he stopped Roldan at the Hilton hotel a year earlier that both Hearns and Leonard were ducking him.

"How long do I have to put out the challenge?" he asked.

Hearns answered the challenge only to go down in the third round of a fight that would become legendary. It seemed that Leonard, though, would stay in retirement and never give Hagler the fight he had craved for years.

Leonard had announced his retirement as the undisputed welterweight champion in November 1982, six months after he underwent surgery to fix a detached retina. Then, amid much public criticism and worry that he would lose his eyesight, he came back in May 1984 to stop journeyman Kevin Howard.

The plan was that the Howard fight would be a tune-up for a challenge to Hagler for the middleweight title. But Leonard again announced his retirement, and the fight seemed doomed.

Two and a half years later, Leonard made a dramatic announcement. He was returning to boxing to fight Hagler on April 6, 1987, at Caesars Palace.

"I don't want a career," Leonard said. "I want one fight."

The two boxers went on a 12-city tour to promote the fight, at one point appearing with Bob Hope at Caesars to listen to the comedian describe the bout as a "fight for the common man . . . two millionaires trying to beat each others' brains out."

During the tour, Leonard was careful not to say anything bad about Hagler. He didn't want to upset him, didn't want to give him a reason to train even harder for the fight.

"I was having fun using psychological warfare," Leonard said. "I never said anything to piss him off or make him dislike me. Fighters like Hagler and Duran must create aggression to get motivated and train hard. If I never activated that, he couldn't feed off of it."

Indeed, Leonard went out of his way to thank Hagler for giving him an opportunity to fight. He called him a great champion and a fine person. Hagler couldn't stand the compliments. He quit the tour, and Leonard was already one round ahead.

The name for the fight was "Destiny at Caesars—The Super Fight," and there was every indication it would be just that.

Hagler had desperately sought the fight, but Leonard wanted it just as much. For once, Leonard was taking less money—$11 million to $12 million for Hagler—so he could have his first megafight since beating Hearns six years earlier.

"It got to a point when I announced I wanted to fight Hagler that people saw it as justification I was crazy and had really lost it," Leonard said. "As time went on and we were promoting the fight people saw I could beat him. Whether I could pull it off they didn't know."

Leonard was moving up in weight and had fought only once in the previous five years. Both fighters were aging, but Hagler still appeared at the top of his game.

Leonard was 41 days shy of his 31st birthday and Hagler was 47 days short from what he

It was to no avail, though, as he fell back and was counted out by referee Richard Steele.

said would be his 33rd birthday, though many felt that Marvelous Marvin was three or four years older.

One interested observer was Hearns, who had lost to both Hagler and Leonard.

Hearns thought there was no way Hagler could be as aggressive against Leonard as he was against him. He also thought he had taken a lot out of the Marvelous One, even by losing.

"Another fight like that would kill him," Hearns said.

The arena at Caesars was jammed full of the usual mix of the beautiful and famous, and Leonard was the clear crowd favorite when he stepped into the ring.

Unlike his fight against Hearns, Hagler came out passive and tried to box with Leonard. As the rounds piled up, it looked like a big mistake.

"I recall going back to the corner after Round 3 and looking at people in the audience and there was a look of amazement I was still there," Leonard said. "Then by the eighth round, they were thinking, holy cow, it could be an upset."

Hagler grew increasingly desperate as the fight went on, chasing Leonard, who landed flurries of light punches to his head. Leonard wasn't hurting Hagler, but he was scoring enough to win rounds.

When it was over, both fighters threw their arms up in victory. The split decision went to Leonard.

Hagler was devastated.

"I told you about Las Vegas," he said. "They stole it."

Hagler would never fight again, taking his riches and moving to Italy to begin a film career.

Marvelous Marvin Hagler's power was just too much for Thomas Hearns, who desperately tried to hold him around the neck, but couldn't escape his right hand in the thrilling middleweight title fight.

Leonard would return for fights against Donny Lalonde and Hearns, but his career had peaked, too.

"It was without question my biggest win," Leonard said. "Tommy Hearns was awesome, but without question that fight was huge for me. It took me to the next level."

Leonard fought only four times in Las Vegas in the '80s, but they were all memorable. Hearns would fight nine times in Fight Town during the decade, twice against Leonard.

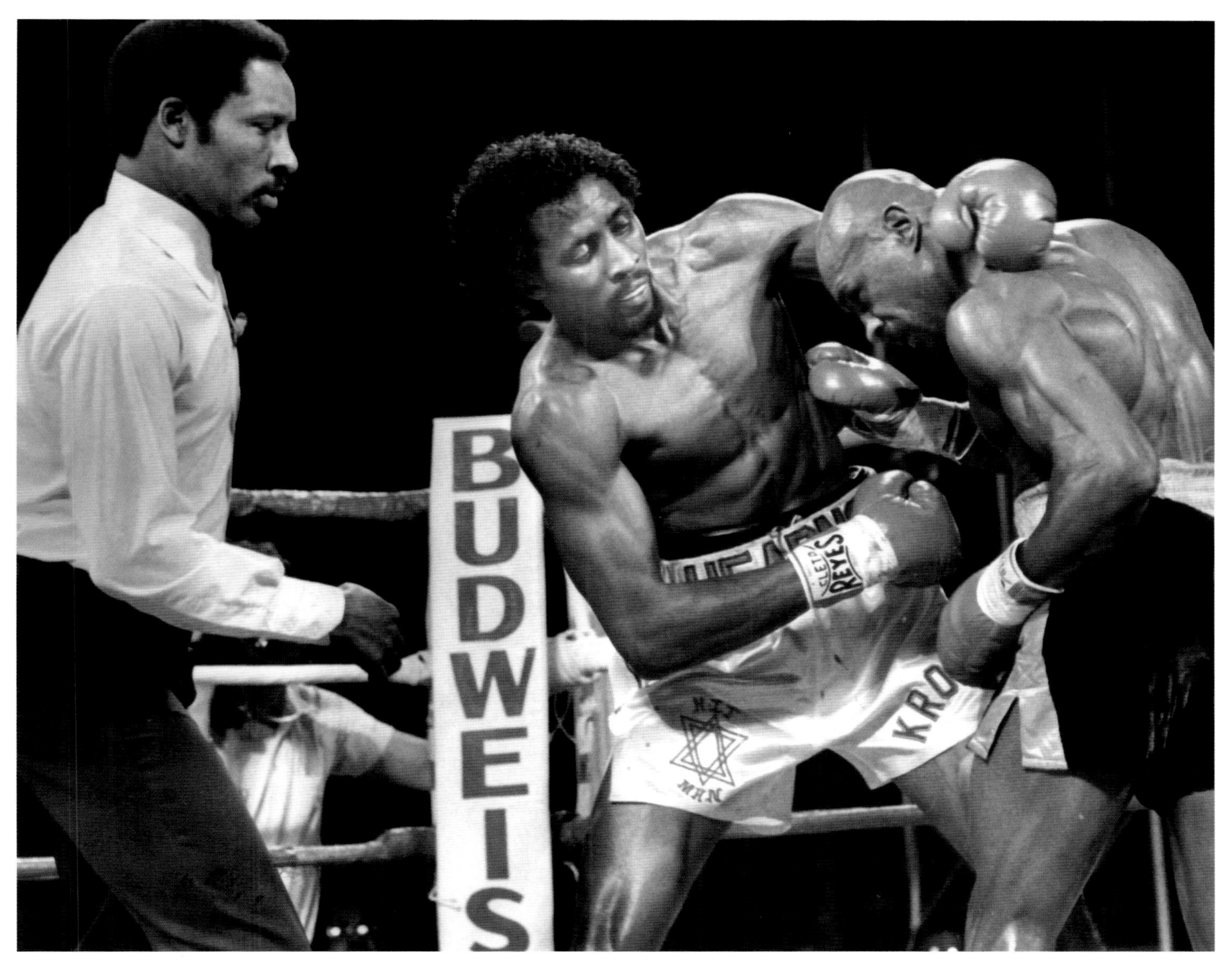

In a decade that saw the rise of Mike Tyson and the dominance of Larry Holmes, the really big fights took place from 147 to 160 pounds. Almost all were in Las Vegas; most under the stars at Caesars Palace.

Among them were:

LEONARD-HEARNS II—Eight years after they first met, Leonard and Hearns got together June 12, 1989, for one last go at each other. Promoter Bob Arum tried to hype the fight by calling it "The War" and showing scenes of war battles during pre-fight press conferences.

If this was war, it was between two aging warriors.

Leonard was a faded fighter, but Hearns was in even worse shape. In his three previous fights, Hearns was knocked out once and hurt badly in the other two.

"There is speculation that Thomas Hearns is shot and Ray Leonard is slower," Leonard said before the fight. He didn't know how accurate the speculation was.

Before a crowd of 12,064 outdoors at Caesars, the two fighters turned back the clock in one last shot at glory. Hearns was desperate to get revenge, and even more desperate to prove he could still fight.

And fight he did, knocking Leonard down in the third and 11th rounds and controlling the fight. But Leonard rallied in the last two minutes of the fight to get a 10-8 round on one scorecard that salvaged a draw.

Leonard had been a 3-1 favorite, but most of those at ringside thought Hearns had easily won. So did Leonard, who embraced his old foe in the ring after the final round.

"Tommy, you won the fight," Leonard said.

"If you think that, why don't you make that public," Hearns replied.

"Don't push it," Leonard said.

LEONARD-DURAN III—The Mirage Hotel and Casino was opening, and there was nothing owner Steve Wynn wanted more than a big fight to kick things off. On a freezing December night, all he got were two big names.

Leonard figured he had one more fight in him and Duran knew he had something to prove, nine years after he said "No Mas" to Leonard in their second fight. Each had won a fight in their prime, but the rubber match would take place long after both should have retired.

TOMMY'S HAIR

Tommy Hearns liked to get his hair done on the day of a big fight. It was part of looking good when he went into the ring. His trainer, Emanuel Steward, never liked it. After losses to Sugar Ray Leonard and Marvelous Marvin Hagler, he began to feel Hearns might be like Samson and lose his strength when he had his hair cut.

For the second fight with Leonard, Hearns had his hairdresser set to come up to his suite at Caesars Palace and do his hair the day of the fight. When he arrived, though, Steward sent him away. "I told Tommy, 'I feel you never had your strength and for whatever reason I don't want you to get your hair cut,'" Steward said. "I gave the guy $200 and said, 'Leave him alone.'" Hearns had one of his better fights that night, knocking Leonard down twice in a fight that was ruled a draw.

When it was over, referee Richard Steele held Hearns and signaled the fight to an end. Hagler was held aloft in victory by his trainers, Pat and Goody Petronelli.

MARVIN'S MONEY

Some fighters blew their money. Marvelous Marvin Hagler had trouble spending any of his.

Hagler would earn more than $10 million knocking out Thomas Hearns in their epic middleweight clash April 15, 1985. You wouldn't have known it by the size of his entourage or his suite at Caesars Palace.

While Hearns arrived early and was seen strolling the hotel grounds with dozens of people wearing gold and red Kronk jackets following him around, Hagler came to Caesars just in time for the final prefight press conference and promptly asked for a room away from everyone and the worst suite in the house.

He got it, in a bank of first floor rooms just off the elevator that were so little used that even Caesars boxing executive Bob Halloran didn't know where they were.

Hagler got a room to himself, but, ever so thrifty, had his trainers, Goody and Pat Petronelli, share one together. Ditto for his two sparring partners. And, just in case they had any ideas, Hagler had the hotel switch off the long distance just in case they tried to do something funny like make a long distance call that might cost him a few bucks.

After winning the biggest fight of his life, Hagler was in a mood to celebrate. A little while later he went down to dance with fans at a party in a hotel ballroom, but now Hagler was with the Petronellis and less than a dozen other people. The spread wasn't much, just a few Diet Cokes and water. Hagler, after all, knew a few things about hotel room service prices.

Halloran came by to congratulate Hagler on his win and thought the champion ought to have a little something more to celebrate with. He picked up the phone, called room service and had them send up six bottles of Dom Perignon for a proper toast to the winner.

While waiting for room service, Hagler handed out rings he had made to the Petronellis. He gave the gloves he used in the fight to Halloran. The champagne came, and there were toasts all around.

"I had no idea this was so good," said Hagler, never much of a drinker.

A month later, Halloran was in his office when the phone rang. It was Hagler, calling from his home and highly agitated.

"I got this bill for $1,300 from Caesars for champagne," Hagler told Halloran. "What should I do? I'm shaking."

Hagler was a multimillionaire, but unlike many fighters he was determined to stay that way. He wasn't about to buy a round of drinks, much less a half dozen bottles of fine champagne.

Marvelous Marvin Hagler lands a right hand as he chases Sugar Ray Leonard around the ring at Caesars Palace. Leonard danced, mugged and fought brilliantly at times, frustrating Hagler to win an upset decision. Hagler was so bitter about the loss that he quit boxing and moved to Italy, where he made Western movies.

Wynn built an outdoor stadium behind the new hotel for the December 7, 1989, fight, but many wished he hadn't. It was so cold the night of the fight that Leonard asked if he could fight in ski pants.

"I've never been so cold," Leonard said. "I didn't even know it got that cold in Vegas. I thought it was the desert."

Leonard came into the ring in a karate-style outfit, with a knit ski hat to keep his head warm. Between rounds, his cornermen piled blankets on top of him as he sat shivering.

"I wanted to say let's cut it short by five rounds," Leonard said. "I think everybody would have agreed with that."

Duran didn't have as much trouble with the cold, but he had plenty with Leonard. Leonard proved in their second fight he could easily outbox and frustrate Duran, and he did it again in the rubber match.

Leonard danced and boxed and moved to pile up points. It was a virtual repeat of their second fight, except this time Duran didn't say "No Mas."

The only real excitement came in the 11th round when Leonard, hearing the crowd booing the lack of real action, mixed it up with Duran and came out of it cut badly around both eyes. Blood flowed down his face and he would need 50 stitches to close the wound.

Leonard wanted to make Duran quit again, but he settled for a lopsided unanimous decision that Wynn topped off with a massive fireworks show above the hotel.

It seemed symbolic for Leonard's last hurrah in a city that meant so much to his career.

"Every one of my big fights was in Las Vegas," Leonard said. "I loved it there."

HEARNS-DURAN—The Hit Man was at his devastating best against a legend who had no answer for his long arms and power.

Hearns was dominating fighters once again after recovering from his 1981 loss to Leonard when he and Duran met June 15, 1984, at Caesars Palace. He towered over Duran and had an 11-inch reach advantage, two things that made him a favorite to keep his WBC 154-

"Every one of my big fights was in Las Vegas," Leonard said. "I loved it there."

pound title.

Hearns smashed Duran to the canvas three times and stopped him at 1:07 of the second round with a sensational right hand.

"What did I do wrong?" Duran asked someone as he left the ring.

It wasn't what Duran did wrong, but what Hearns did right. Hearns hurt him with a minute to go in the first round and then put Duran down for only the third time in his career.

Duran got up but he never stood a chance. He was on shaky legs in the second round when Hearns trapped him in a corner and worked him over, then finished him with a crushing right hand that dropped Duran on his face.

"The right in the second round was probably the best right of my career," Hearns said.

HEARNS-BARKLEY—By the time of this June 6, 1988, fight, Hearns had moved up to middleweight and was the WBC champion. He was a 4-1 favorite over Iran "The Blade" Barkley, and confident he would retain his title at the Las Vegas Hilton.

For two rounds, it looked like an easy night for the Hit Man, who hammered Barkley with left hooks to the body and head, opening up a cut over the challenger's left eye and bloodying his mouth.

Between rounds, Barkley's corner urged him to put more pressure on Hearns, who seemed not to take Barkley too seriously.

"You want me to go for it right now?" Barkley asked his corner, who told him to do just that.

Late in the third round, Barkley countered a left hook with a crushing right hand that landed on Hearns's jaw. Hearns dropped to the canvas, managing to struggle to his feet at the count of eight.

But a Barkley combination put him through the ropes and referee Richard Steele finally stopped the fight at 2:39 of the third round.

"Now I know how my opponents feel when I hit them," Hearns said.

LEONARD-LALONDE—This fight was always more hype than substance, and fans seemed to see through it. There were a lot of empty seats at Caesars Palace on November 7, 1988, when Leonard tried to claim Lalonde's light heavyweight title and a new super middleweight crown at the same time.

Lalonde was promoted as the "Golden Boy" and he looked the part with long, blond hair. He was bigger than Leonard, but he hadn't fought nearly the opposition that Leonard had.

"I'm fighting a welterweight, an old welterweight," Lalonde said.

Lalonde knocked Leonard down in the fourth round, but Leonard came back to knock Lalonde down twice and end the fight in the ninth round.

"That was just to add to my resume," Leonard said later.

Leonard's career ended, for all intents and purposes, when he was badly beaten by Terry Norris. He came back six years later for an ill-advised comeback fight against Hector "Macho" Camacho that went even worse.

Today, he promotes fights and is still sought after by fans. When they talk about his career, though, they don't mention Norris and Camacho.

"This will tell you the impact Vegas boxing history has," Leonard said. "People ask me about my last fight and the first thing I say is it wasn't a good day. They say, 'What do you mean? You beat Lalonde and had a draw with Hearns.' They think those were my last fights because they were in Vegas and Norris and Camacho weren't."

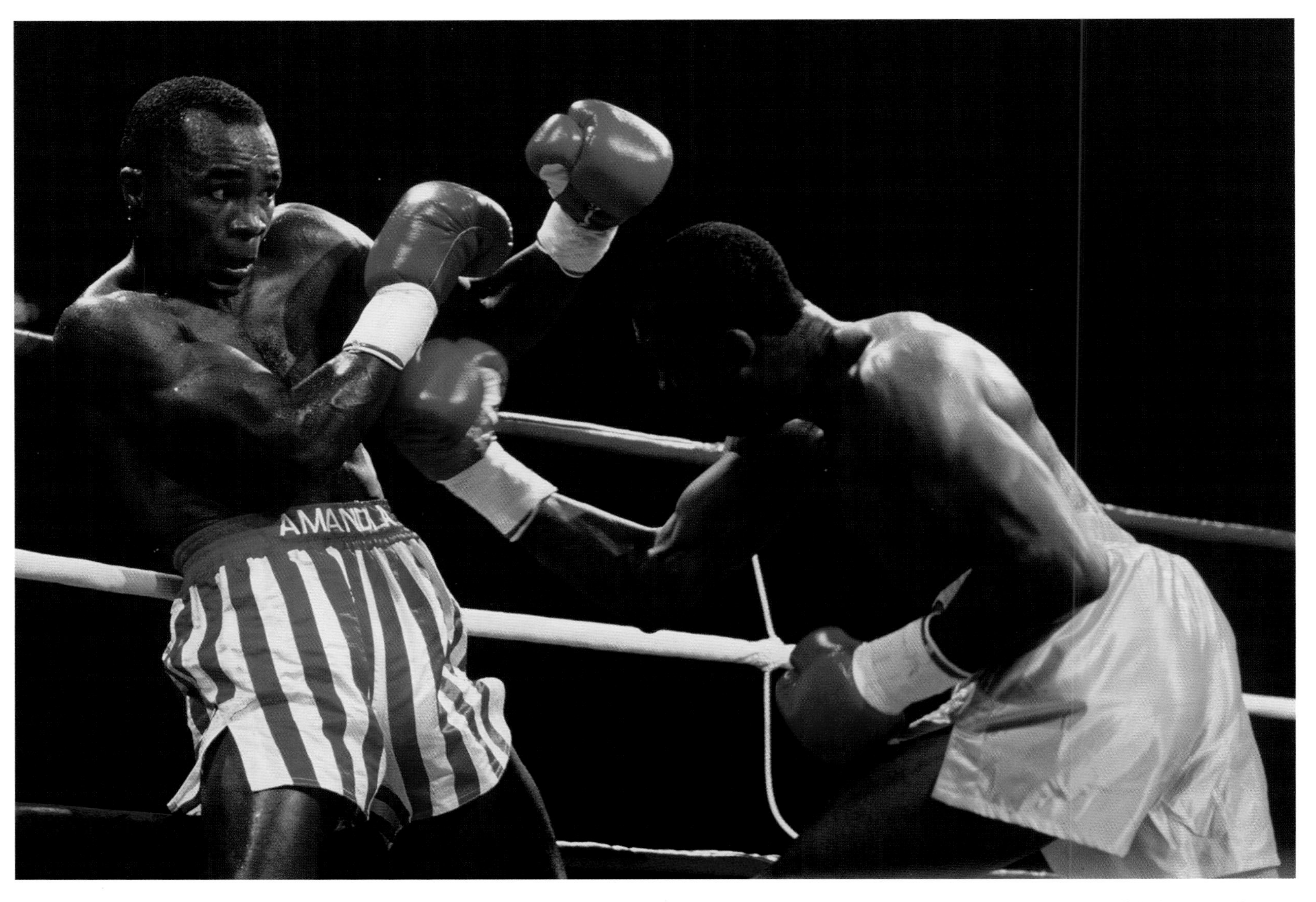

What Thomas Hearns couldn't do the first time they met in 1981, he was more successful eight years later when he knocked Leonard down twice in the fight. Hearns couldn't do what he desperately wanted, though, which was to get a win over his nemesis. Though most in the crowd thought he won the fight, the judges scored it a draw.

LEONARD'S FIGHT FACE

Sugar Ray Leonard was having trouble getting his fight face on. He was due to meet Thomas Hearns for the second time when he heard the news that Hearns' brother had been involved in a shooting in Detroit.

At the weigh-in for the fight at Caesars Palace, Leonard felt he had to say something to Hearns.

"I told him I was very sorry what happened with his brother and, 'God bless you,'" Leonard said. "It was totally out of my character. I was trying not to like the guy and was feeling sorry for him."

Hearns went into seclusion in the days before the fight, but came out and knocked Leonard down twice in a bout that was ruled a draw.

His brother, Henry Hearns, was later convicted of second-degree murder in the shooting of a 19-year-old woman and sentenced to 20 years in prison. Henry Hearns was a security guard at his brother's Detroit home at the time of the shooting.

Tommy Hearns later paid the victim's family $685,000 in a wrongful death suit.

BOOKIES BREATHE EASIER

Sugar Ray Leonard wasn't the only person to breathe a big sigh of relief when the judges gave him a draw in his second fight with Thomas Hearns. Each time Leonard got knocked down, Las Vegas bookmakers feared they would be taking a bath.

Hearns was a 3-1 underdog in the June 12, 1989, fight, which came eight years after Leonard stopped him in the 14th round of their first fight. But a rush of late money, much of it from Hearns's home town of Detroit, was bet on the Hit Man. For its own sake, the sports books needed Leonard to win and badly.

Leonard managed a draw with a 10-8 final round on one scorecard, and bettors lined up to get back the estimated $15 million they had wagered. At the Sands Hotel and Casino, bettors were in line until 2 a.m. getting their money back.

Bookmakers were glad to give out the refunds. If Hearns had won, they would have lost millions. Oddsmakers had learned their lessons. After the fight ended they put up odds making Leonard only a 7-5 favorite if the two boxers met again.

Promoting a fight wasn't always fun and games, and Marvelous Marvin Hagler hated it more than anything. Still, he manages to don a chef's hat and smile while carving a piece of turkey with Sugar Ray Leonard to promote their 1987 fight at Caesars Palace. Hagler wasn't smiling afterward, losing the fight on a disputed decision to Leonard that prompted him to hang his gloves up for good.

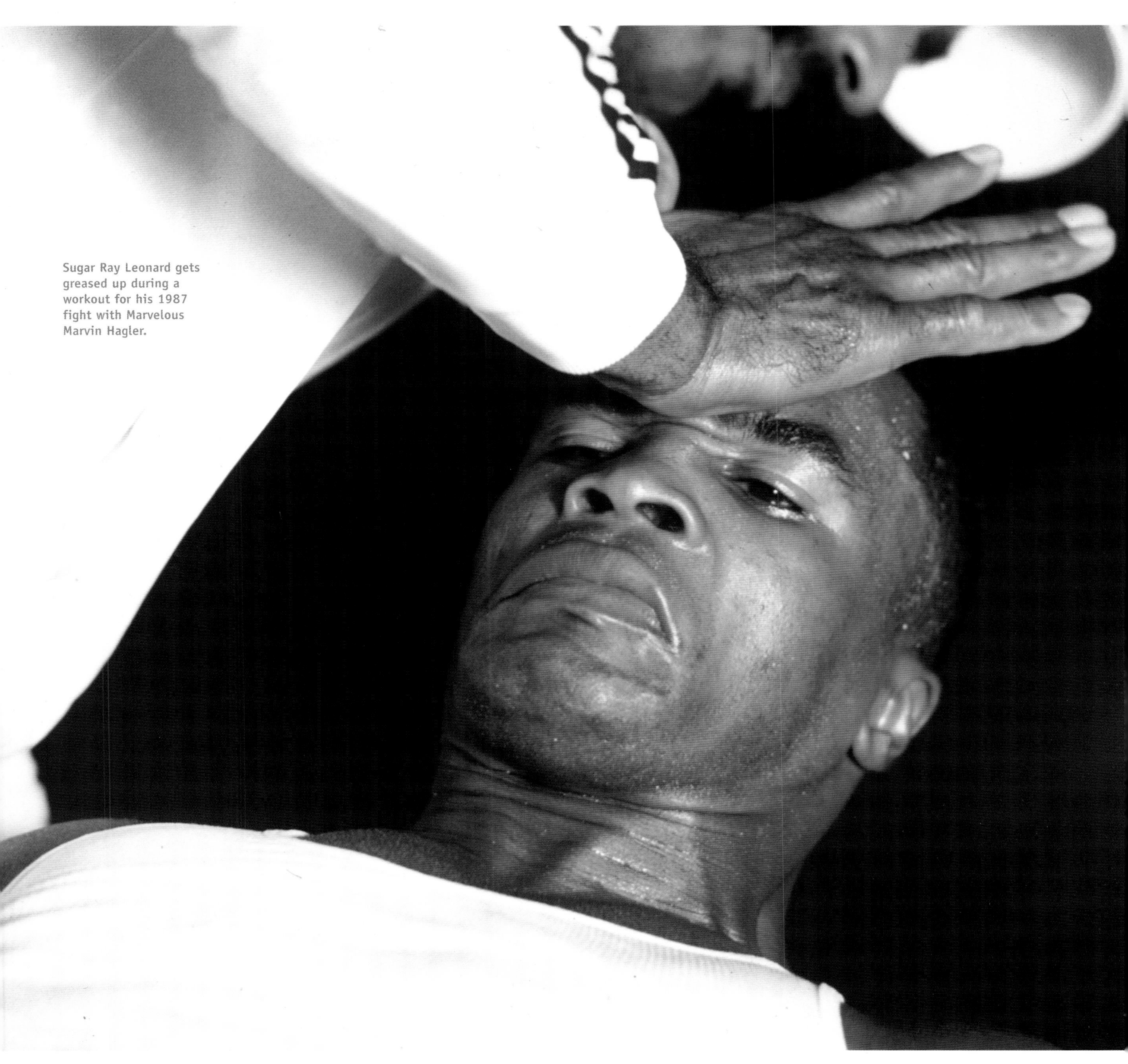

Sugar Ray Leonard gets greased up during a workout for his 1987 fight with Marvelous Marvin Hagler.

6 >> A PLACE TO FIGHT

Don King had just finished promoting a Larry Holmes fight and he and Caesars Palace owner Cliff Perlman were having a few drinks at the hotel's Galleria Bar when talk turned to a possible megafight between Holmes and Gerry Cooney

"This fight will be so big we could put it on the moon," said King, never one to shy away from hyperbole, Perlman hardly blinked.

"Well, Don," he said, "then we'll build you the moon."

Caesars didn't quite reach to the moon, but the hotel did build the biggest outdoor arena ever for a fight in Las Vegas. Muhammad Ali and Holmes drew 24,570 in a temporary arena two years ago, but for Holmes-Cooney in June 1982 Caesars erected bleachers that would hold 30,000.

Every seat was sold, with the crowd of 29,214 setting a record for the biggest Las Vegas fight ever. Hundreds of fans who couldn't get tickets tried to peer into the arena from a nearby freeway interchange, while thousands of others watched the fight on closed circuit in other Strip hotels.

Though the arena was torn down after the fight, it would be replaced by a semi-permanent outdoor arena that seated about 15,000 and would become the place to fight over the next decade with some of the era's greatest fighters performing on its raised canvas.

Sugar Ray Leonard, Marvelous Marvin Hagler, Tommy Hearns, Mike Tyson, Evander Holyfield and others fought beneath the giant American flag that hung down from the adjacent hotel tower. Hagler and Leonard and Hagler and Hearns staged memorable duels, and Oscar De La Hoya became a primetime attraction outdoors on the Strip.

That arena, too, was finally torn down after the De La Hoya-Julio Cesar Chavez fight in June 1996 to make way for an enlarged pool and garden area. With the resort's shed-like but cozy pavilion also demolished, the hotel gradually gave up its spot as the premier place for fights to new indoor arenas built at the MGM Grand and Mandalay Bay.

For nearly two decades, though, Caesars reigned as the epicenter of boxing. It replaced Madison Square Garden as the site of the biggest fights, hosting more than 160 championship bouts.

"They realized with Ali-Holmes and Leonard-Hearns that this was a great, great business," fight promoter Bob Arum said. "The real visionaries were Caesars and Cliff Perlman. Cliff really started the outdoor fights and all that."

Perlman really didn't have much choice. He and his sports director, Bob Halloran, had won the rights to hold the October 2, 1980 heavyweight title fight between Holmes and Ali and they quickly realized that the demand for seats would be far greater than what was available in the small pavilion.

Perlman and Halloran considered the Convention Center rotunda, but that was also too small. They thought of UNLV's football stadium, but it was too far away from the strip to bring gamblers back and forth.

"Let's put it in the parking lot," Perlman told Halloran.

"Great," Halloran said, "I know a guy who can get the bleachers."

Today, building codes probably wouldn't allow the temporary structure. But the fight was simply too big to put anywhere else, and

Legendary trainer Johnny Tocco takes a break ringside at his gym on Charleston Boulevard. The Ringside Gym was tiny, dark and a throwback to boxing gyms of old, but it drew a clientele that included the likes of Mike Tyson, Bernard Hopkins and Marvelous Marvin Hagler. Tocco worked with many world champions, and was close to Sonny Liston, Larry Holmes and Michael Dokes in the 40 years he ran the gym. He died in 1997 at the age of 87, and the city of Las Vegas later honored his memory with a "Johnny Tocco Day."

JEFF SCHEID—LAS VEGAS REVIEW-JOURNAL

BOAT!
STARLING
MORGAN
RINGSIDE

"It was the most unbelievable atmosphere. It was almost like a cock fight atmosphere," Arum said. "Everybody was almost hovered over the ring. The stands were rickety and made noise."

Boxing made strange bedfellows, and it was never stranger when promoters Don King and Bob Arum got together occasionally to make a few bucks. Here, King appears to be making a point to Arum, who has a point or two of his own to answer with. Watching the two biggest promoters is trainer Angelo Dundee. King and Arum didn't do business together often, but did put on a few fights, including the Oscar De La Hoya-Felix Trinidad bout in 1999. Arum always kept a close eye on King, remembering how the spiky-haired promoter tried to climb in the ring and steal his spotlight after Sugar Ray Leonard beat Marvelous Marvin Hagler in 1987, only to have Arum and a security guard throw him out.

Las Vegas wanted it desperately. Caesars built the arena in 30 days at a cost of $750,000, chump change when the tickets were added up and the live gate was $5.7 million—the biggest in the history of boxing up to that time.

Caesars had paid a site fee of around $2.5 million—big money at the time—and Halloran figured that if even half the tickets were sold the hotel would at least break even. The fight hit a home run, and Caesars won both at the box office and in its jam-packed casino.

Much to the relief of everyone, the bleachers stayed up.

"Despite some people's misgivings, the bleachers didn't collapse and there were no accidents or problems," Caesars vice president Harry Wald said a day after the fight.

Caesars liked the arena so much it had Frank Sinatra play there two days later in an outdoor concert, a bonus that kept big gamblers around for the weekend. And gamble they did. During the 30-day period surrounding the fight, Caesars took in $30 million from table games and slot machines, two and a half times the monthly average and more than any similar period in the hotel's history.

Caesars had sent out invitations to 2,000 of its so-called "Noble Friends," high-rollers who could be counted on to spend freely at the table in exchange for a ticket to the fight. Seven hundred of them accepted the offer, and the city's reputation as a boxing mecca was about to be hatched.

The action was so good—with the minimum at blackjack tables raised to $25 and not a seat at be had—that other hotels soon wanted a piece of the action, too. Even the fading Riviera got into the act by building an outdoor arena where Larry Holmes lost his heavyweight title to Michael Spinks.

It wasn't always easy to be outside, though. At the Dunes, which was later imploded to make way for the Bellagio, a series of early 1980s fight cards were memorable only because of the weather.

Ol' Blue Eyes loved a good fight, and like to have fun with fighters. Here, Frank Sinatra playfully jabs with Esteban DeJesus before his January 21, 1978 fight with Roberto Duran for the lightweight title. DeJesus was the WBC champion and Duran held the WBA title when they met in the Caesars Palace pavilion. Duran stopped Dejesus in the 12th round to avenge a loss four years earlier to the Puerto Rican champion. DeJesus would later be ravaged by drugs and AIDS, and died in prison a decade later in Puerto Rico.

"Hot" is how Holmes remembers his fight with Tim Witherspoon at the Dunes on a warm May night in 1983.

Others hotels came and went as challengers to Caesars' reign as a boxing mecca, but for several years the Las Vegas Hilton tried the hardest.

There was nothing better than a big fight to lure big gamblers to the casino, and no one knew that better than Barron Hilton.

Hilton spent millions to get Muhammad Ali to defend his heavyweight title against Leon Spinks in 1978, and landed the 1986 Mike Tyson-Trevor Berbick fight that made Tyson the youngest heavyweight champion ever.

After that fight, the 20-year-old Tyson walked through the Hilton's casino in overalls, with the flashy green WBC belt around his waist.

Promoters knew one thing—it wasn't hard finding hotels eager to try their hand at boxing. Fights generated a buzz and they attracted gamblers. It wasn't unusual for high rollers to bring $1 million in cash to gamble over a fight weekend, and the craps tables and baccarat pits were always busy places.

Over the years, fights were held in parking lots, ballrooms, showrooms, temporary arenas and even the UNLV basketball arena. They were staged in 110-degree heat, pouring rain and winds that sent grandstands rocking.

Nothing compared, though, with the atmosphere inside an oversized metal shed that actually began as an indoor tennis pavilion behind Caesars Palace. Here, some of the biggest fighters in the game engaged in memorable bouts.

The Caesars Sports Pavilion had folding chairs on the floor, roll-up bleachers against the walls and the mixed smell of fighters, blood, perfume and steaming hot dogs wafting around the ring. To find the place in a corner of the hotel's property just off Interstate 15, fans had to walk from the hotel through people sunning at poolside and then past the tennis courts.

The pavilion had nothing, and it had everything. Bare bones and intimate, it was a fight fan's delight. Every fan felt like he was sitting at ringside.

"It was the most unbelievable atmosphere. It was almost like a cock fight atmosphere," Arum said. "Everybody was almost hovered over the ring. The stands were rickety and made noise."

Though it opened in 1975 with Rod Laver playing Jimmy Connors in what was billed the "heavyweight championship of tennis," it didn't take long for the pavilion to find its real role.

George Foreman and Ron Lyle met there on January 24, 1976, in one of the first big fights ever staged at a Las Vegas hotel. Foreman stopped Lyle in the fifth round of a slugfest that not only inaugurated the shed, but set the tone for some great fights ahead.

Two years later, Larry Holmes fought Ken Norton there in one of the great heavyweight title fights ever. Sugar Ray Leonard barely beat Wilfredo Benitez for the welterweight title, while Marvelous Marvin Hagler, Oscar De La Hoya and Thomas Hearns all plied their trade inside a building that barely seated 4,000.

"It was the best place in the world to watch a fight," Arum said. "There was nothing like it before and nothing like it since."

When the fights were too big for the pavilion, Caesars turned it into a training facility and pressroom for the outdoor spectacles. Ali and Holmes trained there before their fight and so did Leonard and Hearns before their first meeting in 1981.

Part of the building's charm was there was no VIP section, no special seating. Everyone sat on flimsy chairs or in the bleachers, while Caesars' top-heavy cocktail waitresses trolled the aisles selling drinks.

"It was a throwback to the old days of boxing when you had what were known as smokers," Halloran said. "You'd smell the smoke, the noise was huge and every seat was a good seat. It was the place where everything started."

A mariachi band blared in the ring before Salvador Sanchez fought Wilfredo Gomez there in one of the first big Latin fights. Roberto Duran fought Ivan DeJesus, and Holmes traded bombs with Earnie Shavers.

The atmosphere was electric, and the fighters rarely disappointed.

"It was just remarkable what they were able to accomplish with what amounted to a storage facility," said matchmaker Bobby Goodman. "It was a closely knit arena without a bad seat. When you think of the big fights they had in there, it was just amazing."

The pavilion was small, but there were fights held around town in a lot smaller places.

At the tiny Castaways, which was later demolished to make room for the Mirage, Bill Miller used to put on the "Strip Fight of the Week" series in the even tinier showroom. The cards didn't last long, though, mostly because the fights in the early 1960s were mismatches.

Times were good when new heavyweight champion Buster Douglas walked through The Mirage with manager John Johnson and hotel owner Steve Wynn.

JIM LAURIE—LAS VEGAS REVIEW-JOURNAL

BURNED BY THE FIGHTS

It's hard to burn a Las Vegas casino, but the fight business can be risky, even for those who make a living off of gambling. The Las Vegas Hilton learned that lesson in 1989 when it spent millions for the heavyweight title fight between Mike Tyson and Frank Bruno.

Tyson was coming off of his savage first-round knockout of Michael Spinks, and the Las Vegas Hilton thought it pulled off a coup when it landed the fight for the pricey sum of $7 million. But the Englishman Bruno wasn't seen as much of an opponent, and only a few thousand people bothered to buy tickets. Hotel executives learned a brutal lesson in fight economics: You can't find enough high-rolling gamblers to cover a $4 million loss at the gate. The experience caused the Las Vegas Hilton to back out of bidding for some fights and scale back the number of fights the hotel had planned to host.

Steve Wynn also found that out when he opened The Mirage and reportedly lost millions in the opening fight, Sugar Ray Leonard's third fight with Roberto Duran. The experience didn't deter Wynn, who wooed James "Buster" Douglas after he shocked the boxing world by knocking out Tyson in Japan. Wynn paid Douglas $24 million, part of $40 million sum The Mirage invested in the October 25, 1990, fight between Douglas and Evander Holyfield.

Wynn envisioned it as a two-fight deal, with Douglas meeting Tyson in a rematch after beating Holyfield. But Douglas came in fat and lazy, and Holyfield knocked him out in the third round with a single punch to the nose. The Mirage lost about $5 million on the promotion, though enough big gamblers turned out to help Wynn justify the cost.

Wynn was so furious with Douglas that he suggested future fights be held as winner-take-all to give a boxer more incentive to win. "I don't think anyone would pay $5 to see him fight again," spokesman Alan Feldman said of Douglas after the fight. The Mirage held some more fights, but it soon tore down the outdoor stadium behind the hotel and got out of the boxing business for good.

A DRINKING MAN'S GAME

If Caesars Palace was the center of the boxing world in its prime, the Galleria Bar inside Caesars was the center of the center of the boxing world.

The Galleria was just inside the main entrance and, like much in real estate, owed everything to its location. To get almost anywhere in the hotel at the time you had to walk by the Galleria, and those in the fight scene were drawn to the bar like moths to a flame.

Don King held court in the back, while boxing writers tossed down drinks up front. To the writers who liked to watch the Caesars cocktail goddesses work their magic from the bar, it was known as the Gonorrhea Bar.

For years King's matchmaker, Bobby Goodman, would meet with Caesars fight honcho Ron Amos in the back of the bar, where there were two stools next to a telephone.

At 5 p.m. sharp every day they would be there to work out some of the thousands of details of a major fight card.

"That would be our office the rest of the day," Goodman said. "We'd resolve a lot of things. We knew what we'd be doing the rest of the day."

One night Goodman and King were drinking at the bar with the late Duke Durden, a member of the Nevada Athletic Commission who hated nothing more than promoters who didn't bring fights to Las Vegas.

The three were discussing a heavyweight title defense by Larry Holmes against Earnie Shavers when King mentioned that he had an offer from Egypt for a fight and perhaps it could be held there.

Durden was drinking a cognac and he swirled it around, threw his head back and took one big gulp before slamming the glass down.

"The closest you motherfuckers will get to Egypt is Cleopatra's Bar (another bar at Caesars)," Durden yelled as he stormed out.

King didn't know it, but Durden hadn't gone far. He ran to a house phone to call Holmes.

"These MFs want to take you away from Las Vegas where you won your title and is like a home for you and take you to fight in Egypt," he told Holmes. "Are you gonna let them do that to you, Champ? You wouldn't let them do that would you?"

A short time later, an unknowing King was on the phone to Holmes.

"Hey, Champ, how ya doing?" King said.

"You ain't taking me to no fucking Egypt," Holmes bellowed.

The Gonorrhea—er, the Galleria—wasn't the only place for boxing sorts to drink.

Down the street, just across from the Desert Inn, was the Flame, where Ferd Hernandez used to tend bar and tell stories of his fight with Sugar Ray Robinson. It was there that boxing writers gathered to drink the hours away the week of every major fight.

The Flame was a classic Vegas steakhouse with red booths and meat the same color. Waiters would parade the raw meat on platters for diners to make their selections.

It wasn't the food that drew the boxing crowd, though. At the dimly lit bar, writers would drink through the night, often joined by trainers, commissioners, former fighters and other hangers-on.

The latest information would be traded and debated. Often the phone would ring at the bar with an out-of-town editor looking for his writer.

It was also there that one of the shortest fights in Las Vegas history took place.

It happened on the eve of the Larry Holmes-David Bey heavyweight title fight in 1984, and the occasion was the 50th birthday party of now-retired Associated Press boxing writer Ed Schuyler Jr.

The bar was packed and drinks were flowing. British writers on liberal expense accounts were ordering bottle after bottle of $100 champagne.

Suddenly, the door opened and in hopped a kangaroo. An acquaintance of Schuyler's had arranged with the Circus Circus hotel to bring its boxing kangaroo over as a birthday gag.

Now, the kangaroo had its red gloves on and was facing off against the inebriated Schuyler.

A couple of punches were thrown on each side, and then it was over. Schuyler was judged the loser by decision.

"I had him beat until I called him an animal," Schuyler said.

Boomer the kangaroo can't wait to get in some licks against Ed Schuyler Jr. (holding dice).

JEFF SCHEID—REVIEW-JOURNAL

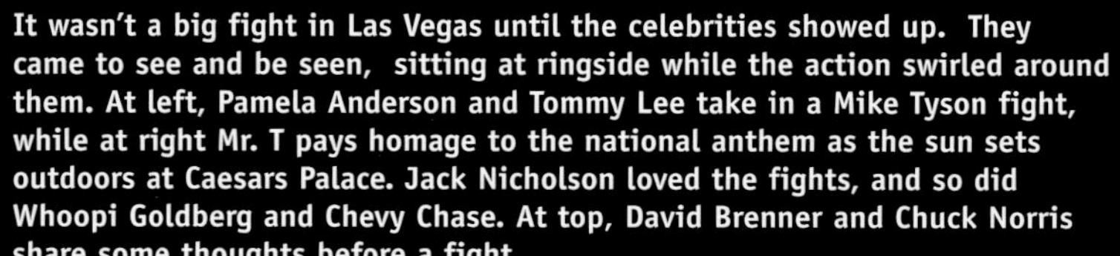

It wasn't a big fight in Las Vegas until the celebrities showed up. They came to see and be seen, sitting at ringside while the action swirled around them. At left, Pamela Anderson and Tommy Lee take in a Mike Tyson fight, while at right Mr. T pays homage to the national anthem as the sun sets outdoors at Caesars Palace. Jack Nicholson loved the fights, and so did Whoopi Goldberg and Chevy Chase. At top, David Brenner and Chuck Norris share some thoughts before a fight.

"The first couple of nights the fights started at 7 p.m. and were over by a quarter to eight," said Art Lurie, who judged more than 200 title fights and served four terms on the Nevada Athletic Commission. "There were four knockouts and the fans weren't happy at all."

One night, Big Train Lincoln and Jimmy Fletcher, both Top 10 heavyweight contenders, met in what couldn't have been more than a 16-foot ring on the showroom stage at the Castaways.

Lincoln and Fletcher were both around 6-foot-5 and 250 pounds, big heavyweights for their day. They looked even bigger in the tiny ring, where the ropes barely reached up to the middle of their backs.

Longtime fight publicist Bill Caplan watched nervously.

"It was a hell of a fight, they went right at each other," Caplan said. "But the ring was shaking and the fear was they were going to flip over the ropes and fall on the people at ringside. You felt like you were watching these two big guys fight in homemade rings in your garage."

Miller eventually moved his weekly Wednesday night fights to the Silver Slipper, where Lurie was working as a food and beverage executive. Lurie couldn't get off to go see the fights at the Castaways, so he talked Miller into moving them to the Silver Slipper.

Casino executives weren't so sure they wanted the fight crowd around, but Lurie persisted and eventually they agreed to one fight card on a trial basis. It was such a success the nightly fights lasted 15 years.

"They would get 700 people and we had the same 700 people every week," Lurie said. "They all had the same seats. Someone had to die before you got their seat."

The first big-name fight in Las Vegas history wasn't held near any casino. It took place May 2, 1955, on the infield at the old Cashman Field just north of downtown, where the city's semipro baseball team played.

In that day it wasn't unusual for ballparks to host fights. Yankee Stadium, the Polo Grounds and Comiskey Park all held title fights on a regular basis. Archie Moore was trying to get

The Castaways and Silver Slipper hosted weekly and monthly fight cards at various times. At the Castaways, fights were held in the small showroom, lending an intimate atmosphere to the whole affair.

George Foreman fights Ron Lyle in the first fight ever held in the Caesars Palace pavilion.

ON THE VERGE OF DISASTER

The first big heavyweight fight at a Strip hotel turned out to be a smashing success. It came close, though, to being a memorable disaster. George oreman was fighting Ron Lyle, Foreman's first fight ince losing to Muhammad Ali 15 months earlier in aire, and Caesars Palace wanted the fight badly.

Hotel executives came up with a plan to stage it in he hotel's new tennis pavilion. A crowd of nearly 5,000 illed the pavilion on January 24, 1976, joined by a ational television audience eager to see if Foreman ould recover from his shocking loss in Zaire. Ali had ecome a fearsome force in the heavyweight division nce again.

The undercard went smoothly enough, up until the last preliminary fight. It was then that the hotel's chief engineer came running up to Caesars Palace publicity director Ron Amos and Jim Deskin of the state's athletic commission at ringside. A main beam holding the ring up on the side of Foreman's corner had cracked, and the engineer wasn't sure it would hold up for another fight. It was too late to find another ring. But canceling the fight wasn't an option, either. ABC was televising the fight and the nation was waiting to watch.

At ringside, they came up with a plan. The final preliminary fight was cut short by a few rounds while three workers crawled under the ring with floor jacks. They stayed under there for the main event, bracing the ring while praying it didn't collapse on top of them.

Lyle soon came into the ring and was jumping up and down in his corner. Then Foreman climbed into the ring and started jumping up and down in his corner. Foreman's trainer, Gil Clancy, looked over at Amos and yelled out, "The fucking corner is going to collapse. What's wrong with it?"

"Nothing," Amos assured him.

Foreman would go on to stop Lyle in a slugfest still regarded as one of the best back-and-forth heavyweight fights of all time. Foreman was knocked down twice in the fourth round only to drop Lyle in the same round. Through it all, the ring held up, but barely.

"We were just praying the whole time," Amos recalled "When the fight ended, Curly, the pavilion engineer, came running up to me and said, 'Thank God. One more round and that ring would have folded up like an accordion.'"

CAESARS PALACE

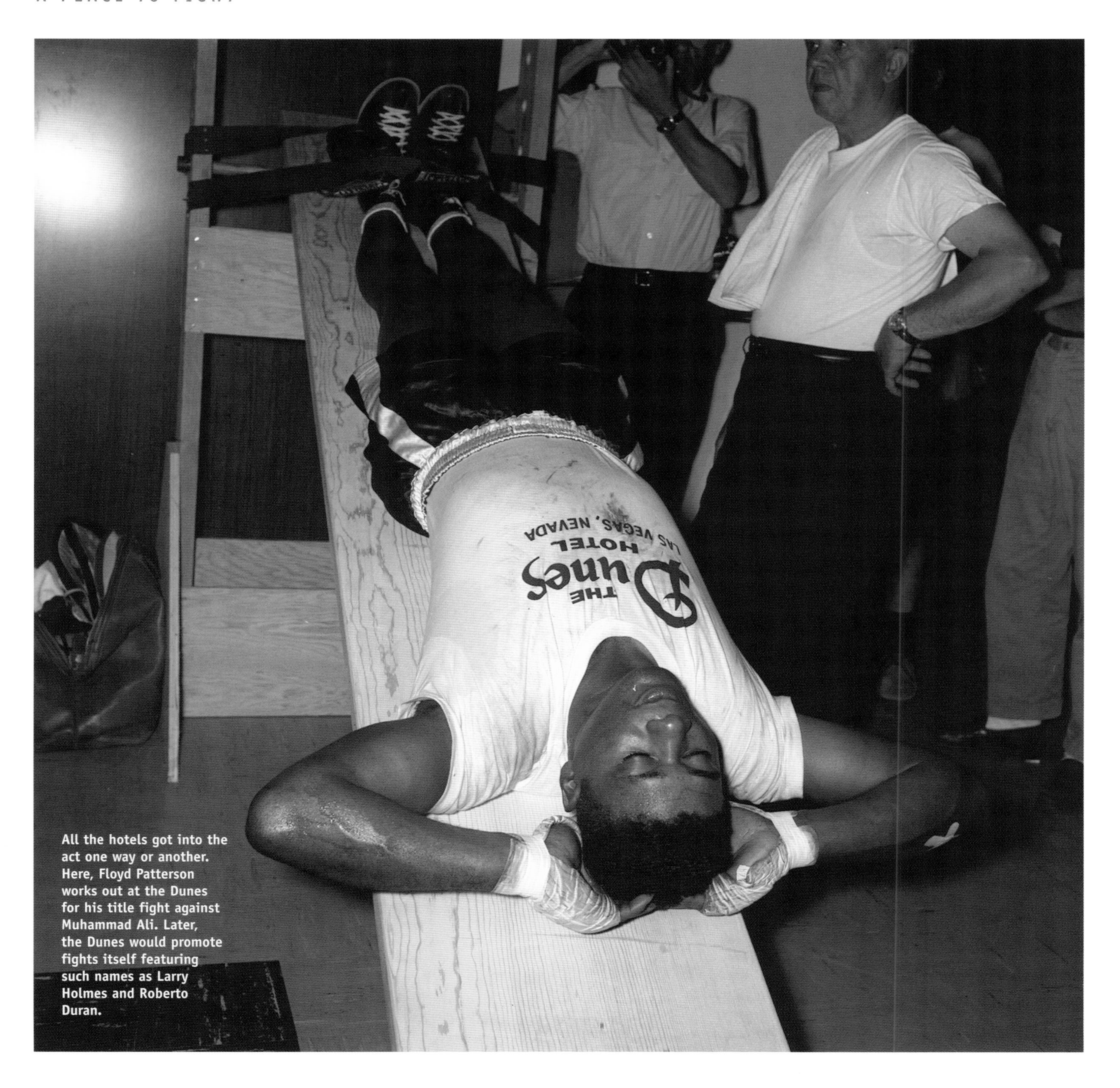

All the hotels got into the act one way or another. Here, Floyd Patterson works out at the Dunes for his title fight against Muhammad Ali. Later, the Dunes would promote fights itself featuring such names as Larry Holmes and Roberto Duran.

LAS VEGAS REVIEW-JOURNAL

a fight for the heavyweight title and he came to Las Vegas a month early to train for his fight with Nino Valdes.

When big-time boxing returned to Las Vegas in 1960 with Benny Paret and Don Jordan, they had moved indoors to the rotunda of the new Las Vegas Convention Center, which seated about 7,500 for fights.

The Convention Center was host to most of the fights of the '60s, including the first appearance of Cassius Clay in 1961 against a large Hawaiian named Duke Sabedong. Ali would later defend the heavyweight title against Floyd Patterson in the same arena.

The Strip hotels wanted to host the fights but had to settle for sponsoring them because they didn't have a place to put them. The idea of building temporary arenas for big events hadn't yet germinated.

It wasn't until Caesars Palace hosted the first USA-USSR amateur dual meet in its showroom in October 1969 that some events began moving to the Strip. A month later, the old International Hotel—now the Las Vegas Hilton—put on a fight between Sonny Liston and Leotis Martin in its showroom.

The fight was on ABC's Wide World of Sports and Howard Cosell was at ringside. On the undercard was a young heavyweight named George Foreman.

Fans sat in old-style red showroom booths watching the fights unfold on the stage where Elvis usually played.

Martin knocked an aging and fading Liston out in the ninth round, while Foreman scored a first-round knockout. The fights were a hit, but it would be nearly a decade before the Hilton would get back in the boxing game.

Meanwhile, the Silver Slipper and Silver Nugget held regular fight cards, and there was even a night of fights held at the old La Vista Supper Club across from what is now the Hard Rock Hotel, where the ring was set up over the pool and would bounce up and down above the water.

Almost every major Las Vegas hotel hosted a fight at one time or another, with some 40-odd fight sites coming and going over the years. There were fights in the showroom of the old Hacienda, fights in a tent at the Tropicana, fights at the Stratosphere and Showboat and fights at The Mirage. The Marina held fights, as did the Imperial Palace, New Frontier and Arizona Charlies.

For a time in the mid-1980s, the Riviera Hotel fancied itself as a fight center, with a series of bouts that culminated with Spinks becoming

ROMAN BOXING EMPIRE

Ron Amos spent a lot of time in the late 1960s trying to figure out how to follow Evel Knievel's motorcycle jump over the fountains at Caesars Palace with another big event. The jump helped put the young Strip resort on the map, and it gave a reputation as a place where things were happening. The trouble was, that there wasn't much happening after that.

The fights at the Las Vegas Convention Center seemed to be petering out, with Dick Tiger's fight against Roger Rouse in November 1967 fading into memory. No hotel, just yet, had figured out how to host a boxing card on property.

Amos was running publicity at Caesars Palace and was a big follower of amateur athletics. At the time, the United States and the Soviet Union were in the Cold War, and he correctly figured a series of fights between the country's amateur teams would be a hot ticket. "It was huge at the time because the Soviets had great fighters, and the U.S. boasted an Olympics where George Foreman won the heavyweight gold medal," Amos said.

The showroom seated only 1,000 or so, and it was a tough ticket. Caesars Palace sent out specially printed Roman-themed invitations to its best gamblers, and ABC was on hand to televise it to the country on *Wide World of Sports*. "We even invited Anatoly Dobrynin, the Russian ambassador, and he came," Amos recalled.

It was the first time ABC had devoted all 90 minutes of its *Wide World of Sports* to one sport. The matches were broadcast live across the United States, Europe, and the Soviet Union, reaching 250 million people. The fights drew the highest rating for a boxing event ever on ABC to date. The Soviets won 7-5, but Caesars Palace had learned something new about promoting big events. "That convinced the owners we should be doing this stuff, and it would work," Amos said. "It was really the kickoff that launched this thing."

That's what happened for the Muhammad Ali-Jerry Quarry fight in 1972, where Ali trained daily to sold out crowds in a ring set up in the hotel's showroom. "It was second only to Sinatra. He was funny, magnetic," Amos said.

Seven years after Caesars Palace brought the amateurs to the showroom, George Foreman fought Ron Lyle in the first pro fight in the hotel's tennis pavilion. More than a quarter century later, Caesars Palace is still solidly entrenched in the boxing business.

Ali managed to shorten the odds, but Holmes made it a long night for the former champion.

A WAGER OR TWO

In the world of sports betting, inside information means everything. And no one over the years knew more about what was going on behind the Las Vegas boxing scene than Lem Banker.

The longtime Las Vegas gambler was Sonny Liston's friend, and also one of his pallbearers. He was close to Joe Louis and Rocky Marciano, counts Mike Tyson among his acquaintances, and knows people who know people.

That paid off handsomely for Banker when Tommy Hearns and Marvelous Marvin Hagler fought for the middleweight title April 16, 1985, at Caesars Palace.

A few days before the fight, a doctor friend of Banker called him with the news that his partner had gone to Caesars Palace to put some stitches on a cut on the inside of Hearns' mouth.

"He said not to say anything but as soon as I hung up I called Hagler's attorney in Boston," Banker recalled. "I told him Hearns was cut inside the mouth and nobody's supposed to know about it. I said tell the Petronelli brothers (Hagler's trainers) to tell him to go after the face."

Hagler probably didn't need the information, but he did go right after Hearns, who responded by bloodying Hagler's face in one of the greatest first rounds ever in boxing.

"Hagler would end up knocking Hearns out in the third round, and Banker had a winner.

"I put a big bet on that fight," he said.

A few years earlier, Banker was a winner in another fight.

Larry Holmes was favored to beat Muhammad Ali, but the odds were closing as the fight drew near and it looked like the 38-year-old Ali had gotten himself into great shape.

"Caesars had just opened the sports book in the round gazebo outside and I was with Gabe Kaplan the comedian, who asked me if I liked Holmes," Banker said. "I said it's probably the best investment of the last 10 years. I knew Ali was taking water pills to get the weight off."

Banker made his way to his ringside seat, where he saw former Kentucky Gov. John Brown sitting with his wife, Phyllis George. They wanted to know whom he liked, and he blurted out, Holmes, before realizing there was a tall black woman standing next to the Browns.

"I look up and realize it's Veronica, Ali's wife at the time," Banker said. "She gives me a dirty look, so I said 'I'm only joking. I love Ali.'"

Banker won a big bet when Holmes stopped Ali in the mismatch, but he wasn't celebrating.

"It ruined the whole thing," he said. ``I should have kept my mouth shut."

Banker's inside information didn't always pay off.

Ali was fighting Patterson in 1965, and Banker figured Ali would win easily. He didn't want to put money on the champion, though, because the price was too high.

The day of the fight, a member of Ali's entourage was in Banker's Sahara Health Club talking to his attendant, Sid Washington. He told Banker he was nervous about the fight and had a feeling something bad was going to happen.

"I'm listening, so I pick up the phone and bet 10 grand on Patterson with mixed emotions," Banker said.

On a rainy night, Banker went to the fight at the Convention Center. Ali toyed with Patterson for 12 rounds before stopping him in a dominating performance.

"I thought maybe he knew something," Banker said. "I guess he didn't."

The worst bets weren't always made on big fights.

One night, Jimmy "The Greek" Snyder was at the monthly Silver Slipper card, where publicist Ron Amos was moonlighting as a judge for a fight for the state lightweight championship.

Snyder and Amos had plans to go to dinner after the fight, on which The Greek had put $1,000.

The fight was a close one, and when the decision was announced it was split. The referee favored one fighter, while one judge had the other winning. Amos was the third judge and he voted against The Greek's fighter.

"He was bitching and moaning all the rest of the night," Amos said. "He couldn't believe I had voted for the other guy."

Former heavyweight champion Joe Louis won a lot of money for bettors, but wasn't particularly astute himself when it came to making bets.

Banker remembers a big gambler, who was one of Louis' friends, seeing the fighter in the casino one Saturday morning and telling him he was going to bet $10,000 for him on the Southern California-Notre Dame football game that day.

The bet was free to Louis. All he had to do was collect the money if he won.

"Who do we have?" Louis asked the gambler.

"Notre Dame," he replied.

"Forget it," Louis said. "I like the other side."

Former light heavyweight champion Archie Moore shares a laugh with George Foreman as they hold up a poster for one of Moore's last fights, a 1962 bout with Willie Pastrano at the Los Angeles Sports Arena. Moore helped put Las Vegas on the map when he fought the city's first big fight with Nino Valdes at the old Cashman Field in May 1955.

the first light heavyweight champion to win the heavyweight title when he beat Holmes in 1985.

The owner of the Riviera at the time was Meshulim Riklis, whose young wife, Pia Zadora, was an aspiring singer and actress. She was eight months pregnant the night of the Holmes-Spinks fight, all the more obvious dressed completely in stretch leather, when she did a bad lip synch that didn't synch to the national anthem – especially when the record stuck!

That wasn't nearly as bad as a fight card promoted in the 1960s at the old Ice Palace skating ring in the Commercial Center.

Boards were put over the ice, and folding chairs placed on top, and the ring was set up in the middle of the rink. During the preliminaries, the ring collapsed and had to be put back together again.

Casino host Ash Resnick's wife, Marilyn, sang the national anthem and forgot the words, just part of an evening in which nothing went right.

"It was like something out of a Mel Brooks comedy," said gambler Lem Banker.

Today, temporary fight arenas are mostly a thing of the past. Caesars built a small one for the David Reid-Felix Trinidad fight in 2000, but just as quickly took it down.

The Caesars pavilion is also history, torn down to make room for hotel expansion, leaving Caesars to either host small fights in its ballrooms or rent the Thomas & Mack Center at UNLV as it did with the Roy Jones Jr.-John Ruiz heavyweight title fight on March 1, 2003.

The Dunes, Hacienda and Silver Slipper are no longer, while hotels like the Riviera long ago quit chasing high-rolling gamblers and began offering cheap shows to lure coupon-happy slot players.

Fights have moved indoors, first at the Thomas & Mack Center and then at the MGM Grand and Mandalay Bay arenas.

The Thomas & Mack was built to house the Runnin' Rebels basketball team, but over the years it has had its share of big fights. Casinos would shuttle their big gamblers in by limo, hoist a tent for them to party in outside and then bring them in for the fight before quickly getting them back to the casino to gamble.

It was at the Thomas & Mack in November 1992 that Evander Holyfield and Riddick Bowe staged an epic war in their first heavyweight title fight before a crowd of nearly 14,000. A few months earlier, Julio Cesar Chavez and Hector Camacho inaugurated the arena's first boxing card with a fight that drew 18,361 fans and was trumpeted as the fastest sellout in boxing history with all tickets gone in 36

Las Vegas fights soon began to attract more than just gamblers and big bettors. Former heavyweight champion Max Schmeling doffs his hat as he gets off a plane at McCarran International Airport.

LAS VEGAS REVIEW-JOURNAL

There were ring girls, and then there were ring girls at Caesars Palace. The same cocktail waitresses who plied their trade inside the hotel were also used to carry ring cards between rounds. This woman is unidentified, but she can claim a footnote in history. She was the first ring girl ever at Caesars Palace, getting her chance after the first round of the George Foreman-Ron Lyle heavyweight fight in 1976.

CAESARS PALACE

hours.

Holyfield and Lennox Lewis also fought their rematch in the arena, and George Foreman lost a fight to Tommy Morrison there.

The minute the MGM opened in 1993 it showed it was serious about landing big fights for its arena and had some of the biggest, including Mike Tyson's two fights with Holyfield. Then the Mandalay Bay opened with its intimidating 12,000-seat arena and began competing successfully with the MGM for fights such as Oscar De La Hoya's knockout of Fernando Vargas.

The indoor arenas were both modern and efficient, but what they made up for in comfort they lacked in charm.

For those who were there, a good hot dog, a folding chair and a night under the stars merely added to the experience.

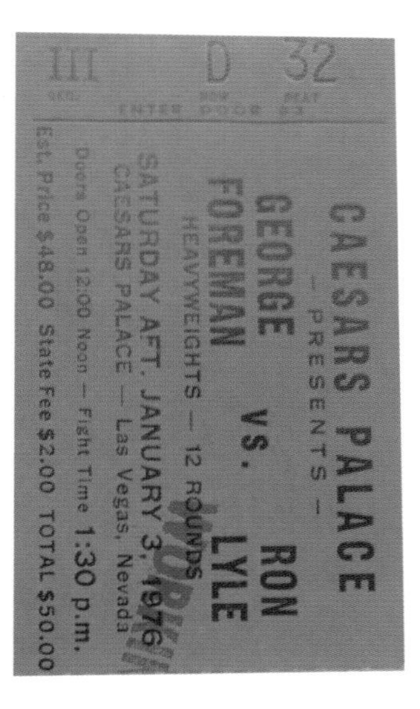

III D 32
CAESARS PALACE
— PRESENTS —
GEORGE FOREMAN vs. RON LYLE
HEAVYWEIGHTS — 12 ROUNDS
SATURDAY AFT. JANUARY 24, 1976
CAESARS PALACE — Las Vegas, Nevada
Doors Open 12:00 Noon — Fight Time 1:30 p.m.
Est. Price $48.00 State Fee $2.00 TOTAL $50.00

GRANDSTAND
SEC. ROW SEAT
IV H 14
JUN 9 1978
ADMIT ONE THIS DATE
CAESARS PALACE AND DON KING PRESENT
Ken Norton vs. Larry Holmes
15 ROUNDS
JUNE 9 1978 FRIDAY
CAESARS PALACE
Las Vegas Nevada
TOTAL $50.00
NO REFUNDS OR EXCHANGES
$50.00
IV H 14

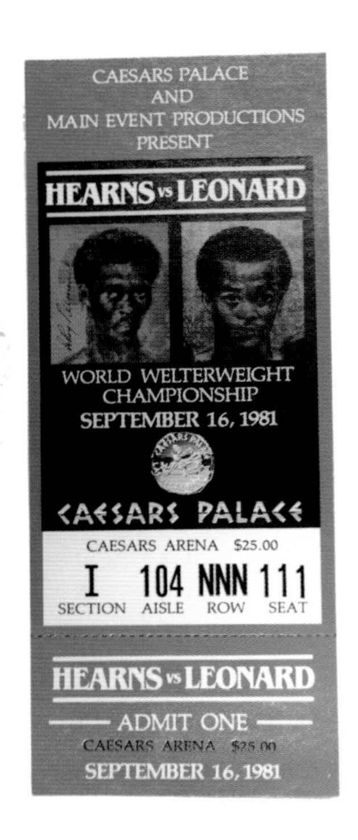

CAESARS PALACE
AND
MAIN EVENT PRODUCTIONS
PRESENT
HEARNS vs LEONARD
WORLD WELTERWEIGHT CHAMPIONSHIP
SEPTEMBER 16, 1981
CAESARS PALACE
CAESARS ARENA $25.00
I 104 NNN 111
SECTION AISLE ROW SEAT
HEARNS vs LEONARD
ADMIT ONE
CAESARS ARENA $25.00
SEPTEMBER 16, 1981

CAESARS PALACE
IN ASSOCIATION WITH
DON KING PRODUCTIONS
& TIFFANY PROMOTIONS
PRESENTS
Holmes vs Cooney
WBC WORLD HEAVYWEIGHT CHAMPIONSHIP
JUNE 11, 1982
CAESARS PALACE
CAESARS ARENA $100.00
I 104 DDD 98
SECTION AISLE ROW SEAT

Don King Productions, Inc.
TYSON VS HOLYFIELD
FINALLY.
MGM GRAND
MGM GRAND GARDEN ARENA
SAT NOV 9, 1996 3:30PM
Section U102 E NVCOMP
Row X $.00
Seat 13 MAYUMI
MGM GRAND GARDEN ARENA
SAT NOV 9, 1996 3:30PM
Section U102 E NVCOMP
Row X $.00
Seat 13 MAYUMI

TOP RANK INC. AND
CAESARS PALACE PRESENT
HAGLER vs HEARNS
THE FIGHT!
World Middleweight Championship
Monday, April 15, 1985
CAESARS PALACE
Caesars Court $600
1 12 B 48
SECTION AISLE ROW SEAT

Dokes vs. Holyfield
AND
Meldrick Taylor vs. Jong-Jong Pareguing
Saturday, March 11, 1989
Caesars Palace Sports Pavilion
CAESARS PALACE
CAESARS COURT
2 4 F 15
SECTION AISLE ROW SEAT

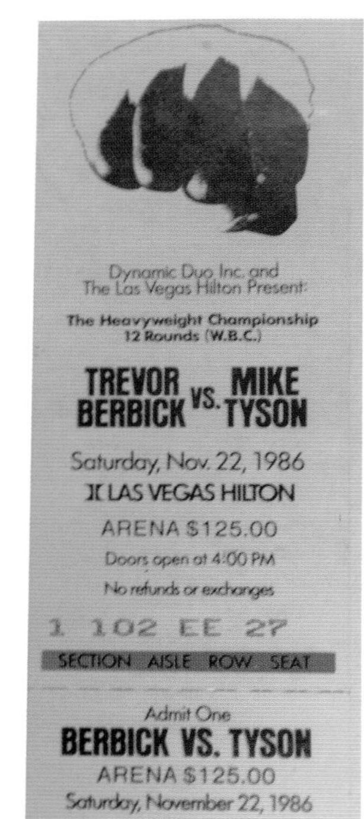

Dynamic Duo Inc. and
The Las Vegas Hilton Present:
The Heavyweight Championship
12 Rounds (W.B.C.)
TREVOR BERBICK VS. MIKE TYSON
Saturday, Nov. 22, 1986
LAS VEGAS HILTON
ARENA $125.00
Doors open at 4:00 PM
No refunds or exchanges
1 102 EE 27
SECTION AISLE ROW SEAT
Admit One
BERBICK VS. TYSON
ARENA $125.00
Saturday, November 22, 1986

THUNDER MEETS LIGHTNING
JULIO CESAR
VS.
MELDRICK
TAYLOR
Saturday March 17, 1990
NORTH LOWER RESERVED $350.00
31 JJ 87
AISLE ROW SEAT

CAESARS PALACE
BOWE HOLYFIELD
REPEAT OR REVENGE
WORLD HEAVYWEIGHT CHAMPIONSHIP NOVEMBER 6, 1993
$800
CAESARS PALACE OUTDOOR STADIUM
TICKET ENTRANCE E
3 9 B 57
SECTION AISLE ROW SEAT

7 >> THE VEGAS TOP 10

Try to sift through hundreds of title fights, thousands of other bouts to come up with the best of the best, and there will always be an argument about what was left out. Picking the top 10 fights in the history of Las Vegas is no exception.

The best fights weren't always the biggest title fights, though they got the most attention. Some might argue for the inclusion of a thrilling 10-round undercard, while others will wince at the exclusion at fights like the first Marco Antonio Barrera-Erik Morales bout or the Sugar Ray Leonard-Wilfredo Benitez fight.

Sometimes it wasn't just the fight, but the event itself. Sometimes it was both of them put together, that rare night when reality lived up to hype.

There's room for argument, but no argument that these were great fights – and made for some great nights.

Here, in no particular order, is the Las Vegas Top 10:

>> GEORGE FOREMAN VS. RON LYLE

JANUARY 24, 1976

Caesars Palace couldn't have picked a better way to get into the fight business. It had been 15 months since Muhammad Ali knocked George Foreman out in the Rumble in the Jungle and Foreman hadn't been in the ring since. There were questions about the future of the once fearsome heavyweight champion, questions that would have to be answered in the first fight ever in the hotel's sports pavilion.

Lyle, meanwhile, had fought Ali the year before in Las Vegas and was winning the fight before being stopped in the 10th round. In his last fight he had come off the canvas to knock out Earnie Shavers.

Lyle was a big puncher with a fragile chin. It was a dangerous combination.

Caesars had been sponsoring fights for years at the Convention Center, but this time hotel executives decided they would convert an indoor tennis center built behind the resort into a boxing arena.

"It was a Quonset hut was all it was," Foreman publicist Bill Caplan said. "But you knew right away it had great atmosphere."

Soon, it had a great fight.

In the first round Lyle hit Foreman so hard that Foreman's trunks drooped down. Stunned, Foreman held on to survive the round, but barely. Foreman returned the favor in the second round, staggering Lyle with a big right hand, but Lyle came right back to jar Foreman with a right of his own.

It only got better in a fourth round that was one of the wildest in heavyweight history.

Moments into the round, Lyle stunned Foreman with a right hand, then landed another left and right that put him down. Foreman got up and Lyle moved in for the kill only to be dropped by a desperate right hand from Foreman.

Now it was Foreman's turn to try and stop the fight and he went for the kill, punishing Lyle against the ropes. Suddenly, Lyle landed two left hands and Foreman went down for a second time, face first on the canvas.

The bell rang as Foreman staggered to his feet, lucky to survive the round.

"I kept getting knocked down and thinking: What will I say to the media," Foreman recalled. "The ropes are loose or there's something in my drink? I had no excuses, so I kept getting up."

The fight couldn't possibly go on at this pace—or could it?

Lyle came out trying to finish Foreman in the fifth round and Foreman landed a couple of shots to the head. A right hand by Lyle staggered Foreman again and the two traded huge punches before a Lyle uppercut hurt Foreman one more time.

Somehow, Foreman stayed on his feet. Somehow, he unleashed a vicious combination to Lyle's head. Suddenly, Lyle was backed into the corner and Foreman pounded on him before Lyle collapsed to the canvas and was counted out.

"Some people think that might be the greatest heavyweight brawl of all time," Caplan said.

"It was the fight of the decade," Lyle said years later.

Howard Cosell climbed into the ring to interview Foreman, and Caplan stood behind him, saying "George Foreman, heart of a lion, heart of a lion." Later, Foreman got a T-shirt printed with the saying on it.

"That fight recaptured something in me," Foreman said. "I felt like now I could get up if I got knocked down. I was restored with confidence. After that I didn't wake up at night with dreams of Ali."

"That fight recaptured something in me," Foreman said. "I felt like now I could get up if I got knocked down. I was restored with confidence. After that I didn't wake up at night with dreams of Ali."

George Foreman takes a wild swing at Ron Lyle in the third round. Lyle knocked Foreman down twice but Foreman somehow managed to come back in the fifth round after being staggered by Lyle and unleash a vicious combination that knocked Lyle out. It was the first fight in the Caesars Palace pavilion, which went on to host some of the greatest fights of the era.

CAESARS PALACE

>> LARRY HOLMES VS. KEN NORTON

JUNE 9, 1978

Larry Holmes had just become the heavyweight champion of the world. Now it was time to celebrate. Still in his boxing trunks, with the gaudy WBC belt around his waist, Holmes ran past startled hotel guests and jumped into the pool at Caesars Palace. Soon, his jubilant trainers, handlers and followers were splashing around with him.

For years, Holmes had to be content to be known as Muhammad Ali's sparring partner. Now he was the heavyweight champion himself, thanks to a thrilling win over Ken Norton that could have gone either way.

The pavilion just past poolside at Caesars Palace had been in use for only two years, but it already had a reputation as a place where heavyweights brawled.

Three months earlier, Holmes had gotten off the canvas to beat Earnie Shavers in the same ring to earn a shot against Norton for the vacant WBC heavyweight title.

Holmes was unbeaten in 27 fights, while Norton was a former champion who had beaten Ali and had a reputation that Holmes had to respect.

They fought for a belt that Ali vacated when he decided to fight Leon Spinks.

"I wasn't supposed to win it," Holmes said. "I was the underdog, but I knew I could whip Ken Norton."

Holmes was confident because of what had happened against Shavers. He had gotten up from a right hand landed flush by one of boxing's biggest punchers and he wasn't going to let Norton get in his way of the title he so badly wanted.

"Everybody was saying Larry Holmes did not have it, that he was just a copy of Muhammad Ali," Holmes said. "I was mainly determined to show them I did have it and I could be heavyweight champion of the world."

Holmes entered the ring to what was to become his trademark ring walk song, "Ain't No Stopping Us Now." And there was no stopping Holmes in a fight he desperately wanted to win.

The fight was a classic battle of left jabs early, but by the middle rounds the two heavyweights were trading big punches. By the eighth round, Holmes was cut inside his mouth and Norton's eye was swelling, but the two kept punching almost nonstop.

Norton worked the body of Holmes while Holmes kept throwing left jabs and right hands to the head of Norton. By the 13th round, both fighters had taken tremendous punishment, but the fight was still up in the air.

"It was just a great battle," said Bobby Goodman, Don King's matchmaker. "After each round you'd wonder how the guy was going to come out of the corner and then he'd come out and turn the tables on the other guy."

Holmes, in intense pain with a bad left arm, stunned Norton in the 13th round and seemed to be taking command, but Norton came back in the 14th round to land some big shots to the head.

The 15th round would be decisive, and both fighters were ready.

Norton landed a big right early in the round, then buckled Holmes' legs with a left hook. The two fighters went at it toe-to-toe in the center of the ring, trading huge shots, and Holmes seemed to hurt Norton with a big uppercut in the final seconds.

Both fighters were so exhausted that neither could raise his arms in victory.

"I fought my ass off," Holmes said.

The final punch may have won the fight for Holmes. Judges Harold Buck and Joe Swessel each gave Holmes the last round and the fight 143-142. Judge Lou Tabat had Norton ahead by the same score.

It was as close as it could be. But by a one-point split decision, Holmes was the new heavyweight champion.

"It was one of the great heavyweight championship fights of all time, if not the greatest," Goodman said. "I think it was the most exciting fight I ever saw in Las Vegas for the sheer ebb and flow and true great fighting."

The fight seemed to take everything out of Norton. He would win only two more fights before retiring after being knocked out in the first round by Gerry Cooney three years later.

Holmes, meanwhile, would hold the heavyweight championship for seven years.

But first he was going to take a little swim.

"Everybody was saying Larry Holmes did not have it, that he was just a copy of Muhammad Ali," Holmes said. "I was mainly determined to show them I did have it and could be heavyweight champion of the world."

Larry Holmes connects with a right hand in his heavyweight title fight with Ken Norton. Holmes may have won the fight with a big uppercut in the 15th and final round, which gave him a split decision and made him a heavyweight champion for the first time. Holmes celebrated by jumping into the pool at Caesars Palace.

AP WORLD WIDE

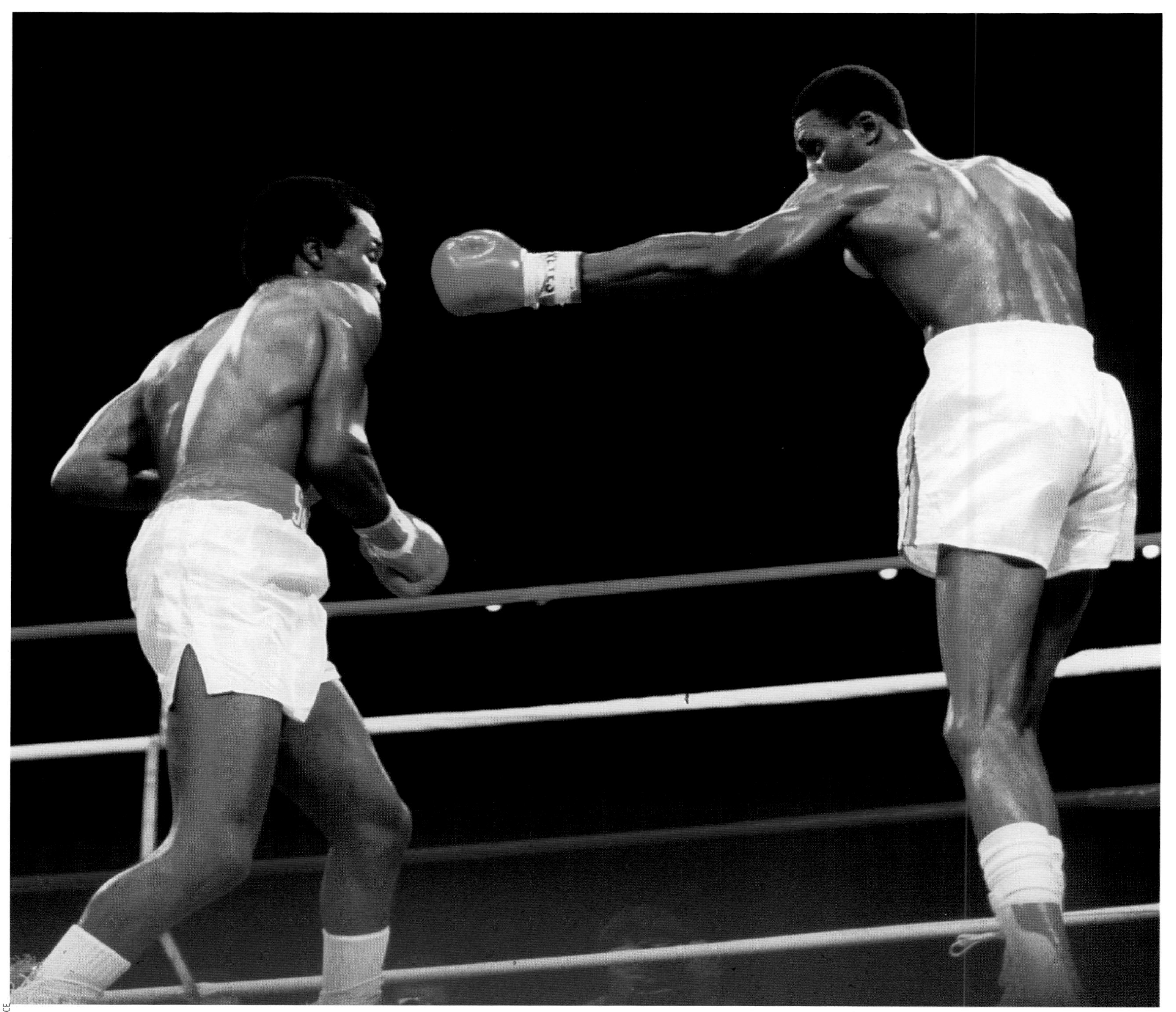

CAESARS PALACE

Thomas Hearns was on his toes in the late rounds, trying to box Sugar Ray Leonard and win a decision. Their welterweight title fight was an epic, won by Leonard when referee Davey Pearl decided he'd had enough in the fourteenth round. The fight was a rare megafight that actually lived up to its hype.

>> SUGAR RAY LEONARD VS. THOMAS HEARNS

SEPTEMBER 14, 1981

Sugar Ray Leonard's left eye was swollen, and he was trailing on the three ringside scorecards. To the astonishment of everyone at Caesars Palace, Thomas Hearns had come back from almost being knocked out to take command of the fight by turning from slugger to boxer.

The celebrity-studded crowd of 23,306 had already witnessed a fight of epic proportions as it moved into the later rounds. Now Hearns was on his pencil-thin legs, boxing circles around Leonard.

"You're blowing it, son. You're blowing it," trainer Angelo Dundee shouted at Leonard after the 12th round.

Leonard knew better. He had wobbled Hearns in the sixth and seventh rounds and he knew it was only a matter of time before he would do it again. The freakishly thin legs that belonged to Hearns were wearing down, and Leonard was waiting for his moment to pounce.

With his eye almost swollen shut, he just had to hope it would come before the bell sounded to end the 15th round.

"I couldn't touch him when he turned boxer," Leonard recalled. "He had that lateral movement and long left jab. My eye was practically closed." The great ones, though, somehow find a way to reach down inside for something extra when they need it. Leonard would show on this sultry night in the desert that he belonged in that group.

"My gas tank had gotten low, but I had what I called a hidden reservoir of strength," Leonard said. "I just had to find it."

The fight wasn't supposed to go like this. In the massive buildup in the weeks before the two met at the outdoor stadium at Caesars, the talk was all about Leonard's boxing abilities and Hearns' great right hand.

If boxing is a game of styles, these two provided the greatest contrast of any two welterweights ever.

Hearns was the undefeated Hit Man, whose vaunted right hand was feared throughout the division. Leonard was America's gold medal hero, with a flashy smile and flashier ring skills that won him fans even outside boxing.

He would earn boxing's biggest purse ever—$12 million—while Hearns got $5 million.

Caesars Palace had hosted its first megafight a year earlier with a fading Muhammad Ali and Larry Holmes. That was a show. This was a great fight.

"It was two guys at their very best in the prime of their career," Leonard said. "One guy was a total exterminator, a freak of nature at 147 pounds. He was big, destructive, fast and confident against me, a guy who had commercials and a little kid with a picture of his wife on his sock. It was almost blue collar against white collar. Ray could fight, but Ray couldn't take Tommy's power."

Leonard had been through big fights before, including two with Roberto Duran. For Hearns it was a new experience, and he paid the price.

"I hate to say it was because of the magnitude of the fight as one of reasons we lost, but it was the first time we had been in such a big event," said Emanuel Steward, Hearns' trainer. "The enormity of the fight had such an effect on everybody. The tension was unbelievable. I still haven't found anything to compare it to."

In the corner after the 12th round, Steward knew his fighter had lost even though he was comfortably ahead on points. In the 13th, Leonard hurt Hearns with a right to the head midway through the round. Leonard drove Hearns through the ropes with a barrage of punches, but referee Davey Pearl ruled he was pushed. With 28 seconds to go, Leonard drove Hearns to the ropes with another barrage, and Hearns sank to a sitting position on the second strand from the bottom.

Pearl ruled it a knockdown, and though Hearns got up at two, he was still hurt when the bell sounded to end the round. Leonard was nothing if not a great finisher, and he came out in the 14th round to land a looping right to the head that hurt Hearns badly.

Finally, at 1:45 of the 14th round, with Hearns taking blow after blow to the head, Pearl decided he had had enough.

Rich Rose, who would later become Caesars' director of sports, was sitting on a crate in Leonard's corner watching the look on the faces of people in the crowd.

"You saw everything from disbelief to excitement," he said. "If you ever got the Webster's dictionary and looked up boxing, that picture would be there. It was so entertaining back and forth, It was just remarkable."

They fought in 100-degree heat, and both gave it everything they had. Leaving the ring, Hearns fell down the steps, while Leonard had to be supported by two aides and came to the post-fight press conference in dark glasses. His wife, Juanita, wept.

If Hearns could have stayed upright in the face of Leonard's onslaught, he likely would have won the fight. Judge Duane Ford had him ahead 124-122, while Chuck Minker had it 125-121 and Lou Tabat scored it 125-122, all in favor of the Hit Man.

The late Cus D'Amato had predicted the fight might unfold like it did. He saw past Leonard's flashy smile, all-American ways and star power to see something vicious inside America's darling.

"Leonard won't let (Hearns) get away," said D'Amato, who was at the time raising future heavyweight champion Mike Tyson. "Leonard is one hell of a finisher, like (Sugar Ray) Robinson."

The win defined Leonard's career, cementing his growing legend. The loss haunted Hearns for years to come, and he admitted as much when he and Leonard met in the rematch eight years later.

"It's been a definite nightmare thinking about it over and over again," he said.

CAESARS PALACE

>> LARRY HOLMES VS. GERRY COONEY

JUNE 11, 1982

If Larry Holmes was the heavyweight champion, Gerry Cooney might have been even bigger—he was The Great White Hope. Outside the ring, Holmes didn't stand a chance. Even though he was the champion, he had to accept the same purse as Cooney—$10 million.

Inside, it was another matter.

Holmes was defending his title for the 12th time, and he counted an aging Muhammad Ali among his victims. But this would be his biggest fight ever, a spectacle made even bigger by an undercurrent of racism from the moment it was announced.

"Everything was Gerry Cooney, Gerry Cooney. It was not Larry Holmes," Holmes said. "Larry Holmes didn't even exist."

Caesars Palace built its biggest outdoor arena for the fight, and nearly 30,000 people bought tickets to see if the 6-foot-5 Cooney, owner of a vicious left hook, could withstand the piston-like jab of Holmes and win his 26th straight fight.

The fight wasn't just the talk of the town. It was the buzz all around the country.

Don King was the promoter and he knew how to make every last buck out of a promotion. But even King's people were taken aback by the racial overtones.

"We weren't selling it as white versus black, but when we came to Caesars Palace they had changed their logo to Kelly green," said King matchmaker Bobby Goodman. "It seemed like they wanted to make it where Cooney was their fair-haired darling."

Cooney's skin color and popularity meant something to a country starved for a white heavyweight champion. King claimed there was even a phone installed in Cooney's dress-

Gerry Cooney gave Larry Holmes all he had — and more. But it wasn't enough as Holmes weathered a series of low blows to stop Cooney in the thirteenth round. The fight, which had racist overtones that were exploited by promoter Don King, drew a record crowd of nearly 30,000 to Caesars Palace.

CAESARS PALACE

ing room so President Reagan could call him if he won. There was no phone in Holmes' dressing room.

"They took the fight out of our hands and made it what it was whether you wanted it to be or not," King said. "The fight cut right into the fervor of America. It was white and black."

King said he found out while touring with Cooney to promote the fight how much it meant to white America, whether they were fight fans or not.

"We got off an airplane somewhere and a little white lady walks up to Gerry and squeezes his hand. She says, 'Gerry, do it for us, do it for us, Gerry,'" King said. "This is a grandma who has to be 80-years-old. She's grandma and apple pie and she didn't even know who I was. Gerry Cooney was the white hope and she squeezed him with reverence."

The night of the fight, the crowd was so thick and the atmosphere so tense that the fighters needed police escorts to get to the ring from the dressing room.

Although Holmes was the champion, he was introduced first. Cooney was introduced second, as if he were the champion.

Mills Lane was the referee and he was eager to try out a new slogan.

"Let's get it on," he barked at the two fighters after giving them instructions.

Holmes was as ready as he had ever been for a fight. He started the jab early and often and soon Cooney's face was turning red. In the second round, he dropped the challenger with a short right hand to the chin. Cooney, for some reason, was trying to box with Holmes instead of attacking him. It wasn't working.

"America needs you," Cooney's manager, Dennis Rappaport, yelled to his fighter between rounds.

It was a wakeup call for Cooney, who came back in the third and fourth rounds to land his trademark left hook often. Holmes didn't back off, but the punches were taking a toll.

"Gerry hurt me and to this day he doesn't know he hurt me," Holmes said. "He hurt me a number of times to the body but I hid it."

It was Holmes doing the hurting in the sixth

CAESARS PALACE

round, when he staggered Cooney with a right and an uppercut that knocked his mouthpiece out, then pummeled him across the ring.

Cooney came back strong in the next two rounds, but it was hot and Holmes' persistent jabs kept finding the mark. Cooney's left hook began landing lower and lower, and in the ninth round he hit Holmes with a low blow that had him wincing in pain.

"Twenty years later, I can still feel it," Holmes said.

At ringside, WBC president Jose Sulaiman jumped up and demanded to Lane that he start deducting points. He did in the 10th and 11th rounds before Holmes finally stopped Cooney in the 13th round.

Even though Cooney was penalized three points for low blows, Holmes was only leading by two points on two of the three ringside scorecards and six on the third.

"Gerry Cooney could fight, but the white folks didn't give him any credit after I beat him," Holmes said. "He fought a good fight, as good as anyone out there could have fought me at the time."

The fight did huge business for Caesars Palace, but the hotel's fight director, Bob Halloran, wasn't entirely pleased. No one knew it at the time, but Halloran had gone down to Mexico earlier and met with Cuban boxing officials who agreed to allow Olympic star Teofilo Stevenson to fight once as a pro should Cooney win. They didn't want Stevenson to face Holmes, but thought he could handle Cooney.

"I never pulled for fighters, but in the back of my mind I'm thinking it might be great if Cooney had won," Halloran said.

Cooney didn't, disappointing Americans who wanted a white heavyweight champion. And unfortunately, in the end, Holmes never got credit for what should have been the defining fight of his career.

JIM LAURIE—LAS VEGAS REVIEW-JOURNAL

>> EVANDER HOLYFIELD VS. MIKE TYSON

NOVEMBER 9, 1996

Evander Holyfield wasn't supposed to beat Mike Tyson. There were some who feared he might die trying. Nevada boxing regulators were so worried about Holyfield's health that they put him through a battery of specialized tests at the Mayo Clinic before allowing the fight.

They had good reason to worry. Holyfield had lost two of his last four fights and retired briefly after Riddick Bowe stopped him in the eighth round because of what doctors at the time said was a heart abnormality.

Holyfield always felt he and Tyson were destined to someday meet in the ring, from the time they were both trying to make the Olympic team in 1984. The two heavyweights were to have fought five years earlier, on November 8, 1991, at Caesars Palace, but the fight seemed like it would never happen after Tyson pulled out in training with a bad back and then was sent to prison for three years for rape.

Tyson's handlers, though, sensed an opportunity to make millions on what they thought would be an easy mark. Holyfield was 4-3 in his last seven fights, and was coming off a fight against Bobby Czyz in which he looked slow and easy to hit. Tyson, meanwhile, was 15 months into his comeback after serving a three-year prison term for rape and had already won the heavyweight title back.

To Tyson, it was a simple matter of economics.

"All I know is that Saturday I'll pick up $30 million," Tyson said the week of the fight, "then Monday I'll sign up for another $ 30 million."

Oddsmakers opened the fight with Tyson a 22-1 pick. Though he had fought less than eight rounds in his comeback, Tyson seemingly had his confidence back and was intimidating other fighters once again.

Holyfield, it turned out, wasn't so easily intimidated.

"The only person who hit me that I couldn't hit back was my momma," he said.

Tyson found that out soon enough. As the bell sounded to end the first round, Tyson landed a shot after the bell and Holyfield responded with a right to the head. With one punch, he showed Tyson he would have to find someone else to bully this night.

Holyfield controlled the tempo in the first four rounds, but Tyson landed a right uppercut early in the fifth that wobbled Holyfield. It was Tyson's best round, but Holyfield would not let him enjoy it.

Early in the sixth round, Tyson was cut over the left eye from a head butt. Then Holyfield brought the sellout crowd of 16,325 at the MGM Grand Garden to its feet when he knocked Tyson down with a left hook.

With the crowd chanting, "Holyfield! Holyfield!" the challenger kept up the pace. By the end of the 10th round it was obvious Tyson was beaten. He had been driven to the ropes by a left hook with 20 seconds remaining and then battered by a dozen head punches.

The bully was getting bullied, and it was only a matter of time before it ended. Tyson came out for the 11th round in a daze and was hit by nine straight punches. With only 18 seconds gone in the round, referee Mitch Halpern stopped the fight.

In a tumultuous press conference afterward, Tyson buried his head in a towel while his handlers proclaimed loudly that he would be back. Holyfield, meanwhile, basked in the glow of becoming the only fighter other than Muhammad Ali to be heavyweight champion three times.

"I don't even remember the fight from the third round on," Tyson said. "He hit me in the third or fourth round and I just whacked out. I don't remember being knocked down."

Almost immediately, Holyfield agreed to a rematch. It would be the most eagerly anticipated heavyweight showdown in years and set box office records. Tyson was such a presence that he was even favored in the rematch, despite taking a beating.

"'I know you don't think no little defeat can discourage Mike Tyson," Tyson said.

The lore of the rematch seven months later will always live in history because Tyson did the unthinkable and bit off a piece of Holyfield's ear.

As the years go by, that one act of ring madness threatens to overshadow a great performance by a man who proudly wore "Warrior" on his trunks. Those who were there to see it, though, will never forget.

Mike Tyson was as fearsome as ever early on, landing a good right to the head of Evander Holyfield. But Holyfield did something few other fighters were brave enough to do against Tyson — fight him back. He did it so well he stopped Tyson in the eleventh round, leading to a wild celebration and the raising of the winner's hand by referee Mitch Halpern.

The promotional picture for the fight seemed to promise something from two proud warriors who didn't know how to step backward. It delivered in a fight that was most memorable for a first round considered by many in boxing to be the best ever in a major title fight.

CAESARS PALACE

>> MARVELOUS MARVIN HAGLER VS. THOMAS HEARNS

APRIL 15, 1985

Big fights seldom live up to their expectations. This one lasted only eight minutes and one second, yet exceeded them all. On a warm desert evening, the movie stars and high rollers had barely settled into their ringside seats when a first round so furious it will live long in boxing legend erupted before their disbelieving eyes.

Most boxing experts had expected Hagler to box and move against Hearns, whose fearsome right hand had put many opponents to sleep. But he came out and went right after Hearns, who responded by landing a flurry to the head, including a big right hand that shook Hagler and opened a big cut on his nose.

The fight was on. And, oh what a fight it would be!

No less an expert than Sugar Ray Leonard predicted a few days before the fight that the fighter who wanted it most would probably lose. He thought it might be Hearns, and he was right.

"The outcome of the fight will be determined by who wants it too much. By that I mean one fighter will be quicker to leave his game plan, because he desperately wants to beat the other guy," Leonard said. "The one who does that will make more mistakes and lose, and I think it will be Hearns. Tommy wants to knock Marvin out so bad it will harm him."

The two middleweights went at it toe-to-toe the first 45 seconds. Midway through the round, a short right hand by Hearns buckled Hagler; Hearns then threw a right that opened a cut over Hagler's right eye. Blood was flying everywhere, but the action didn't slow. Hagler came back to pin Hearns on the ropes and they went at again, and this time it was Hearns who was hurt near the end of the round.

"He hit Hagler in the head and split his head with his right hand. I never have seen that before," referee Richard Steele recalled. "And you know what? Hagler didn't move at all. It didn't hurt Hagler at all. He just shook his head and kept on coming."

Publicist Rich Rose was in his seat at ringside. As usual, his practice was to look at his digital stopwatch near the end of the round so he would be ready between rounds to keep photographers from standing in front of spectators at ringside.

"I had it down so I could look at my watch and it would be right near the end of the round," Rose said. "I'll never forget. Three times that round I looked at my watch thinking the round should be over. But it just kept going. Nobody threw any jabs, they just went and beat the hell out of each other. The sheer intensity of that I will never forget."

The sellout crowd of 15,008 was roaring and on its feet as the second round began with the same fury. Hagler was wearing Hearns down, exposing his frail legs as he got inside the right hand to land big shots to the head.

Worse yet, Hearns had broken his right hand with a shot to the top of Hagler's bald head in the first round.

"I couldn't believe how hard the man's head was," Hearns said.

Hagler had blood streaming from cuts over both eyes in the third round, and it was flowing in huge rivers down his nose and the side of his face. Steele momentarily halted the fight to let the ring doctor look at the injury.

"I had no intention of stopping the fight, but my job was to get a medical opinion," Steele said.

Hagler thought otherwise.

"I'm not going to let you stop this fight because of a cut," he told Steele.

Desperate to end the fight, Hagler went back and finished Hearns off, landing a big right hand that sent Hearns reeling and then dropping him with a volley of blows.

Hearns struggled up to beat the count, but Steele looked into his glazed eyes and stopped the fight.

As Hagler celebrated, a Hearns cornerman picked up the challenger like a broken rag doll and carried him back to his corner.

"I told you I was going to eat him up like Pac Man," Hagler said.

Hagler connected on 96 of 173 punches thrown; Hearns on 94 of 166. Hagler won the first two rounds on two scorecards, while Hearns won them both on the third.

After the fight, Hearns came into Hagler's dressing room to congratulate him.

"Marvin, you hit so hard you should move up to light heavyweight," Hearns told him.

A short time later, Hagler would be dancing in a ballroom at Caesars Palace at his victory party. Now, the two warriors stood giving each other respect. Hagler had his baseball hat with the word "War" on it, and a bandage over his eye.

The late columnist Jim Murray marveled at what he had seen, while at the same time wondering what possessed Hearns to try and trade punches with Hagler.

"Hurling yourself on Marvelous Marvin Hagler is heroic," Murray wrote. "You don't have to do it. Marvin will come find you. And when he does, chances are you'll find yourself wrapped in the arms of a referee who is asking you what day it is, and you can't remember. It was magnificent. But so was the Titanic hitting the iceberg."

The strategy may have been flawed, but the fight wasn't. It was brief, filled with violence and may have had the greatest first round ever.

By the third round, Hearns's legs were shot and he was in deep trouble. Hagler was relentless, going straight after Hearns, who tried to backpedal on his spindly legs. Hagler caught up with him, though, knocking him down and ending the fight in the third round. It was Hagler's greatest win, though he would suffer his greatest disappointment in the same Caesars Palace ring two years later when he lost a controversial decision to Sugar Ray Leonard.

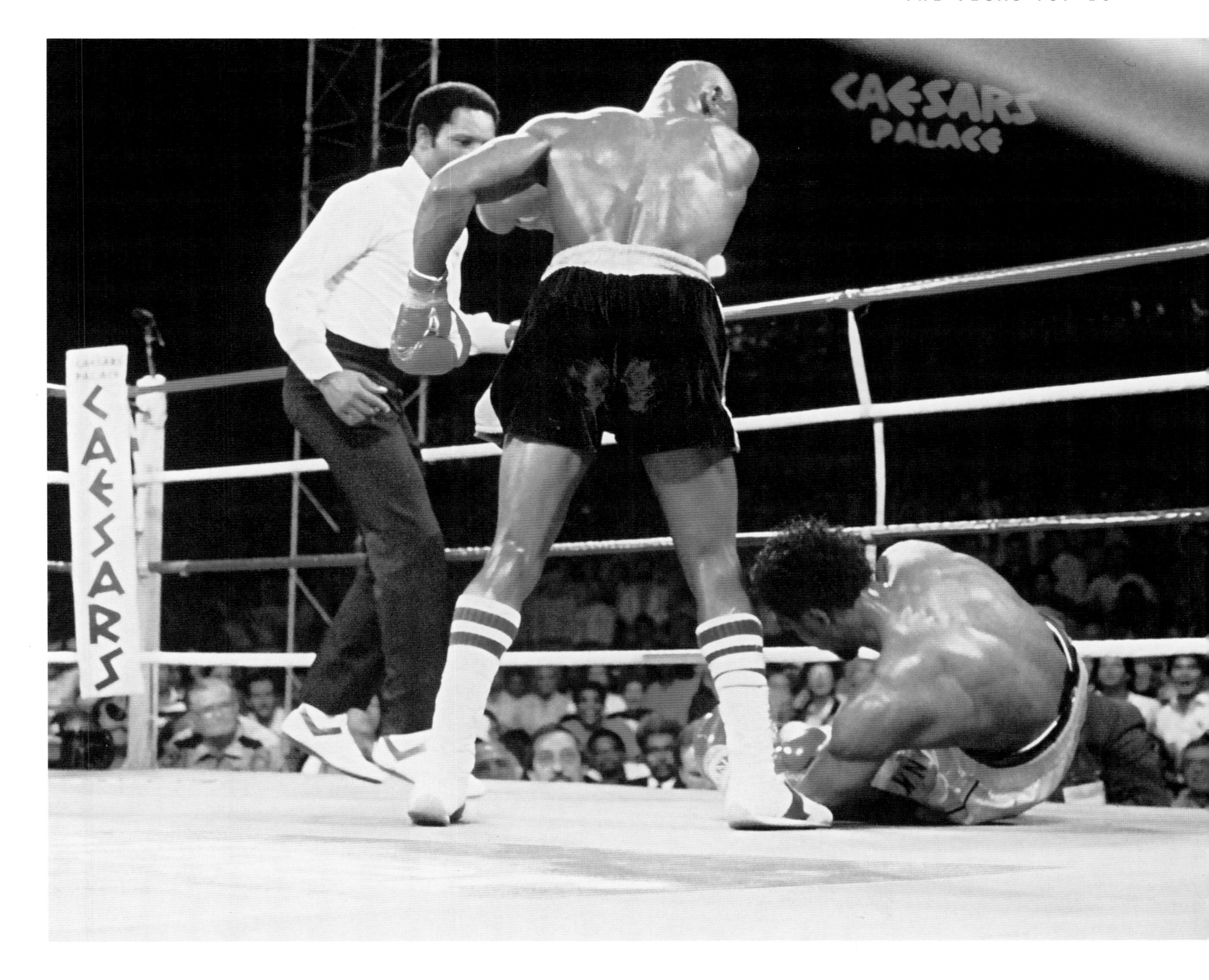
CAESARS
PALACE
CAESARS

>> EVANDER HOLYFIELD VS. MICHAEL DOKES

MARCH 11, 1989

Evander Holyfield was fighting as a heavyweight for only the third time in his career, and there were questions about his punching power. They were answered in a brutal slugfest at Caesars Palace that established Holyfield as a legitimate heavyweight presence.

Evander Holyfield was fighting as a heavyweight for only the third time in his career, and there were questions about his punching power.

They were answered in a brutal slugfest at Caesars Palace that established Holyfield as a legitimate heavyweight presence for the first time.

Dokes was a former WBA champion who had kicked a cocaine habit and was determined to win a title again. Holyfield was an up-and-coming 208-pounder who even then was chasing a title fight with Mike Tyson.

From the opening bell, the two heavyweights fought with the fury of men half their size. Dokes used a punishing body attack while Holyfield landed frequently with sharp combinations and opened cuts above both of the former champion's eyes. The tone of the fight was set early when Dokes caught Holyfield below the belt with a few hooks in the first round.

Near the end of that round, Holyfield retaliated by drilling a hook hard against Dokes' protective cup, and referee Richard Steele allowed Dokes time to recover. "You're a dog, a lousy dog!" Holyfield trainer Lou Duva screamed at Dokes. At the end of the round, the referee told the fighters, "OK, you guys are even on low blows. From now on, anything low I deduct a point."

Neither fighter gave any ground in a savage battle, and the fighting continued in several rounds even after the bell. In the sixth, Steele caught Dokes hitting low again and took away a point. A moment later, Holyfield opened up a cut over Dokes' left eye. The eighth round was especially vicious with the two trading fearsome head punches. But Holyfield was relentless and never let up, finally catching Dokes with two big hooks to the head that left him helpless along the ropes at 1:41 of the 10th round.

"Throughout the fight, I'd shake him with one punch, but he'd be able to shake it off," Holyfield said. "I didn't want him to shake it off and come back again."

The 30-year-old Dokes was behind by three to seven points on the scorecards of the three ringside judges when the end came.

"I wasn't at the Thrilla in Manila, so I don't know," promoter Dan Duva said afterward. "But this is the greatest heavyweight fight I've ever seen live."

Evander Holyfield was moving up in weight and trying to establish himself as a contender for the title. Michael Dokes was on the comeback trail, having kicked a cocaine habit and ready to make his mark again. The two engaged in a slugfest so intense that it seemed both would be badly hurt. Holyfield was relentless, finally wining it in the tenth round when two big hooks left Dokes helpless along the ropes.

"Throughout the fight, I'd shake him with a punch, but he'd be able to shake it off," Holyfield said. "I didn't want him to shake it off and come back again."

Few in the crowd of 3,497 would argue that. They got their money's worth and more from two fighters who refused to budge an inch.

"I couldn't tell if it was a great fight or not," Holyfield said. "I just knew it was the toughest fight of my life."

Despite the loss, Dokes received a hero's welcome two weeks later when he appeared at Madison Square Garden at a Buddy McGirt fight.

"It's very seldom these days you can have a match where the loser comes out better than most winners," matchmaker Bobby Goodman said. "This was like when Leonard and Duran went to war in Montreal. Red Smith wrote, 'This was the night a boy became a man and a man became a legend.' "

The effort briefly revitalized Dokes career, and he would go on to fight Riddick Bowe for the heavyweight title a few years later, only to be knocked out quickly. Holyfield thought the fight would put him in line to challenge Tyson for his heavyweight title, and his manager, Ken Sanders, promptly offered Tyson a $25 million winner-take-all bout. "We want to do it now, while he (Tyson) is alive," Sanders said. "We're concerned about what Tyson is going to do next (outside the ring)."

It turned out Sanders had reason to worry. Tyson would lose to Buster Douglas and then injure himself while training for his scheduled November 8, 1991, fight with Holyfield. The two wouldn't meet for seven years.

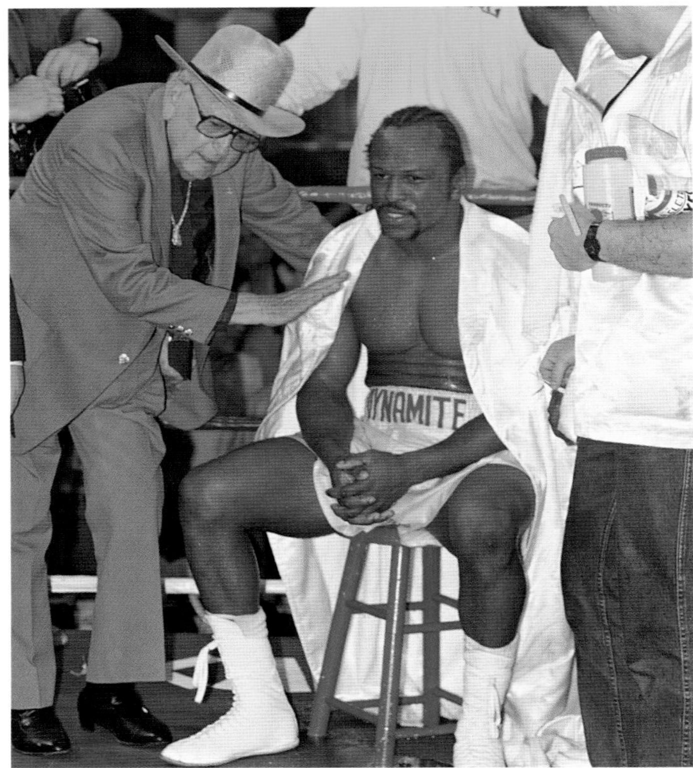

JIM LAURIE—LAS VEGAS REVIEW-JOURNAL

Mike Tyson was only 20 years old, but his reputation had already spread. Never before had there been a puncher of this intensity in the heavyweight division. Trevor Berbick was the WBC champion, but not for long as Tyson hurt him in the first round and dropped him in the second at the Las Vegas Hilton to become the youngest heavyweight champion ever.

"I was throwing hydrogen bombs out there," Tyson said.

>> MIKE TYSON VS. TREVOR BERBICK

NOVEMBER 22, 1986

Mike Tyson was always in a hurry to become the heavyweight champion. It took him 20 years, 4 months and 22 days to fight for the title, and only five minutes and 35 seconds to win it.

Trevor Berbick was the WBC heavyweight champion, but Tyson's reputation as a fearsome puncher was so great that he was a 4-1 favorite to beat Berbick and become the youngest heavyweight champion in history.

Before the fight at the Las Vegas Hilton, Berbick scoffed at the young pup's chances.

"I love breaking those bubbles that have never been busted," Berbick said. "I'm going to give him a good whipping, then knock him out."

Tyson was undefeated in 27 fights, and had knocked out 25 of his opponents, 15 of them in the first round. He was determined to do things his own way, even paying a $3,000 fine for wearing his traditional black trunks into the ring when he was supposed to wear a different color than the champion.

Tyson had gone only 10 rounds twice in his career, but this fight was never going to go the 12-round scheduled distance.

Tyson overwhelmed Berbick from the start, hurting him with a combination late in the first round. Fifteen seconds into the second round, he knocked him down with a right hand, then dropped him later in the round with a crashing left hook to the jaw.

Berbick struggled to his feet but fell into a corner. He tried once again to rise but once again fell.

Finally, he got up at the count of nine. But he was wobbling like a drunk and referee Mills Lane stopped it.

"I was throwing hydrogen bombs out there," Tyson said.

After the fight, the young champion dressed in denim and wearing the heavyweight championship belt walked proudly around the casino at the Hilton.

He couldn't know what was in front of him, or the bizarre turns his life and career would take over the ensuing years. He just knew he was happy for himself and his late mentor, Cus D'Amato.

"This is a moment I've been waiting for all my life," Tyson said.

Tyson overwhelmed Berbick from the start, hurting him with a combination late in the first round. Fifteen seconds into the second round, he knocked him down with a right hand, then dropped him again with a crashing left hook to the jaw.

>> JULIO CESAR CHAVEZ VS. MELDRICK TAYLOR

MARCH 17, 1990

For 35 minutes and 58 seconds, this fight between unbeaten 140-pound champions could have been remembered as a classic battle of strength, courage and style.

But it was what happened with two seconds left that will always live in boxing history.

Meldrick Taylor was a 1984 Olympic gold medalist and had never lost as a pro when he stepped into the ring at the Las Vegas Hilton for a unification fight with the legendary Julio Cesar Chavez.

Taylor had speed and he had style. He could move and he could punch. But he was facing a Mexican champion who was 68-0 and was relentless in wearing down opponents in the ring.

"I don't look at him as a legend," Taylor said before the fight. "I look at him as just a fighter."

For much of the early fight, Chavez appeared to be just that as he tried to catch the faster Taylor, who kept getting the better of Chavez in exchanges and then managed to get away before Chavez could catch him.

The fight gradually built in intensity until the 10th round when the two went at it toe-to-toe, with Taylor throwing more punches but Chavez landing the cleaner and sharper blows. Chavez shook Taylor with a four-punch combination early in the round and with another with about 30 seconds left.

Taylor, though, had the edge in the 11th round, and as the fight entered the final round he was ahead by six points on one card and five on another. The third judge had Chavez winning by a point.

Taylor had taken some punishment, though, to get his lead. His left eye was nearly closed, his face was swollen and lumpy and his white satin trunks were stained with his own blood. Still, all Taylor had to do was survive the final round to win.

With a minute left in the fight, HBO announcer Jim Lampley proclaimed "'It doesn't appear at this moment that Chavez has the stuff to get it done."

Then Chavez badly hurt Taylor with a right to the head. In the final seconds, he was crumpled in the corner by another right.

Taylor got up at five and referee Richard Steele counted to eight. Only two seconds separated Taylor from victory, but Steele was getting no response from the fighter.

"Are you all right?" Steele asked Taylor, who was looking toward his corner, where trainer Lou Duva was inexplicably up on the steps ready to charge into the ring.

"Are you all right?" he asked again—still no response.

Steele waved the fight to a close as Duva charged from the corner in protest. The trainer leapt through the ropes and went racing over to confront Steele. "Unbelievable! Unbelievable! What the hell are you doing?" he yelled. "What did you stop it for? He was on his feet at five!"

Steele did not respond. He simply turned and walked away. As security guards climbed into the ring to protect the fighters, the spectators stood by their seats and applauded for several minutes in a moving tribute to the fighters.

The next day, Taylor faced the press behind dark glasses after spending the night in Valley Hospital. His face was swollen and bruised and he had a small fracture in the bone behind his left eye. He had received two pints of blood to replace what he lost, and said he had blurred vision from the third round on and had been unable to see Chavez's right.

He had to talk doctors into releasing him from the hospital so he could have his say.

"He had a blowout fracture of the left eye," Nevada state Athletic Commission doctor Flip Homansky said. "He also swallowed a lot of blood, plus he was badly dehydrated. He vomited a number of times and his blood count dropped over two points, which meant he lost about two pints of blood. He had blood in his urine. He was pretty beaten up. As I understand it, he was released against the doctors' wishes."

Still, Taylor wanted to make his point.

"My head was really clear," he said. "I wasn't wobbly. It was a very traumatic thing for me. It was ludicrous."

Steele was unapologetic.

"I'm not the timekeeper," Steele said. "When a man is hurt, I stop the fight."

Midway through the twelfth round, Chavez badly hurt Taylor with a right to the head. Then, in the final seconds, he was crumpled in the corner by another right.

Meldrick Taylor was way ahead on the scorecards but Julio Cesar Chavez never quit, finally catching up with Taylor in the final round and winning when referee Richard Steele stopped the fight with two seconds left.

>> RIDDICK BOWE VS. EVANDER HOLYFIELD I AND II

NOVEMBER 13, 1991
NOVEMBER 6, 1993

Pretend the Fan Man never happened and these were still two great championship fights between two heavyweights in their prime. Add the Fan Man in, and the mystique simply grows. Holyfield was the undersized heavyweight who knocked out Buster Douglas in October 1990 to win the title. Bowe was big and strong at 6-foot-5 and 235 pounds and had been carefully groomed for the opportunity since winning the silver medal in the 1988 Olympics.

They met at the Thomas and Mack Center on the UNLV campus. Almost immediately, it was clear Holyfield would have his hands full with a fighter who was not only bigger and stronger, but just as quick.

Holyfield couldn't match Bowe's power, but he did match his courage as the two heavyweights engaged in a series of toe-to-toe exchanges throughout the fight. Bowe appeared on the verge of ending it in the 10th round when he hit Holyfield with a right uppercut that sent him reeling and followed it with a barrage of 41 punches.

Holyfield came back at the end of the round, though, to land several head blows, and as the bell sounded they were winging huge punches at each other.

"In the 10th round, he was knocking me from pillar to post," Holyfield said. "But I thought I got him. He thought he got me."

Bowe knocked Holyfield down in the 11th round, and as he went back to his corner at the end of the round, he played to the crowd by pretending to adjust the heavyweight title belt around his waist.

One round later it was his, and a joyous celebration erupted in a corner that included his volatile manager, Rock Newman, and aging trainer Eddie Futch. But he and Holyfield were far from through.

They met again a year later outdoors at Caesars Palace, and for a time it looked like the rematch would be even better. Bowe was landing his jab well, but Holyfield was getting inside and getting the best of toe-to-toe exchanges in the early rounds.

In the seventh round, Bowe was finding his range, though he was cut in two places. Then, the Fan Man shockingly parachuted into the ropes in Bowe's corner and the fight would never be the same.

Both fighters went cold while waiting 21 minutes on the cool November night until order was restored. Bowe put on a stocking cap as he sat on his stool getting his cuts attended to, while Holyfield was covered in blankets in his corner.

Bowe's pregnant wife, Judy, had fainted at ringside and was taken to a hospital.

The fight ended on a chaotic note, too. The two fighters attacked one another after the bell and Holyfield's trainer, Emanuel Steward, tackled him to keep them apart.

"I thought we'd won a decision, but I didn't know," Steward said. "They broke into fighting and I went running across the ring. I didn't want to tackle Bowe because Evander might get disqualified so I tackled Evander."

In the confusion, the 82-year-old Futch, became dizzy and had to be taken to the hospital.

On one of the strangest nights in boxing history, Holyfield would be awarded a majority decision to become heavyweight champion for the second time.

Holyfield couldn't match Bowe's power, but he did match his courage as the two heavyweights engaged in a series of toe-to-toe exchanges throughout the fight.

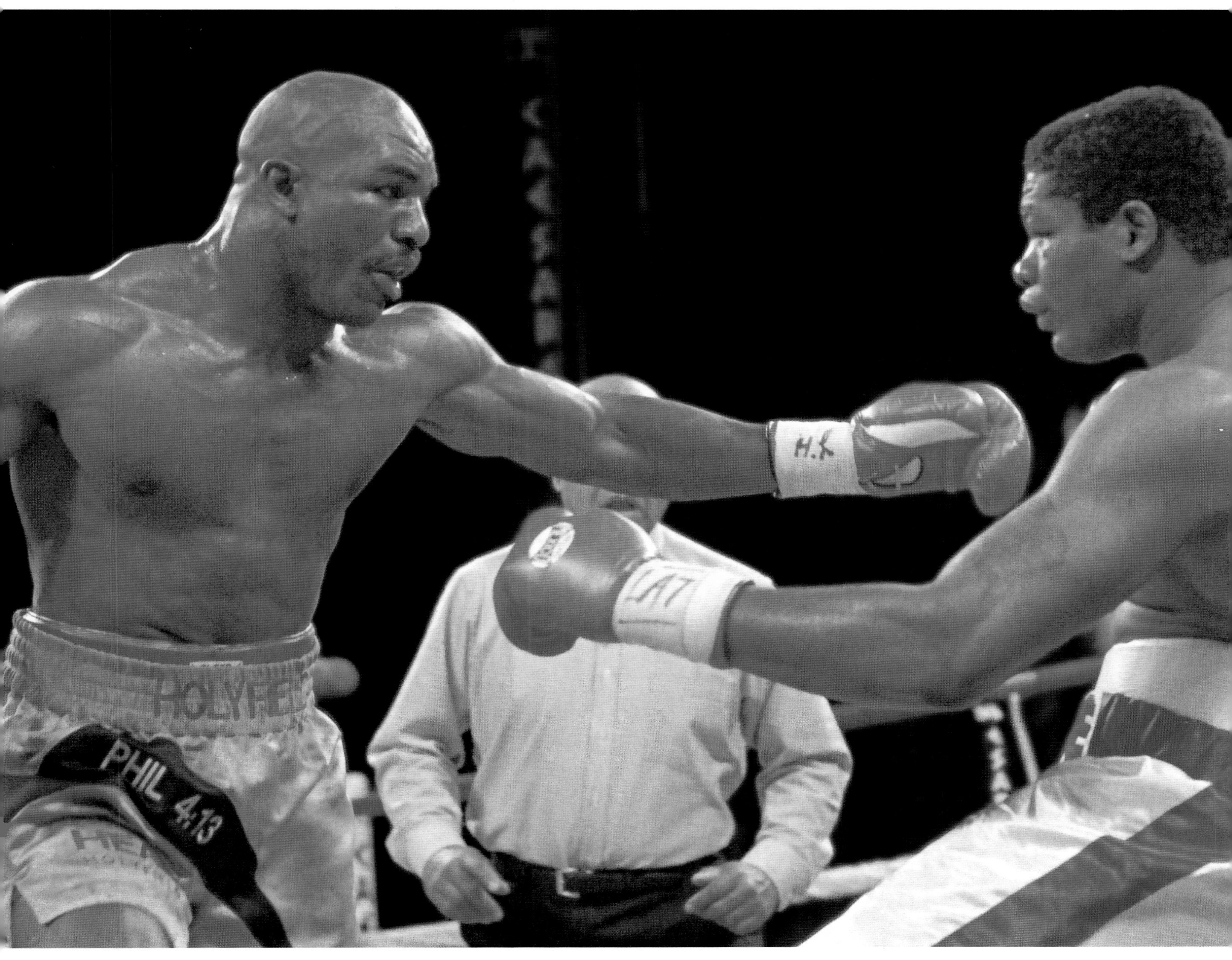

Evander Holyfield lands a left to the head of Riddick Bowe. Bowe beat Holyfield in their first fight to win the heavyweight title, then lost the second, which became infamous for the "Fan Man" dropping in.

CAESARS

8 >> ONLY IN VEGAS: THE WACKY AND WEIRD

THE NIGHT THE FAN MAN DROPPED IN

At the time, Riddick Bowe thought it was just really weird. The more time he's had to think about it, the more he believes it was something more sinister behind a night that will forever live in boxing history.

The Fan Man didn't just ruin a great fight. He may have cost Bowe his heavyweight title.

Bowe and Evander Holyfield were going at it in the seventh round of their title rematch in the outdoor arena at Caesars Palace when, suddenly, a dark figure swooshed into the arena and impaled himself on the ringside ropes near Bowe's corner.

The two fighters stopped trading blows and stood looking, astonished. Bowe's wife, Judy, fainted in her seat. Bedlam broke out in the arena.

Members of Bowe's entourage—fearful that the Nation of Islam's Louis Farrakahn or the Rev. Jesse Jackson were being attacked—began hitting the parachutist over the head with the large cellular phones of the day.

The Fan Man tries to untangle himself from the ropes after smashing into them during the seventh round of the heavyweight title fight between Riddick Bowe and Evander Holyfield. James Miller had circled the outdoor arena at Caesars Palace before aiming his motorized hang glider into the ring in one of the most bizarre scenes of a sport which has seen more than its share.

What may have hurt Bowe the most was that he had seemingly gained the edge and was winning the round when James Miller flew in on his motorized paraglider.

Over the years, he's thought about it long and hard.

"It was a conspiracy from day one," Bowe said. "What happened was they knew eventually Evander Holyfield would fade at some point in the fight. They had this cat up in the air waiting for him."

Fight writer Ed Schuyler Jr. of The Associated Press was at his usual place at ringside, phone in one ear, dictating the round-by-round of the fight to his desk in New York City when Miller flew in.

On the other end of the line some 3,000 miles away, deputy sports editor Ron Sirak looked over the shoulder of the person taking Schuyler's dictation to see what was happening.

"Bowe landed four punches to the head plus a stiff jab, then another, then two more," he read. "Bowe was finding the range with his jab."

What Sirak saw next caused him to think perhaps Schuyler had been drinking. The veteran writer had been known to have a taste or two.

"A man in a parachute fell into the ring," Schuyler dictated, "and the fight was stopped."

In a sport where the bizarre is sometimes normal, this was the most bizarre thing that had ever happened.

Schuyler hadn't been drinking, and he wasn't seeing things. In a sport where the bizarre is sometimes normal, this was the most bizarre thing ever.

A few seconds earlier, Bowe and Holyfield had been fighting a hotly contested rematch for the heavyweight championship of the world. Now, chaos ensued.

"There was a sound in the crowd so you knew something was happening," recalled Marc Ratner, who was at ringside for the Nevada Athletic commission. "It was the different noise. I heard the sound but I didn't see him until his feet were hanging between the ropes in the ring."

Caesars Palace sports director Rich Rose did see it from his third row seat, though he couldn't comprehend what he was seeing.

"I always sat with a monitor and a headset and I've got one eye on the ring and the other on the monitor," Rose said. "I look up and all of a sudden out of the corner of my eye I see something and it's getting closer. I said he's going over and going to land on the roof."

Lennox Lewis celebrates while Oliver McCall is walked back to his corner by referee Mills Lane after one of the strangest heavyweight title fights ever. At right, McCall stands sobbing between rounds as trainer George Benton, left, implores him to stop crying and start fighting.

JEFF SCHEID—LAS VEGAS REVIEW-JOURNAL

Then Rose saw he would miss the roof and was aiming toward the ring.

"I thought he had no shot of making the ring and I was hoping he didn't get caught in the lights and a fire start," he said. "I stood up literally as he hit he canopy."

Holyfield was in a clinch and facing Bowe's corner when the helmeted man harnessed to the propeller-powered paraglider crashed into the ropes. His first thoughts were of tennis star Monica Seles, who had recently been stabbed by a disturbed fan.

"It was scary," Holyfield said.

Bowe thought it was something more.

"Evander Holyfield could barely breathe and they told this guy to come in the ring and disrupt the fight," Bowe said.

Security guards quickly intervened and began disentangling the man from between the ropes, while Ratner and referee Mills Lane debated what to do.

If the fight was going to go on, the fighters would have to stay warm in the cool November night. Bowe had a knit hat while Holyfield sat in a corner underneath a blanket.

Ring announcer Michael Buffer tried to calm the crowd.

"I stood in the cold a half-hour while he had a quilt," Bowe said. "How did they get the quilt so fast? Why would that be in the corner? It was all a conspiracy."

The parachutist was finally freed from the ropes and his contraption, handcuffed and led away.

Twenty one minutes after he interrupted the seventh round, it resumed.

"At that point I'm pretty much out of the fight, and I'm so cold," Bowe said.

Though the round resumed, the problem was trying to figure out how to score it. Ratner went around to his judges reminding them to think about what happened in the first 1:10 of the round in what seemed like an awfully long time ago in scoring the completed round.

One judge scored the round for Bowe, one for Holyfield. The other scored it even.

Holyfield went on to win by a majority decision so slim that if the judge who had scored the round even had given it to Bowe, the fight would have been a draw and Bowe would have retained his heavyweight title.

The Fan Man had done his best to disrupt one of the best heavyweight title fights of the era. Later he would be arrested for dropping onto the roof of Buckingham Palace in London. For this, he got a night in jail and a fine, but there weren't many laws about flying into a fight.

Ironically, the fight ended on a chaotic note, too, with Bowe and Holyfield attacking each other after the bell and Steward having to tackle his own fighter to separate them.

"I thought we had won the decision, but I didn't know," Steward said. "They broke into fighting and I went running across the ring. Mills couldn't hold them off and a guy hit my leg as I was approaching them and I was falling and crashed into Evander and he went down. I was afraid it would be a disqualification for both of them."

Bowe's trainer, Eddie Futch, fainted in the commotion. Both he and Judy Bowe were released from the hospital the next day.

It was a night of triumph for Holyfield, who regained the heavyweight title for the second time. And it was the only loss in Bowe's career.

It was also a night where boxing managed to triumph over the bizarre.

DON'T CRY FOR ME

There's no crying in boxing. At least not during the middle of a heavyweight championship fight.

The scene that unfolded one night early in 1997 at the Las Vegas Hilton proved otherwise.

There was Oliver McCall, the one-time heavyweight champion of the world, standing in his corner after the fourth round with tears running down his face. The round before, he had refused to throw punches and at times turned his back on a befuddled Lennox Lewis.

With his trainer looking on in disgust, McCall went out for the fifth round and took a few more punches to the head before referee Mills Lane finally stopped the fight at 55 seconds of the fifth round.

McCall stormed from the ring in tears, only

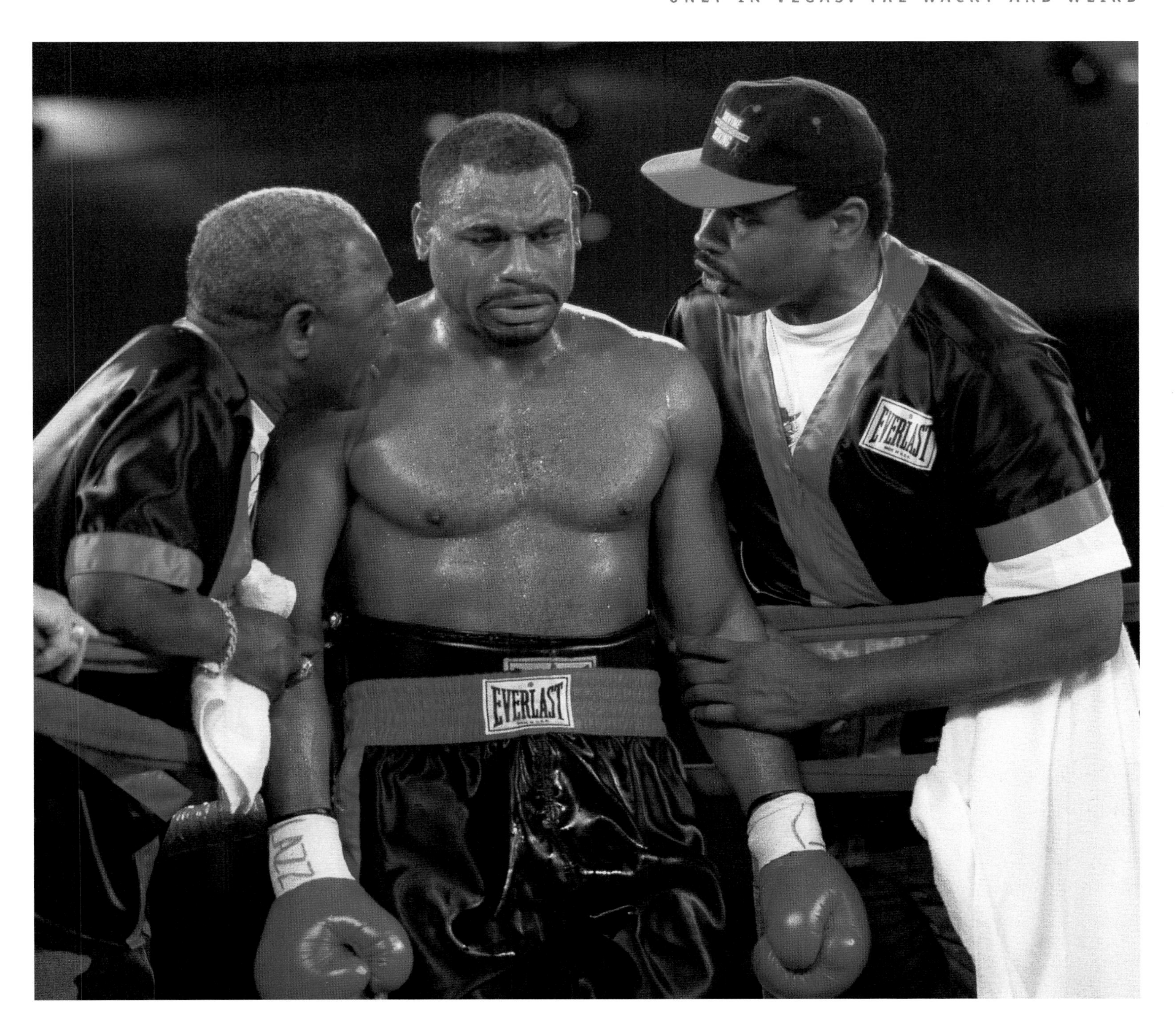

JEFF SCHEID—LAS VEGAS REVIEW-JOURNAL

THIRD MAN IN THE RING

Richard Steele had a memorable career as the third man in the ring for 167 world title fights. He was in the ring for some legendary battles, including the night Marvin Hagler and Thomas Hearns waged war for the middleweight title. For a long time, though, fight fans remembered him for only one fight—and they never let him forget it—Taylor vs. Chavez.

"Taylor was winning the fight, but he was taking a beating doing it," Steele said. In the final round, Chavez landed a crashing right that wobbled him. He landed another right, and Taylor dropped to the canvas.

Taylor was up at the count of five and holding onto the ropes. Steele was right in front of him, asking him if he could go on. "If he could have given me any kind of clue he could continue, I would have let him," Steele said. "I asked him twice if he was okay. He couldn't say anything. He couldn't nod his head, lift his hands, do anything. That was all he had to do." Steele waved the fight to a close with two seconds left.

Taylor's trainer, Lou Duva, leaped into the ring and went ballistic. The crowd booed and chanted obscenities. But Taylor was too far gone to complain. Taylor was taken to the hospital where he was treated for a fracture of his eye socket and severe dehydration. He had swallowed two pints of blood in the fight and was incoherent from his lack of fluids. "He went to the hospital for four days," Steele said. " The doctors later explained to me the reason he couldn't answer me was he was so dehydrated he didn't know where he was. "Still, boxing fans blamed Steele for not allowing the final two seconds to tick off.

Steele wasn't the only referee to take the heat for a decision made in a fight. Joey Curtis was considered one of Nevada's top referees until he prematurely stopped the WBA heavyweight fight in 1982 between Michael Dokes and Mike Weaver only 63 seconds into the first round. Dokes had swarmed all over Weaver and was hitting him with unanswered blows, but Weaver didn't appear hurt when the fight was stopped.

Curtis's career never recovered from the decision, and he was booed roundly everywhere he went. Steele, though, returned to the ring right away although he had to endure the boos. "People inside of boxing eventually came to realize I did the right thing," Steele said. "I'm proud of what I did."

SCOTT HENRY—LAS VEGAS REVIEW-JOURNAL

Sometimes it was the fighters who were goofy. John "The Beast" Mugabi is on queer street after Marvelous Marvin Hagler hits him in their 1986 fight. Hagler would stop Mugabi in the 11th round in his last successful title defense.

to claim later that he was playing possum and had a fight plan.

If he did, his own trainer George Benton didn't know anything about it.

"Lennox was in there with a lunatic," Benton said. "Any man in his right mind wouldn't act like that."

Lewis had been knocked out by McCall in 1994 to lose the heavyweight title, and he thought McCall might be pulling some sort of trick. Lewis gingerly went after him, but his heart didn't seem in it.

"McCall is just plain mad," Lewis said.

Nevada boxing authorities knew McCall had a checkered emotional past, and had sent him to a doctor before sanctioning the fight. He passed, and seemed fine at the weigh-in.

Just before the fight, basketball player Charles Barkley visited McCall in his dressing room and found him in high spirits.

"He looked fine," said Marc Ratner, director of the Nevada Athletic Commission. "We didn't know he didn't want to fight. It was very sad."

Lewis won the vacant WBC title by disqualification, while McCall was eventually fined $250,000 and suspended for a year by Nevada boxing authorities for refusing to fight.

Worse yet, the fight's promoter sued McCall over his $3 million purse, claiming he didn't fulfill his contract to fight.

McCall would later be put in a mental hospital after his wife took out a restraining order on him, and served a year in prison on drug charges.

He would return to fight again, but he could never shake his image as the heavyweight who cried.

I'M TAKING MY GLOVES AND GOING HOME!

Nevada boxing officials sometimes came about their reputation for firmness the hard way. Victor Galindez found that out, much to the displeasure of thousands of fight fans who had come to watch him fight Mike Rossman one Saturday afternoon in 1979.

Rossman had stopped Galindez the year before to win the WBA light heavyweight title, and the two were supposed to meet in a nationally televised rematch from the Caesars Palace Pavillion. But the WBA got into a dispute with the Nevada Athletic Commission over the judges and Galindez refused to come out of his dressing room, claiming Nevada judges would be biased against him.

Promoter Bob Arum was livid with the commission for not agreeing to use WBA judges, yelling at one point that "the inmates are running the asylum." Fans who crowded into the arena were just as unhappy, screaming for refunds.

"I had to get Arum out of there or there would have been a riot," said Art Lurie, who was on the Nevada commission at the time.

While Galindez refused to get in the ring, Rossman came in and posed for a picture. It wasn't just to record the moment. He was

Evander Holyfield grimaces after being bitten for the first time by Mike Tyson in their heavyweight title fight. Next page, Tyson gestures to his head, trying to tell referee Mills Lane that he acted only after being head-butted by Holyfield.

JOHN GURZINSKI—LAS VEGAS REVIEW-JOURNAL

insured by Lloyds of London for his $100,000 purse, and used the picture to collect from the insurance company.

Galindez and Rossman eventually met later that year, but it was in New Orleans, far from Las Vegas. It turned out Galindez didn't need the judges, knocking Rossman out in the 10th round to regain his title.

Sometimes, the fighter is the last to know when his fight is called off. Terry Norris was in his Caesars Palace hotel suite the night of September 26, 1992, getting ready to go downstairs, walk past the crowd milling at poolside and enter the sport pavilion to defend his WBC super welterweight title against Simon Brown.

The only problem was Brown wasn't going to show up. He was at Valley Hospital, where he had gone after complaining of dizziness the afternoon of the fight.

While the crowd at Caesars waited for the fight, and HBO went on the air to explain why it wasn't going to show it, Norris was left to explain to boxing writers how the fight would have gone if he had a chance to fight.

"Round one, I would have outboxed him," Norris said. "He's a slow fighter, slow hand speed. Then I would have dropped bombs on him. I would have taken him out in seven or eight rounds."

Brown was diagnosed as having a possible viral infection, but not before it was revealed that he had gone to see Dr. Elias Ghanem the Tuesday before the fight complaining of severe chest pains and shortness of breath. Ghanem was a member of the Nevada Athletic Commission, but apparently didn't tell anyone of the visit.

Brown's medical problems launched one boxing-related career, though. Dr. Margaret Goodman, a neurologist, was watching HBO at home waiting for the fight to come on when she heard announcer Jim Lampley say she was being called in to examine Brown. Goodman took to the sport so quickly she later became the chief ringside physician for the Nevada Athletic Commission.

A year later, it would be Brown making Norris dizzy. The two finally met in their

CLINT KARLSEN—LAS VEGAS REVIEW-JOURNAL

postponed fight, this time in Puebla, Mexico, and Brown gave Norris a beating before stopping him in the fourth round to take the light middleweight title.

BITE THIS!!!!

Mike Tyson was safely back in his dressing room, away from Evander Holyfield and angry fans who screamed and pelted him with things as he left the ring.

Back in the arena, a worker at the MGM Grand Hotel was examining the ring canvas and found the treasure he was looking for—the piece of Holyfield's ear that Tyson had bitten off a few minutes earlier.

As the worker carefully wrapped it in a piece of plastic, an angry and disconsolate Tyson tried to contemplate what he had just done.

"It's over. I know it's over," Tyson kept repeating. "My career is over."

As it turned out, it wasn't. Tyson would fight again, but only after he served an 18-month suspension and only after he was embarrassed even further when his psychological records were made public.

When he returned to the ring it was more freak show than feared former champion. People still wanted to see Tyson, but now it was to see a train wreck in the making.

It all happened on a night when 16,279 packed the MGM Grand Hotel arena for the biggest rematch of all time and a fight that promised to be spectacular. The day of the fight the lobby and casino of the MGM Grand was so packed with players, drug pushers, pimps and hookers that it was hard to even move.

Holyfield had upset Tyson to win the heavyweight title seven months earlier. Now Tyson was in shape, cocky and eager to show the world he was still the heavyweight king.

There was an excitement in the air that only Tyson could bring. Celebrities crowded ringside, every seat was sold, and a record two million homes spent $49.95 for the pay-per-view telecast.

"I don't know about this being the greatest fight ever, but I know it's been built up as the greatest fight ever," Tyson said as the fight approached.

Tyson had been a 20-1 favorite in the first

Tyson was actually holding his own, and had a good second round before the bite heard around the world. Next page, Holyfield leaves a local hospital after getting stitches in his ear.

JIM LAURIE—LAS VEGAS REVIEW-JOURNAL

fight, but was stopped in the 11th round. Still, he was a 2-1 favorite for a rematch that would pay Holyfield $35 million and Tyson $30 million.

If ever a fight was hotly anticipated, this was it. It figured to be even better than the first.

In less than three rounds, it all evaporated in two chomps of Holyfield's ears.

Before a frenzied crowd, Holyfield won the first round, while Tyson seemed to come back and fight well in the second. But Tyson was getting increasingly frustrated because he felt Lane was allowing Holyfield to head butt him.

A sellout crowd was chanting Tyson's name as he rallied in the third round to bring the fight to Holyfield.

Suddenly, he snapped.

In a clinch with Holyfield, their two heads together side by side, Tyson bit a gash out of the right ear of the champion, sending him leaping in the air in anger and pain.

At ringside, it was hard to figure out what had happened. After all, no one had bitten off an ear in the ring before.

"I thought he got kneed or his cup was pinching him," Nevada Athletic Commission director Marc Ratner said.

Blood began flowing down the side of Holyfield's face as he headed to his corner. Tyson watched for a few seconds, then rushed across the ring and pushed Holyfield in the back.

Lane stopped the fight and went over to Ratner and told him Tyson had bitten Holyfield and he was going to disqualify him.

"Are you sure?" Ratner asked, wanting to give Lane a few more seconds to think about what he was going to do.

Lane took Holyfield over to ring doctor Flip Homansky to show him the wound, which Homansky said wasn't serious enough to stop the fight. Four minutes had elapsed by the time Lane motioned for the fighters to finish off the 33 seconds left in the third round.

An angry Holyfield immediately landed a vicious left hook. The two clinched again, and then the unthinkable happened.

Tyson spit his mouthpiece out and took a bite of Holyfield's other ear.

Once again, Holyfield jumped in the air. This time, though, Lane didn't appear to see it and let the two fight the final seconds of the round. Finally, he went over to Tyson's corner, lectured him briefly and disqualified the fighter.

"There's a limit to everything, including bites," Lane said. "How many times do you want him to get bit?"

The Fight of the Century ended in bizarre fashion, with Holyfield minus an inch-long gash of his ear but still the heavyweight champion.

In the casino that night there was panic and a near riot as excited and frustrated masses roamed about.

Already, Ratner was second-guessing himself over the decision to let the fight go to a second bite.

"There's a lot of what-ifs, especially if Tyson would have won after biting him," Ratner said. "Maybe I'd do it different today. But it's something you'd never dream would happen."

A contrite Tyson apologized two days later,

MIKE SALSBURY—LAS VEGAS REVIEW-JOURNAL

saying he had just snapped. It wasn't enough to stop him from being banned from boxing and fined $3 million of his $30 million purse.

He would be reinstated 18 months later, but not before being humiliated and embarrassed by a psychological report ordered by Nevada authorities that concluded he had a "constellation of neurobehavioral deficits."

The team of doctors who examined Tyson said he threatened them on several occasions but concluded the "risk of another major boxing offense is low."

Still, Las Vegas wasn't done with Tyson yet.

Four years later, Tyson would be banned from fighting in Nevada again, after a series of incidents culminated with a brawl with Lennox Lewis at a New York press conference followed by an obscenity-laced tirade.

No one wanted boxing in Las Vegas to be like Mike.

Sugar Ray Leonard, shivering between rounds.

MOTHER NATURE'S TURN

The problem with holding fights outdoors is that Mother Nature doesn't always cooperate. Caesars Palace had more outdoor fights than anybody, and there were many memorable evenings where the sun was setting gently behind the mountains, the night was warm, and there was excitement in the air. There were also nights like March 10, 1986, when Marvelous Marvin Hagler defended his middleweight title against John "The Beast" Mugabi.

The night before, Hagler's half-brother, Robbie Sims, had knocked out John Collins in the same outdoor arena on a beautiful spring night. But a storm came in overnight, and it rained most of the day. It was still raining at 5 p.m., an hour before the card that also featured Thomas Hearns against James Shuler was to begin. Fans covered up as best they could, shivering in the wet, cold night.

The VIPs and celebrities had to be kept dry, though, and a call went out to the hotel for large garbage bags. They found 1,500 of them, and soon began passing them out at ringside. It was so wet that Hearns had a cornerman named Hollywood carry him into the ring so his boxing boots wouldn't get wet. He barely needed them, knocking out Shuler in the first round.

More often, heat was the major problem outside in the desert, particularly for those fighting on the undercard before the sun went behind the mountains. Irish featherweight champion Barry McGuigan was never the same after being knocked down twice in the fifteenth round and losing his title to plumber's helper Stevie Cruiz on June 23, 1986, when temperatures at ringside neared 110 degrees. McGuigan was taken on a stretcher from the arena and spent the night in a hospital. He fought only four more times before retiring.

But, it can also get cold at night in the desert. Riddick Bowe and Evander Holyfield found that out when the Fan Man parachuted into the ring's ropes one November night and interrupted the fight for several minutes. Sugar Ray Leonard, in his fight against Roberto Duran, asked if he could wear ski pants at the chilly December opening of The Mirage. Between rounds, cornermen piled blankets on Leonard and put a knit cap on his head. "It was freezing," Leonard said. "I've never been so cold."

The fight will always be known for the Fan Man, but it got ugly after the bell sounded to end the 12th round and the two fighters kept at each other. Referee Mills Lane tries to break it up, while Holyfield's trainer, Emanuel Steward rushes across the ring to try and separate the two big men.

WBC

9 >> A FIGHTER'S KIND OF TOWN

"When I train my boxers today, my whole mindset is how he is going to hold up when we hit Vegas at the Mandalay Bay Resort and Casino, Caesars Palace, or the MGM Grand Hotel and Casino," Steward said.

Larry Holmes thought he had it made when he came to Las Vegas in 1975 to fight Ernie Smith on the undercard of the Muhammad Ali-Ron Lyle heavyweight title fight. Holmes was Ali's sparring partner and had won all thirteen of his pro fights. It was enough to get him on the Strip, but just barely.

Larry Holmes thought he had it made when he came to Las Vegas in 1975 to fight Ernie Smith on the undercard of the Muhammad Ali-Ron Lyle heavyweight title fight.

Holmes was Ali's sparring partner and had won all 13 of his pro fights. It was enough to get him on the Strip—but just barely.

Ali was ensconced at Caesars Palace, which was training headquarters for the fight at the Convention Center. Holmes was relegated to the Tahiti Motel, where rooms could be rented in three-hour increments and X-rated films played on the TV.

It looks like a double knockdown, but it wasn't. Evander Holyfield and Lennox Lewis get tangled up and both go down together in their undisputed heavyweight title fight at the Thomas & Mack Center. The UNLV campus arena was the site of many big fights, including Holyfield's loss to Riddick Bowe in 1992.

In later years, Holmes was accused of having a chip on his shoulder about a number of things. It might have started with his room at the Tahiti.

"It was a little whorehouse on the corner," Holmes said. "It was mind-boggling. I thought I was something but they wouldn't even give me a room at Caesars Palace."

Seven years later, Holmes would fight Gerry Cooney in the biggest heavyweight fight of its time at Caesars, but for now he was a 10-round undercard fighter and promoters weren't going to spend much on him.

"They didn't want to treat me like a pro fighter. They treated me like a chump," Holmes said. "That's one of the things that hurt me. I thought I was king out here."

The Las Vegas that Holmes first saw was a town still trying to make a name for itself as the place for big fights. Ali would fight at the Convention Center against Lyle, Joe Bugner and Jerry Quarry, but his big fights went elsewhere.

Ali fought Ken Norton at Yankee Stadium, George Foreman in Zaire and Joe Frazier at Madison Square Garden, Kuala Lumpur and the Philippines.

When hotels figured out a way to stage fights on property, though, things began changing.

Ali and Leon Spinks met in 1978 in the first heavyweight title fight at a Las Vegas hotel inside a pavilion built at the Las Vegas Hilton. Caesars began putting title fights in its pavilion, and in 1980 Ali and Holmes met in the first outdoor megafight at Caesars.

Suddenly, fighters didn't have to fight in Yankee Stadium or Madison Square Garden to know they had it made.

By the '80s, Las Vegas was firmly entrenched as the boxing capital of the world. Mike Tyson won his first heavyweight title at the Hilton, Cooney and Holmes fought outside at Caesars and Marvelous Marvin Hagler, Sugar Ray Leonard, Thomas Hearns and Roberto Duran kept fighting big fights against each other.

"It was a magical time. They had the four horsemen, Hagler, Leonard, Hearns and Duran," promoter Bob Arum said. "Most of the fights with those guys fighting each other

KEITH SRAKOCIC—THE ASSOCIATED PRESS

took place in Vegas."

Leonard was one of the stars, but even he would marvel at what the fights brought to the town.

"The big fights were always in Vegas because they knew how to host a boxing event," Leonard said. "It was the pizzazz, the personality, the attitude. It was the cars parked at Caesars Palace a couple days before the fight. They didn't drive them so they would stay clean. It was an amazing thing."

Emanuel Steward first hit it big in Las Vegas as Hearns's trainer. He would go on to train Evander Holyfield, Lennox Lewis, Oscar De La Hoya and dozens of others.

He still has only one thing in mind for all of his boxers today.

"When I train my boxers today, my whole mindset is how he is going to hold up when we hit Vegas and he's at the Mandalay Bay, Caesars Palace or the MGM," Steward said. "I don't even get excited about people winning a fight until they get to Vegas. My goal for every fighter I get involved with is to prepare him to hit Las Vegas and have his name up there."

Fighting in Las Vegas made some fighters, and it broke others.

Holyfield thrived on it, making the most of his big chance when he knocked Buster Douglas out with one good right hand in the third round to win the undisputed heavyweight title.

Of course, it didn't help that Douglas weighed a blubbery 246 pounds and trained more at the Mirage buffet line then he did in the gym.

"We're home! We're home!" Holyfield trainer Lou Duva shouted when Douglas's weight was announced at the weigh-in.

Holyfield would go on to battle Riddick Bowe in three fights, including the infamous Fan Man fight, and fought—and beat—Mike Tyson twice at the MGM Grand Garden arena.

Holyfield was 7-4 in heavyweight title fights in Las Vegas during the 1990s, a decade that for him ended on a losing note when Lennox Lewis won a decision and the heavyweight title on November 13, 1999. Still, he made tens of millions of dollars in the city—$35 million for his second fight with Tyson alone.

George Foreman's career in Las Vegas spanned four decades, from his December 1969 first-round knockout of Bob Hazleton to his April 1995 disputed win over Axel Schulz. That fight was the only defense Foreman made of the heavyweight title he won a few months earlier on a one-punch knockout of Michael Moorer to become the oldest heavyweight champion ever.

Foreman wasn't too happy with Las Vegas before the fight. He was in his dressing room before the Moorer fight when Nevada athletic commission officials came in and told him there was no three- knockdown rule.

"I realized then if I knocked him down I'd have to keep him down so I didn't want to go for the quick knockout," Foreman said. "Still, I knew I could knock him out."

Foreman lost almost every round before he did just that, landing a crisp right hand that flattened Moorer. When the champion couldn't get up, the 45-year-old Foreman raised his hand in victory, then went to his corner, knelt and prayed.

Foreman had yet to sell a grill, but the fans cheered the roly-poly champion who poked fun at himself and never refused to give an autograph.

It was a far cry from his younger days when Foreman tried to emulate Sonny Liston and scare people off with his stare.

"When I was heavyweight champion of the world, I'd run people away," Foreman said. "Sometimes you get a second chance."

While Foreman made history as the oldest fighter to win the heavyweight title, Tyson made it as the youngest.

At dusk, the crowd gathers for the Larry Holmes-Gerry Cooney fight at Caesars Palace. The fight was held in an outdoor arena that seated nearly 30,000, but it was later torn down and a smaller arena was built for outdoor fights at the hotel.

CAESARS PALACE

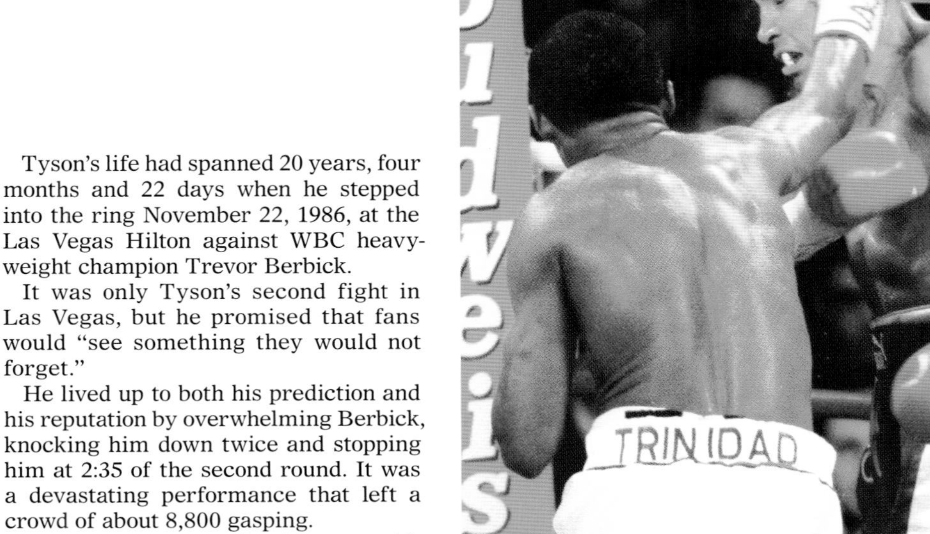

Felix Trinidad lands a right hand to the head of Oscar De La Hoya in their 1999 fight. Trinidad won the fight on a decision after De La Hoya faded and fought only sparingly in the final rounds.

Tyson's life had spanned 20 years, four months and 22 days when he stepped into the ring November 22, 1986, at the Las Vegas Hilton against WBC heavyweight champion Trevor Berbick.

It was only Tyson's second fight in Las Vegas, but he promised that fans would "see something they would not forget."

He lived up to both his prediction and his reputation by overwhelming Berbick, knocking him down twice and stopping him at 2:35 of the second round. It was a devastating performance that left a crowd of about 8,800 gasping.

"I'll fight any man alive," Tyson said.

Tyson would go on to not only fight in Las Vegas, but move to the gambling city, where he bought a house behind Wayne Newton's estate near the airport. There he kept lions and tigers and an assortment of cars that he used to frequent strip clubs about town.

Even though he was banned twice from fighting by Nevada boxing authorities—once for biting Holyfield's ear and a second time for brawling at a press conference with Lennox Lewis—Tyson would prove the greatest continuing box office attraction in Las Vegas.

Four of the top six grossing fights of all time in Las Vegas involved Tyson—including his two fights with Holyfield.

Tyson's first comeback fight after being released from prison against Peter McNeeley was the fourth-largest grossing fight of all time in Las Vegas—with fans spending $1,500 for ringside seats and ticket sales of $13,965,600.

They didn't get much for their money. McNeeley may have been promoter Don King's greatest sales job, but he wasn't much inside the ring.

Tyson needed only 89 seconds to stop McNeeley, who had been knocked down twice but was on his feet at the time his manager climbed into the ring midway through the first round.

Tyson got $25 million for the effort, though it was later revealed that King and Tyson's comanagers kept more than half of his money for themselves. McNeeley's purse was $540,000, and it was withheld from him until manager Vinny Vecchionne explained his actions.

"Mike, who will your first opponent be," was one sarcastic question Tyson and his people left unanswered at the post-fight news conference.

It wasn't just the heavyweights who made the big money. Leonard and Hearns got rich in Las Vegas, and Oscar De La Hoya showed what could be done with good looks, a flashy smile, an Olympic gold medal and plenty of talent.

De La Hoya made his Las Vegas debut in 1993 when he stopped Jeff Mayweather in only his fifth pro fight. The gambling town and De La Hoya were an instant marriage, and he soon became a regular in the outdoor arena at Caesars Palace and then later at the Mandalay Bay.

De La Hoya's disputed loss to Felix Trinidad in September 1999 was the biggest grossing non-heavyweight fight in Las Vegas history, with a crowd of 11,184 at the Mandalay Bay paying $8,871,300 to see it.

"A great percentage of the fan base is now Hispanic," Arum said. "They won't go to see Lennox Lewis fight, but they'll go to see Oscar."

De La Hoya proved that again when he stopped Fernando Vargas before a sellout crowd at Mandalay Bay on September 14, 2002, a fight that may end up being the defining moment of his career.

It was only fitting that he did it in Las Vegas, where the great fighters fight and the great fights are held.

Holmes knew that even when he was staying at the Tahiti Motel.

"I was really crazy about Las Vegas. It was a place I always wanted to be," Holmes said. "I used to take less money to go there."

The problem, Holmes said, was promoter Don King knew that.

"Don King used to tell me when I eat steak everyone eats steak," Holmes said. "I found out that wasn't true. I was eating pork chops, some chitlins."

Holmes would go on to lose his heavyweight title to Michael Spinks in September 1985 outdoors at the Riviera Hotel, an upset that not only cost him his championship but a chance to tie Rocky Marciano's record of 49-0.

Holmes remains bitter today about a town where he began with nothing and left with a bad taste in his mouth.

"Vegas changed. It became a lot of petty bullshit," he said. "I was too long as champion and it was time for me to move on and let somebody else have it. They did everything they could to get me out."

Strange words, for a town that tried to get every fighter in.

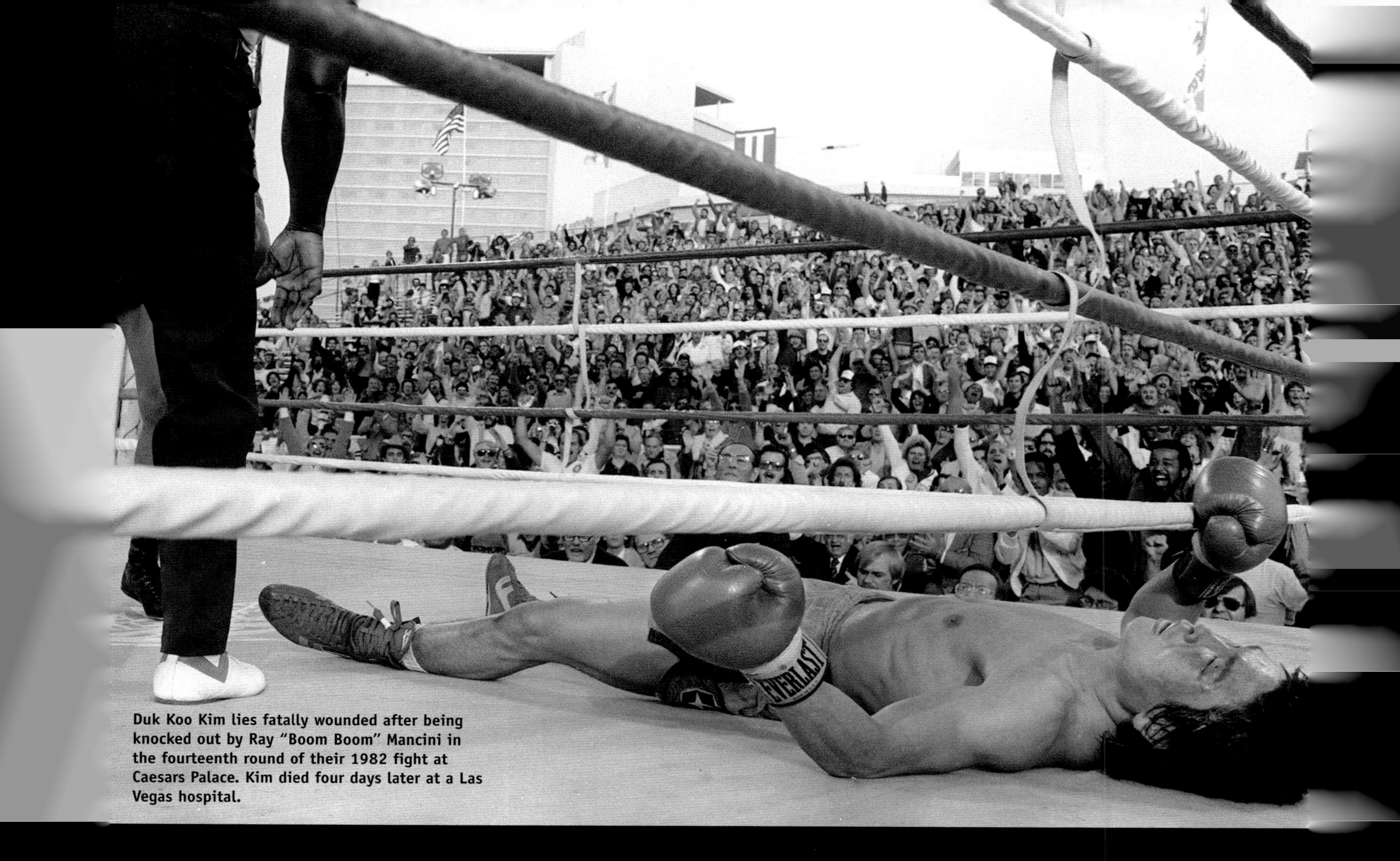

Duk Koo Kim lies fatally wounded after being knocked out by Ray "Boom Boom" Mancini in the fourteenth round of their 1982 fight at Caesars Palace. Kim died four days later at a Las Vegas hospital.

TRAGEDY IN THE RING

On the same night he beat Jimmy Garcia, Gabriel Ruelas went to visit him in the hospital. He knew Garcia was badly hurt, but when he got there he found out just how badly. "The way I saw him, I really saw a dead body in front of me," Ruelas said.

The 23-year-old Garcia had come from Columbia to fight Ruelas for the WBC super featherweight title. He reportedly had to lose 30 pounds in two months before the May 6, 1995, fight at Caesars Palace to make the 130-pound weight.

Garcia was battered throughout the fight and seemed to have little punching power. He made it into the eleventh round before the fight was stopped and then collapsed in his corner. He was rushed to University Medical Center, where he underwent neurosurgery within 35 minutes of his collapse. Doctors held out some hope, but thirteen days later life support systems were disconnected, and he was

An autopsy showed Garcia suffered slow bleeding from a vein in his head, bleeding which probably began sometime during the fight. When the pressure built up to a high level, it moved his brain, causing his collapse.

The death was one of five ring injuries in Las Vegas boxing history. The state has a medical advisory board, and its ringside physicians are trained to leap into the ring at any sign of injury, but ultimately, boxing remains a brutal and dangerous sport.

Even the survivors didn't come out unscathed. Ruelas was never the same, losing his title in his next fight and never winning a championship again. He talked about coming to grips with the fact he killed someone in the ring, but never fought at the top level again.

The same thing occurred to Ray "Boom Boom" Mancini after he stopped Duk Koo Kim in the fourteenth round of their 1982 lightweight fight, only to see him carried out of the ring on a stretcher. Kim died four days later at a Las Vegas hospital. Mancini won only four more fights in his career. "I

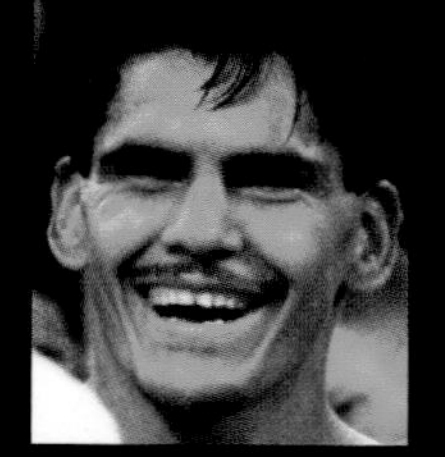

"The way I saw him, I really saw a dead body in front of me."
GABRIEL RUELAS

'HE COULDN'T CARRY MY JOCK'

Larry Holmes meant what he said—he just didn't understand what his words would come to mean. Bitter and frustrated after losing his heavyweight title to Michael Spinks at the Riviera Hotel and Casino, Holmes lashed out at the judges, the media, and everyone around him. It was when he spoke of Rocky Marciano that he made his biggest mistake.

Holmes was attempting to tie Marciano's 49-0 record. He not only didn't do that, but he lost the heavyweight title he had held for seven years and became the first heavyweight champion to lose to a light heavyweight champion.

"Rocky Marciano couldn't carry my jock," Holmes yelled out at the post-fight press conference.

Later, up in Holmes's room, British writer Colin Hart told Holmes he should have kept quiet. "You screwed up," Hart said.

Holmes was always bitter and never got the recognition he deserved as a great champion. He won no fans by beating a faded Ali, and trashed the Great White Hope, Gerry Cooney, in 1982. But to disparage the great Marciano cost him even more fans.

I didn't know what I was saying was going to affect anybody," Holmes said. "I was just saying that because of the way I grew up. It was not a slam against Marciano. It was just something that I felt I was as good as anybody on God's' given earth."

It wasn't just the Marciano comment that got him into trouble. He also claimed the judges "must have been drunk" to score the fight for Spinks, words that came back to haunt him in the rematch when he lost a split decision in a fight most at ringside thought he had won.

"I don't regret saying that. They had to be drunk to score it that way," Holmes said. "I hurt him and slacked up a little bit because I felt sorry for him. I should have tried to kill him because that's what people wanted."

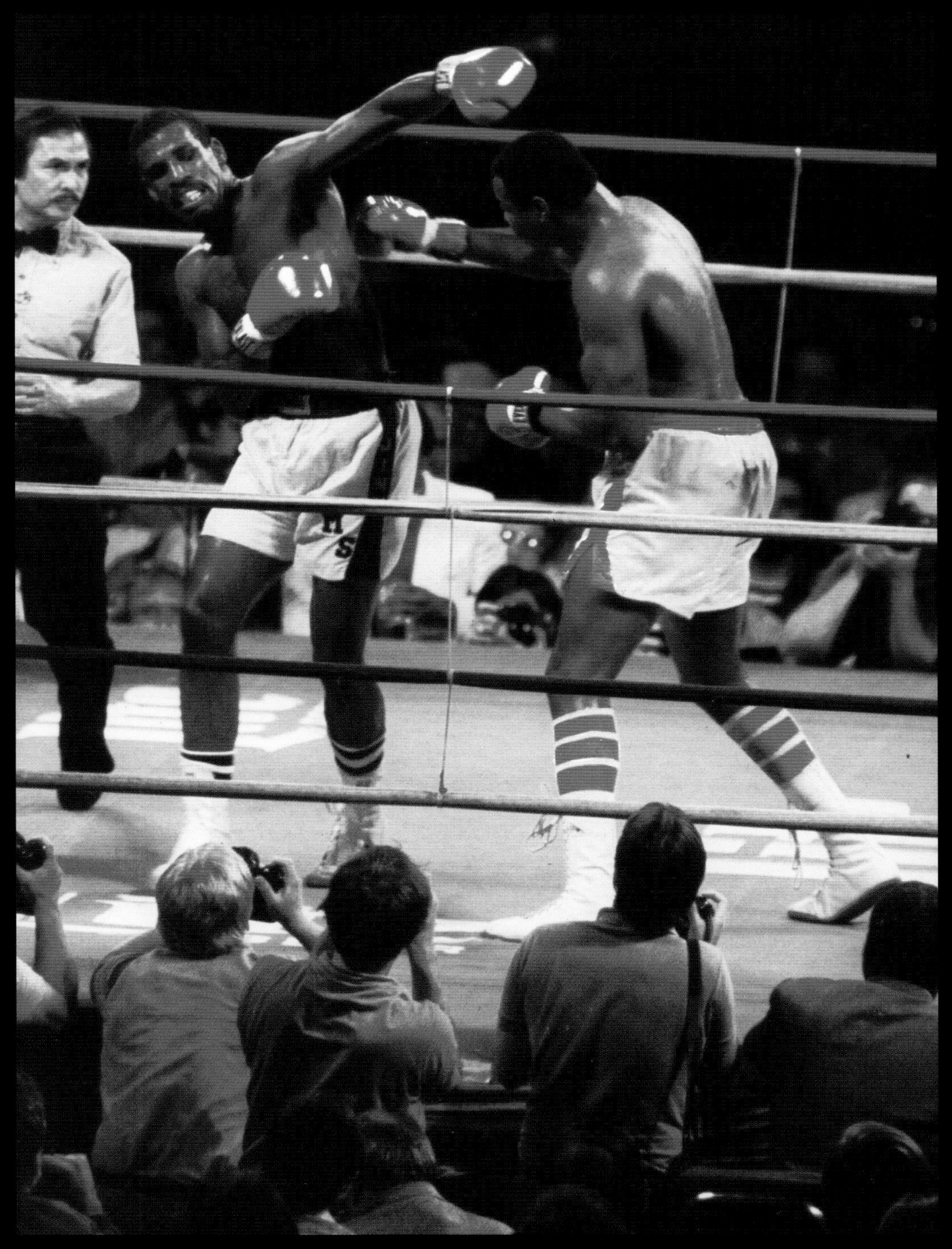

Holmes, in action against Spinks, and later, above left, at an indignant press conference.

JEFF SCHEID—LAS VEGAS REVIEW-JOURNAL

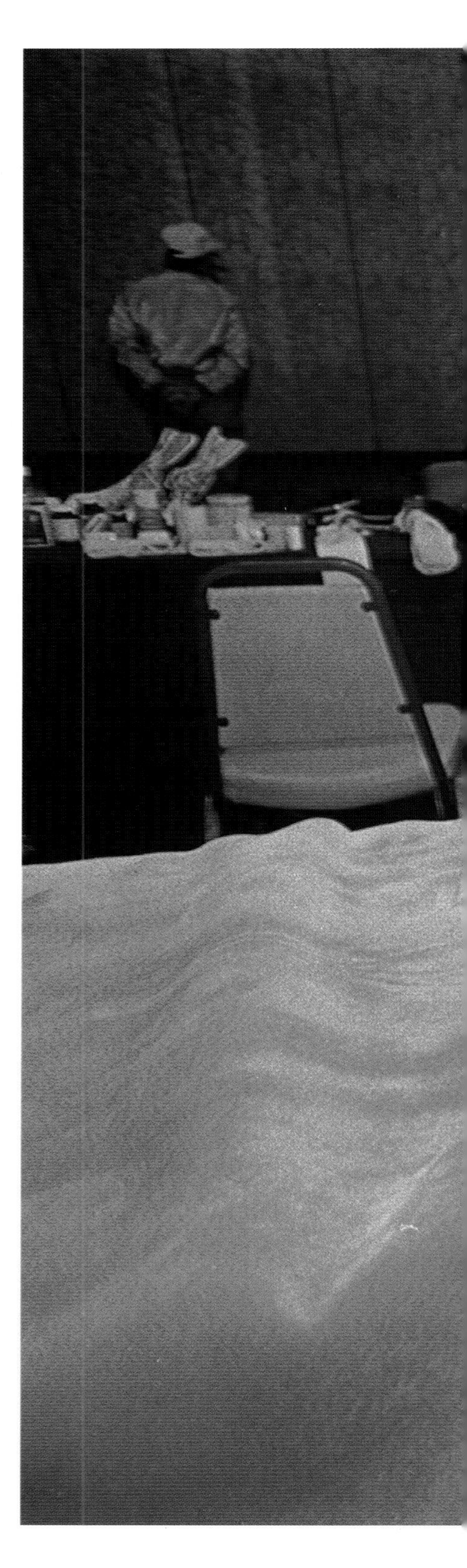

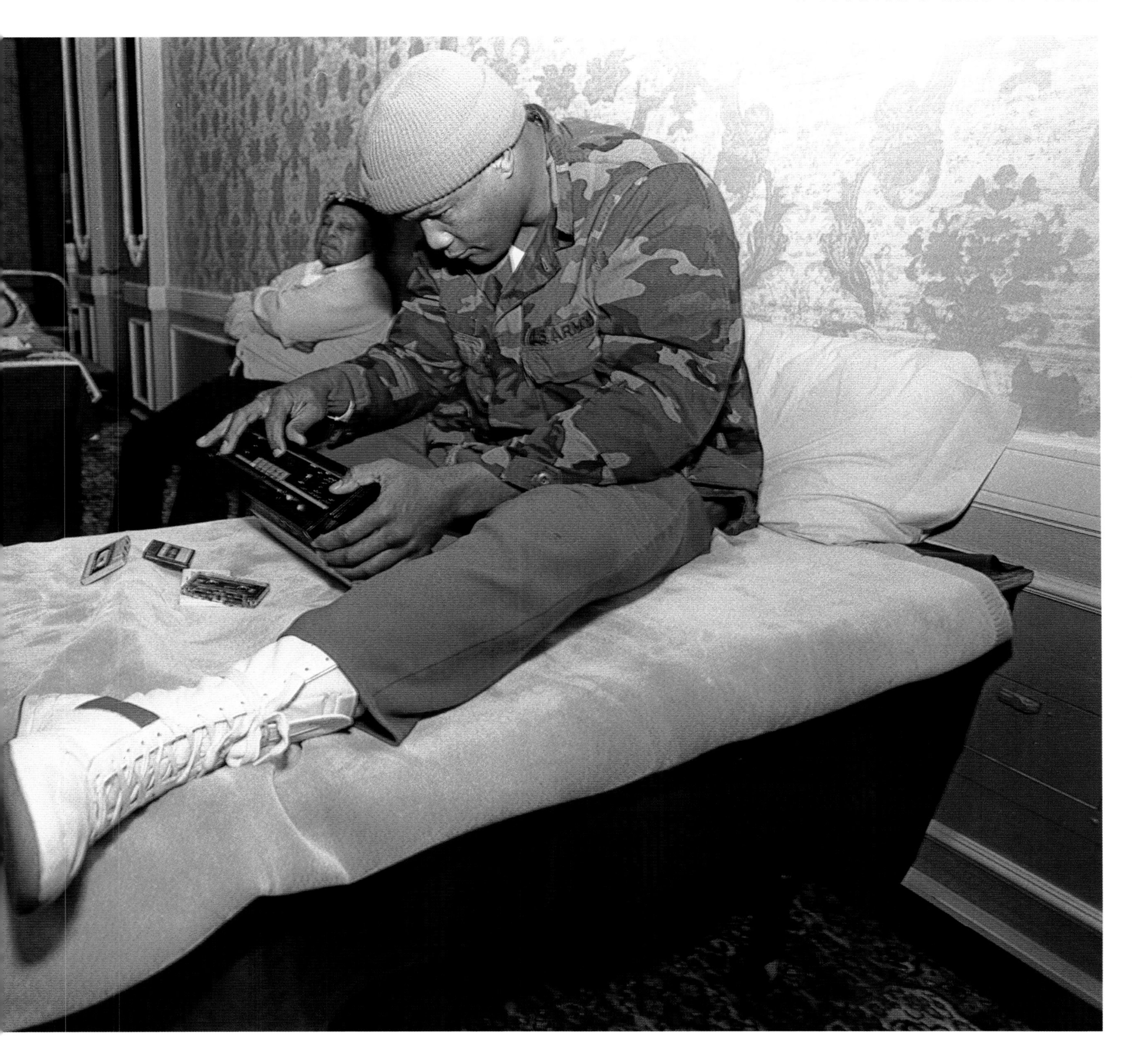

JEFF SCHEID—LAS VEGAS REVIEW-JOURNAL

JEFF SCHEID—LAS VEGAS REVIEW-JOURNAL

JEFF SCHEID—LAS VEGAS REVIEW-JOURNAL

BROWN BOMBER

Larry Holmes was defending his heavyweight title against Trevor Berbick and the cozy sports pavilion at Caesars Palace was packed with more :han 4,000 fight fans. The loudest cheers of the night, :hough, weren't for the fighters. They were reserved or an old man sitting in his wheelchair at ringside, drool running from his mouth over his chin.The crowd stood as one to cheer on Joe Louis, who responded vith a slight wave and the makings of a small grin.

Louis never fought in Las Vegas. The city's emergence as the fight capital of the world took place long after he had left the ring. But he grew to ove the city, hanging around with his friends and benefactors at fights in the '60s and later working as greeter at Caesars Palace to pay off debts to the IRS.

Louis never seemed to need an introduction when ne attended a fight in the city. The crowd always sensed his arrival.That's the way it was the night of April 11, 1981, when Holmes and Berbick met behind Caesars Palace in its outdoor ring. As Louis was wheeled to his ringside space, the crowd stood training to see, then broke into cheers for the former neavyweight champion. Between fights, Louis received another ovation when his presence was announced rom ringside.

Fourteen hours later, the Brown Bomber was dead. The 66-year-old Louis had been in declining health for years. He had suffered a stroke and was confined to a wheelchair after undergoing heart surgery in 1977.

But Louis continued to show up at the fights and work at the hotel. People came by to pay their respects, talk with Louis about their favorite fights and get their picture taken with the former champion. Muhammad Ali was in the middle of his boxing tour around the world at the time, and he couldn't get over how many people talked to him about meeting Louis at the Strip resort. "If all the people who said they met Joe Louis at Caesars Palace were there, they wouldn't be able to get anyone in the door," Ali said.

Louis was seduced by the Las Vegas lifestyle. He still owed the government a bundle, but he would stay up all night shooting craps if he had a bit of money in his pocket. High-rolling gamblers would slip him cash on the side, then spend the night gambling with the former heavyweight champion.

The morning of Sonny Liston's funeral, Louis was in the casino at Caesars Palace where he saw one of his gambling friends. The gambler was shooting craps for big money, and jokingly called Louis over to the table to tell him he could have a piece of the action. "I'll be late for the funeral," Louis said, eyeing the chips and thinking about what he should do. "But, Sonny would understand."

One day, Louis was the honorary referee at the weekly fights at the Silver Slipper. He was also scoring the four-rounder and at the end he turned in his card. Louis had one fighter winning three rounds to two.

"But it's only a four-rounder, Joe," someone said.

"Hey, that's the way I see it," Louis replied.

The weekend before Louis died, a sellout crowd of more than 1,500 attended a "Salute to Joe Louis" at the Frontier Hotel sponsored by the National Veterans Boxing Association. Holmes was there and paid $1,500 for two Louis fight posters that were auctioned. "Joe means a lot to me and always has," Holmes said.

A few days after Louis died, a bronze coffin was placed inside a wreath-filled boxing ring in the same arena where Holmes and Berbick fought. Thousands filed past the bier in the now somber and darkened arena. Many were tourists clad in shorts, others were dressed in the uniforms of various Strip hotels.

The next day, the Reverend Jesse Jackson eulogized Louis as a hero who lifted the spirits of a nation and beat down Adolph Hitler's notion of German racial supremacy. Frank Sinatra was one of the pallbearers, along with promoter Don King and two of Louis' most memorable opponents, Jersey Joe Walcott and Billy Conn. In the crowd of nearly 3,000 were Muhammed Ali, Larry Holmes, Floyd Patterson and Sugar Ray Robinson.

"There's not much that can be said about this," Sinatra said. "He was a dear friend of mine."

Louis was later buried at Arlington National Cemetery, but the boxing world didn't forget him in Las Vegas. At Caesars Palace there is a 7-foot-6 solid marble statue weighing 4,500 pounds that is a tribute to the late, great champion. It sits just outside the resort's sports books, where fans come to get their picture taken and playfully exchange jabs with the likeness.

One day, a fan was crouched by the statue having his picture taken and got up only to run into Louis' marble left hand and fall down unconscious. Even from beyond, the Brown Bomber was still knocking them out.

The elite of boxing turned out for the services for Joe Louis. Don King, Larry Holmes, Frank Sinatra, and Muhammad Ali were among the pallbearers. His old foe, Max Schmeling, would pay for the funeral

Lite
Lite
Lite
EVERLAST

10 >> IRON MIKE

Mike Tyson probably thought he had sunk as low as he could go. The three years in prison for rape were bad enough. Trying to beat up two men following a fender bender was merely Mike being Mike. Biting Evander Holyfield's ear, well, that certainly didn't do much for his reputation but didn't hurt his box office appeal.

But now Tyson was being labeled something even worse—a ferret abuser. Now, he had enraged even the animal lovers.

A pair of ferrets who lived in a custom-built maze in the weight room in Tyson's house weighed only half of their normal two pounds when a Tyson assistant called a ferret rescuer to come and get them in December 1999. The rescuer screamed abuse, which was almost too much for a guy with such a soft spot for animals that he kept lions and tigers at his sprawling home behind Wayne Newton's estate near McCarran International Airport.

A Tyson assistant quickly covered up for the boss, claiming responsibility for the ferrets and saying all the heavyweight fighter wanted was for them to be happy and well.

"If we were neglecting or abusing them we could have just thrown them over the fence into (neighbor) Wayne Newton's yard," was Darryl Francis' way of explaining things.

In his prime, Mike Tyson was an intimidating presence, the most feared fighter around. Before his life grew so complicated he went into the ring clad simply in black trunks with a cut out white towel over his shoulders. Here, he gets some last minute advice from former trainer Kevin Rooney beore going out to demolish Trevor Berbick at the Las Vegas Hilton and become the youngest heavyweight champion ever at the age of 20.

From the time he became the youngest heavyweight champion ever by knocking out Trevor Berbick in the second round at the Las Vegas Hilton in February 1986 to the time 13 years later when boxing regulators finally decided they'd had enough and suggested it was time for Tyson to ride out of town, Tyson loomed larger than life in a city where legends are made and fortunes won and lost.

Tyson was never formally charged with ferret abuse, one of the few victories outside the ring he could claim in his turbulent life in his adopted hometown. Tyson and Las Vegas were made for each other like no other, but he had a love-hate relationship with the city.

Las Vegas was the city where Tyson had won his first title. It was also the place he suffered his greatest embarrassment.

Tyson made tens of millions of dollars inside boxing rings on the casinos that litter the Las Vegas Strip. It was there where he fought his greatest fights, and there where high-rollers and gang bangers alike paid big money for tickets to see the spectacle that only a Tyson fight could provide.

The city remained his home even as his fighting days dwindled, and he filed for bankruptcy, citing $27 million in debts. Tyson had made several hundred million dollars—much of it in Las Vegas—but he had few assets other than his two Las Vegas homes.

From the time he became the youngest heavyweight champion ever by knocking out

The punches came from everywhere, with stunning quickness and with bad intentions. Tyson made his Las Vegas debut in this September 6, 1986, fight, stopping an intimidated Alfonso Ratliff in the second round at the Las Vegas Hilton. Two months later, Tyson returned to the same ring to knock out Trevor Berbick and win the WBC heavyweight title.

Trevor Berbick in the second round at the Las Vegas Hilton in February 1986 to the time 13 years later when boxing regulators finally decided they'd had enough and suggested it was time for him to ride out of town, Tyson loomed larger than life in a city where legends are made and fortunes won and lost.

Like a big-time gambler who couldn't get enough of the action, Tyson won and lost fortunes in the city he found irrestibile. He oogled dancers at the city's strip clubs between fights, bought cars by the handful at local dealerships and spent money like it would never stop coming in.

In the heady days following his release from prison in 1995, Tyson bought the 11,000-square foot home on Tomiyasu Lane that would be his headquarters, then dispatched some of his minions to go next door and offer to buy the neighbor's house, too, so Tyson would have a place to house his entourage.

Not being too worldly in the ways of real estate, they sat down at the neighbor's dining room table and asked him if he wanted to sell. When he declined, they pulled out a briefcase and opened it. Inside was $1 million in cash, an offer the neighbor also declined.

There was plenty of cash to go around. Tyson came out of prison with a $120 million contract to fight for Don King, who promptly signed a six-fight deal with the MGM Grand for a series of Tyson fights that would bring both fame and shame to the hotel and the fighter. The MGM was so eager to get Tyson that it made King a major stockholder, giving him 618,557 shares of hotel stock with a guarantee that it would double in value to $30 million by the time the fights were over.

It was under this deal that Tyson made his eagerly anticipated return to the ring August 19, 1995, fighting for the first time since he had beat Razor Ruddock outdoors at the Mirage hotel-casino four years earlier. His opponent was Peter McNeeley, a little-known white heavyweight who King managed to build up as the next Rocky Marciano, and who for

Tony Tucker was undefeated in 35 fights and held the IBF heavyweight title when he met Tyson at the Las Vegas Hilton on August 1, 1987. Tucker secured a psychological victory by managing to last all 12 rounds with Tyson, but when it was over Tyson had won a lopsided decision and was now the undisputed heavyweight champion of the world.

When Tyson threw the right hand, it was usually trouble for the other guy in the ring. Here, he snaps back the head of Donovan "Razor" Ruddock at the Mirage hotel-casino. Tyson was in the midst of his first comeback after losing to Buster Douglas when he stopped Ruddock in the seventh round in March 1991. The two met three months later, and Tyson knocked Ruddock down twice en route to a unanimous decision win.

Two greats meet outside the ring and out of harm's way when Tyson and Sugar Ray Leonard do a bit of commentary at ringside for a Las Vegas fight. Between the two of them, they were responsible for the biggest fights of the '80s and '90s in a city they helped become Fight Town.

It what became a familiar sight to fight fans, Tyson stands over a fallen Trevor Berbick in their November 1986 heavyweight title fight. Berbick, who went down twice in the second round, managed to stumble to his feet twice after the second knockout, only to fall to the canvas again from the delayed impact of Tyson's right hand.

$540,000 was more than willing to play the part of obliging opponent.

For the 16,143 who packed the MGM Grand Garden arena, it wouldn't have mattered if the opponent was Wayne Newton. For as much resistance as McNeeley put up, it might as well have been. They paid $1,500 to sit ringside and be part of the spectacle. Iron Mike was back, and prison had done nothing but whet the public's appetite to see the fearsome former champion do his devastating thing in the ring once again.

"The Vatican sent me a special crew to redo the resurrection," King chortled years later. "For a man coming out of prison for the most heinous of crimes, to be greeted like a conquering hero was simply an amazing accomplishment."

Tyson was to be paid $25 million for the comeback fight, though it would later be revealed that he would get only $8 million or so of that after his managers and King took their hefty cuts. Still, it was a lot of money for what turned out to be only 89 seconds of work.

Celebrities like Jerry Seinfield, Michael Jackson, future California Governor Arnold Schwarzenegger, Jim Carrey and Eddie Murphy were at ringside, and the buzz reached a fever pitch when Tyson walked into the ring in black trunks with a cutout towel over his head. Tyson was ready to fight, and so was McNeeley, who came right after him, throwing wild haymakers that Tyson answered with crashing punches of his own. McNeeley was knocked down twice and his cornerman Vinny Vecchione jumped into the ring to bring the figiht to a close before it reached the halfway point of the first round.

The crowd booed, and even Tyson wasn't sure

what was happening. "What?" he asked referee Mills Lane, as he waved the fight to a close. "I didn't think I hit him that hard," Tyson said later.

King insisted everything was on the up-and-up, and even those conned into paying heavyweight championship prices for what amounted to little more than a glorified exhibition didn't seem that upset. At least they had gotten a chance to see their hero in action again.

"This was not a ripoff," the spiky haired promoter insisted. "If McNeeley's trainer didn't jump into that ring with the towel it would have been one of the most talked about fights ever. He cheated McNeeley of that glory. McNeeley did not run from Tyson, but to Tyson."

The next time Tyson fought in Las Vegas, it would be for a world title, against Frank Bruno, a fighter he had already knocked out seven years earlier in the fifth round at the Las Vegas Hilton. Bruno was intimidated before he even got into the ring, walking stiffly into the arena and fighting even more stiffly once he got there. Tyson knocked him out in the third round to win the WBC title, then added the WBA belt with a knockout of Bruce Seldon six months later. Rapper Tupac Shakur was at that fight along with many of the hip-hop culture that followed Tyson, and later that night he was shot to death in a drive-by ambush that was never solved.

By then, boxing fans were certain this was the Tyson of old, a menacing figure who would frighten opponents and then waste little time in knocking them out. Next up was former champion Evander Holyfield, who had looked so bad in his previous fight against Bobby Czyz that King and Tyson's handlers figured he was washed up enough for Tyson to handle without

Peter McNeeley comes in swinging wildly as Mike Tyson looks to counter in the first round of their August 1995 fight. McNeeley took the fight to Tyson, but it was a mistake on his part as Tyson landed some big punches before McNeeley's corner threw in the towel after only 89 seconds. The fight was Tyson's first since being released from prison, and a capacity crowd paid up to $1,500 for ringside seats for the mismatch.

Referee Mills Lane points to a neutral corner for Mike Tyson after he knocked Peter McNeeley down early in the first round. McNeeley was handpicked as the first comeback opponent for Tyson after he served three years in prison for rape, and it was easy to see why. He tried to fight, but was overwhelmed by Tyson and the fight ended when his corner threw in the towel.

A decade after he became heavyweight champion, Tyson was back fighting in Las Vegas, this time at the MGM Grand as part of a lucrative contract he signed after getting out of prison on a rape conviction in 1995. The hotel was different, but the results were much the same as Tyson, at left, stops a stiff Frank Bruno in the third round in March 1996 to become the WBC heavyweight champion once again. Six months later he won the WBA title by knockout out Bruce Seldon in the first round, at right.

any difficulty. The Nevada Athletic Commission was so worried about Holyfield that it ordered the 34-year-old to undergo a series of tests at the Mayo Clinic before allowing him in the ring with Tyson.

Oddsmakers saw it the same way, making Tyson a prohibitive 25-1 pick when betting opened, though ominiously bettors who liked Holyfield came in with enough cash to narrow the odds to 5-1 by fight time.

What followed was one of the biggest upsets in boxing. Holyfield didn't just beat Tyson, he dominated him, knocking the former champion around the ring at will before finally stopping him with a nine-punch barrage at 37 seconds of the 11th round. Afterward, Tyson would say he didn't remember anything from the fourth round on, and the sight of him holding his head in a towel in despair at the post-fight press conference was almost as shocking as the way Holyfield bullied him around the ring.

"I take my hat off to him," Tyson said. "I look forward to a rematch."

Holyfield seemed to almost feel sorry for Tyson, who was surrounded by handlers but seemed very alone after taking his beating.

"I just feel Mike needs someone around him who loves Mike for Mike," Holyfield said.

The fight set a new record for live gate in Las Vegas, $14,150,700. While the MGM was happy, bookmakers up and down the Las Vegas Strip weren't. They lost millions but were more careful for the rematch seven months ever, making Tyson a 2-1 favorite in what became the richest fight in boxing history. It also became perhaps the most infamous, the 'Bite Fight" that got Tyson banned from boxing for 18 months and

left Holyfield without a chunk of his right ear.

In just a few short months, Tyson had gone from returning hero to nasty villain once again, and he would not fight again until he apologized repeatedly, acted as contrite as possible and underwent a series of embarrassing psychological tests that portrayed him as an immature person with low self esteem and a massive ego.

"I'm no Mother Teresa," Tyson said when asking for his boxing license back. "I'm not Charles Manson either. Just treat me equal."

When Tyson was finally allowed back into the ring, the anticipation had built almost like a few years earlier when he returned from prison to fight McNeeley. Holyfield was defending his undisputed heavyweight titles against Lennox Lewis around the same time, but Tyson was making more money—$20 million—to fight a South African named Francois Botha—aka the White Buffalo. Tyson immediately went out and tried to break Botha's arm in the first round, then showed he had learned nothing in his next fight by hitting Orlin Norris after the bell ended in the first round.

By then, the MGM was trying to figure out a way to get out of the last fight of the six fight contract and Las Vegas had finally had enough with Tyson and the problems he brought to the ring. Boxing regulators suggested Tyson hit the road if he wanted to fight again.

"I'm not so sure we need him in the state of Nevada any longer," commissioner Lorenzo Fertitta said.

It turned out they weren't bluffing.

Tyson still lived at the house behind Wayne Newton, and he still trained off and on at the Golden Gloves gym just past the left field wall of Cashman Field. But he would have to go elsewhere to fight and he did, traveling overseas for fights in England and Denmark and meeting Andrew Golota in Detroit.

When it came time for his megafight with Lennox Lewis, though, it seemed all would be forgiven. Tyson would be contrite and ask for his license back, and there was so little doubt he would get it that the MGM Grand bought the fight and began making plans to promote it like no other. But Tyson then brawled with Lewis at the press conference announcing the fight in New York, and suddenly things didn't look so good in Las Vegas for Iron Mike.

Summoned to a licensing hearing, Tyson said he had stopped taking his antidepressants and was no longer undergoing psychological counseling. He sat in the front row, indignant that he was being subjected once again to lectures from commissioners.

"We don't want you to be an animal in the ring," commissioner Amy Ayoub told him. "We want you to be a professional."

The words fell on deaf ears. Tyson was out the door getting into a waiting limousine by the time the commission voted 4-1 not to give him a license. It would be five months later before he and Lewis finally met in Memphis, where Tyson took a beating worse than Holyfield gave him in their first fight.

In all, it was a long and tortuous road for Tyson in Las Vegas, one that began when he ran out of Caesars Palace in tears in 1984 after losing a spot in the Olympic box-offs, only to return two years later and win the heavyweight title from Berbick.

The night he beat Berbick as a 20-year-old he was blissfully unaware of the turbulent future ahead of him as he proudly walked around t Las Vegas Hilton lobby with the gaudy plast WBC heavyweight title belt around his waist

"I just wanted the world to say, `Look at m Tyson said.

The world looked indeed, in fascination, h ror and indignation over the years. With Mi Tyson it was hard not to look, even in a ci where the bizarre is sometimes confused wi reality.

Mike Tyson didn't make boxing in Las Vega though he certainly added to the city's lore. I

The most anticipated heavyweight title rematch ever took place in June 1997 at the MGM Grand, drawing a sellout crowd and making both Mike Tyson and Evander Holyfield some $35 million each. Despite being stopped seven months earlier in a huge upset, Tyson was favored in the rematch, and he scored effectively in the opening two rounds. In the third round, though, Tyson was at the center of one of the most bizarre events ever in boxing, when he bit Holyfield's ear. Referee Mills Lane penalized Tyson but allowed the fight to continue, and Tyson bit the other ear, taking off a piece of it and causing Lane to disqualify him.

Mills Lane calls time out as Holyfield holds his right ear and Tyson appears to want more. At right, Lane examines the ear before stopping the fight.

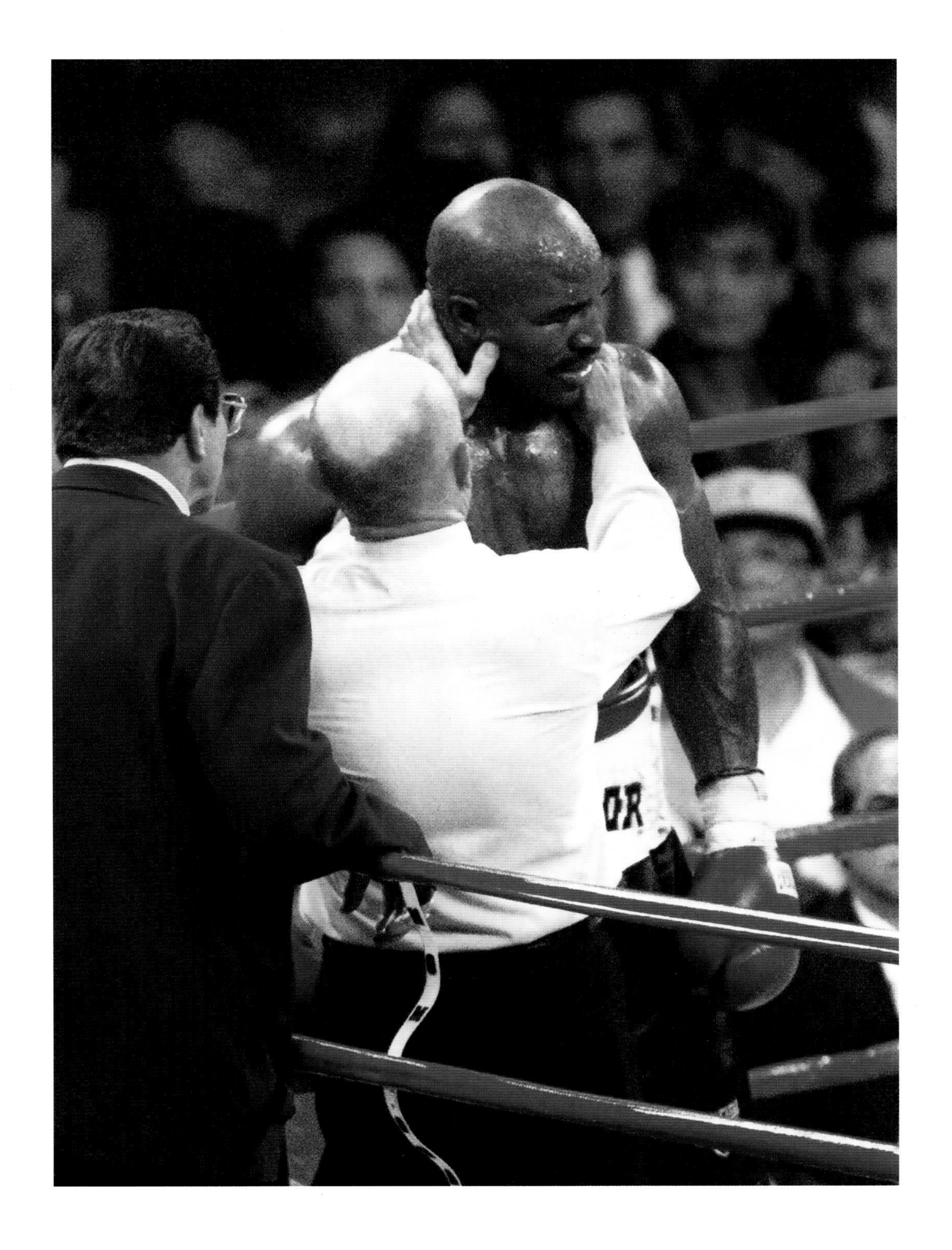

The fight ended in turmoil with Tyson taking a punch at a police officer and trying to get across the ring to get to Holyfield. Later, Holyfield shows off his damaged ear.

GRAND GARDEN
SECURITY

In what would become a familiar scene, Tyson appears before the Nevada Athletic Commission to explain his actions. The commission banned him from boxing for 18 months for biting Holyfield, and later refused to allow him to fight Lennox Lewis in Las Vegas after he bit Lewis at a press conference in New York announcing the fight. An aging and more reflective Tyson is shown at right, his face marked by years of battles in the ring and a facial tattoo he received just before his 2003 fight with Clifford Etienne. Despite his troubles, Tyson's love affair with his adopted home town of Las Vegas continued. Despite filing for bankruptcy, he still lived in the Las Vegas house he bought after being released from prison and was a regular at fight cards held around town.

In all, it was a long and tortuous road for Tyson in Las Vegas—one that began when he ran out of Caesars Palace in tears in 1984 after losing a spot in the Olympic box-offs, only to return two years later and win the heavyweight title from Berbick. He was blissfully unaware of the turbulent future ahead of him as he proudly walked around the Las Vegas Hilton lobby that night in denim overalls with the gaudy plastic WBC heavyweight title belt around his waist. "I just wanted the world to say, 'Look at me," Tyson said.

EVERLAST
BOWE

11 >> THE FAB FOUR OF THE STRIP

The Mirage had just opened and Las Vegas was searching for a new era of stars as the '90s dawned on a desert city about ready to explode in a new wave of megaresorts.

Frank Sinatra was aging and rarely played the Strip. In the showrooms, a new generation was taking over for The Chairman of the Board, Robert Goulet and Dean Martin.

In the ring, it was much the same. Larry Holmes had faded, Sugar Ray Leonard was at the end of the line and Marvelous Marvin Hagler had hung up his gloves in disgust. Boxing needed something, and so did the city that was dependant on big fights to feed the appetites of millions of annual visitors.

It found it among an unlikely quartet of boxers who had little in common except some Olympic trinkets that all could hang around their necks.

Oscar De La Hoya was the Golden Boy with the movie star looks, a matinee idol who could also fight with the best of them. Riddick Bowe was the prototypical new heavyweight, a giant at 6-5, 235 pounds who could punch with both hands and move. And Evander Holyfield was the heavyweight with the oversized heart who would never quit.

Finally, there was hamburger chompin' George Foreman, engaged in the most improbable comeback the sport had ever seen after a decade away from the ring that transformed him from an angry and bitter young fighter to America's jolly grillman.

Together they helped carry Fight Town through the '90s, making history and filling both the venerable outdoor arena at Caesars Palace and the new arenas erected for just their kind of fights at MGM Grand and Mandalay Bay.

Without them, Las Vegas would likely have struggled during a time when the city was trying to reinvent itself as a playground for both adults and children. With them, a new chapter in the city's boxing lore was written with their names splashed across the marquees where the names of Leonard, Hearns, Holmes and Hagler once were.

At the top of any of those marquees was De La Hoya, the only American boxer to win Olympic gold in Barcelona in 1992 and the first Mexican-American looking to capitalize on his crossover appeal and become a multimillion-dollar fighter. De La Hoya did that and more, with megafights against the likes of Julio Cesar Chavez, Felix Trinidad and Shane Mosley. He packed arenas on Mexican holiday weekends and smiled his way through fight promotions to sell his bouts to millions of households around the country on pay-per-view.

By the time he fought—and lost—to Mosley on September 13, 2003, De La Hoya had starred in four of the 10 biggest fights ever held in Las Vegas. In a sport dominated by heavyweights, he did heavyweight numbers, and his loyal fans rewarded casinos by making De La Hoya fight weekends some of the biggest of the year in Las Vegas. His top four fights alone grossed more than $40 million in ticket sales at the gate, and total revenues for his career were approaching the $500 million mark by the time he fought Mosley at the MGM Grand Hotel.

"I represent an image," De La Hoya said. "The fan behind me is the fan that works hard and appreciates life and wants to succeed in life. That's my fan."

De La Hoya was still in search of those fans when, as a skinny 130-pound 20-year-old, he first arrived in Las Vegas in 1993. It was just his fifth fight as a pro, but was something of a coming out party for a fighter who would become one of the biggest stars in town. At the top of the card at the Las Vegas Hilton the night of March 13, 1993, Michael Carbajal and Humberto Gonzalez engaged in a seven-round war that had a crowd of about 6,400 in a screaming frenzy, but De La Hoya wasted

The Fab Four having fun, celebrating after wins in Fight Town, clockwise from top left: Oscar De La Hoya, George Foreman, Evander Holyfield and Riddick Bowe.

little time in getting noticed himself.

De La Hoya was supposed to go to school for eight rounds against veteran Jeff Mayweather, but he dismissed class early, knocking Mayweather down with a left hook to the head and stopping him at 1:35 of the fourth round.

"I think he has what it takes to become a world champion," Mayweather said afterwards.

Mayweather knew what he was talking about. By the time De La Hoya won a decision over Javier Castillejo eight years later at the MGM Grand, he had won titles in five different weight classes. De La Hoya won all but one of them in Las Vegas, where he fought almost nonstop through the '90s.

It was in Las Vegas where De La Hoya beat and bloodied the great Chavez before finally stopping him on cuts in the fourth round June 7, 1996, at Caesars Palace. The fight gave De La Hoya the 140-pound title, but more importantly established him as a legitimate champion and someone who could draw a sellout crowd of 14,738 outdoors at Caesars. It took De La Hoya longer to win over some of the crowd, which cheered Chavez who offered himself as a true Mexican as opposed to the more Americanized De La Hoya.

"I'm an authentic Mexican. He's not a true Mexican," Chavez said. "He has American nationality."

De La Hoya would earn $9 million for the win, but it wasn't until he showed true warrior instincts in knocking out Fernando Vargas six years later that De La Hoya would finally win over the Hispanic fight fans who saw him more as a pretty boy than a fighter who deserved their respect. Ironically, he seemed to know before the Chavez fight that his time was coming when he looked ahead to the future and saw many more big fights.

It was a familiar scene in the '90s in Las Vegas. Oscar De La Hoya on the ring post after yet another big win.

"I'm facing a great champion, but there will be bigger events out there for me," De La Hoya said.

Indeed there were, as De La Hoya showed

his drawing power in fights against Pernell Whitaker, Hector Camacho, Ike Quartey and in a rematch with Chavez that was even more lopsided than the first fight. He seemed almost unbeatable when he signed for what would be his biggest fight—a welterweight unification bout with unbeaten power puncher Felix Trinidad that would take place September 18, 1999, at Mandalay Bay.

It was a fight so eagerly anticipated that many thought it would rival the first fight between Thomas Hearns and Sugar Ray Leonard. Much like that fight, it matched a big slugger in Trinidad against the boxer-puncher De La Hoya, who never seemed to physically overwhelm his opponents but always found a way to win. If that wasn't enough, it featured a fighter of Mexican origin against a Puerto Rican in a huge title fight, a combustible mix the likes of which hadn't been seen since Salvador Sanchez stopped Wilfredo Gomez in the eighth round of their featherweight title fight in August 1981 at Caesars Palace.

"If I box well and win a decision, I'll make myself happy," De La Hoya said. "When I fight I'm always in a no-win situation. If I get a one-round knockout it's because he has a weight problem and no chin. If I win a 12-round decision, people will say I wouldn't stand in front of him, that I was afraid of him."

Unfortunately for De La Hoya, his words were eerily prophetic. In what became the biggest non-heavyweight fight in the city's history, he dominated Trinidad in the early rounds and seemed on his way to an easy win. But in the ninth round he began backpedaling, and gave away the final three rounds by refusing to engage Trinidad. In his corner, they had told him he had the fight won, but it was a crucial tactical mistake and the crowd booed as De La Hoya moved away, and the anticipated brawl moved toward an anticlimactic finish that led to the first defeat of De La Hoya's pro career. He was stunned afterward, feeling the sting of defeat that even a $21 million payday couldn't ease.

"I thought I had it in the bag. I swear, I really did," De La Hoya said.

The damage had been done to both his career and his reputation. But De La Hoya would return to the same arena three years later to win a thrilling slugfest with Fernando Vargas that reestablished his credentials, only to fail in his rematch against Mosley when he lost a decision so disputed that promoter Bob Arum suggested Nevada athletic officials had fixed the fight. For a few days, the Golden Boy had become the Golden Baby, saying he couldn't get a fair decision in Las Vegas. Calmer heads finally prevailed, though, and De La Hoya vowed to fight on, most likely in the city where he won his biggest fights and where he was bigger than any of the stars of the Strip.

"I love boxing and I love fighting," he said. "We'll see what happens with the rest of my career."

Deep in thought, Riddick Bowe takes a break from training for his first rematch with Evander Holyfield.

Put Evander Holyfield or Riddick Bowe in the ring in the 1990s and you had something special. Put the two of them in together and it was magical.

HEAVYWEIGHTS OF THE STRIP

Put Evander Holyfield or Riddick Bowe in the ring with anyone in the 1990s and you had something special. Put the two of them in together and it was magical.

They fought a trilogy of bouts in Las Vegas, two of them with the heavyweight title on the line, and a third with nothing but the pride of two fine warriors at stake. They fought their way through the infamous "Fan Man" spectacle and engaged in one of the best heavyweight title rounds in their first fight in 1992. And even when both weren't at their best, they managed to give fans their money's worth in their final fight in November 1995 when Holyfield knocked Bowe down in the sixth round only to lose when Bowe dropped him twice in the eighth.

In each fight they were both cheered on by sellout crowds thrilled to see two top heavyweights in their prime unafraid to take risks even with millions of dollars and the undisputed heavyweight title at stake.

Nowhere was that more evident than during the tenth round of their first fight at the Thomas & Mack Center when Bowe battered

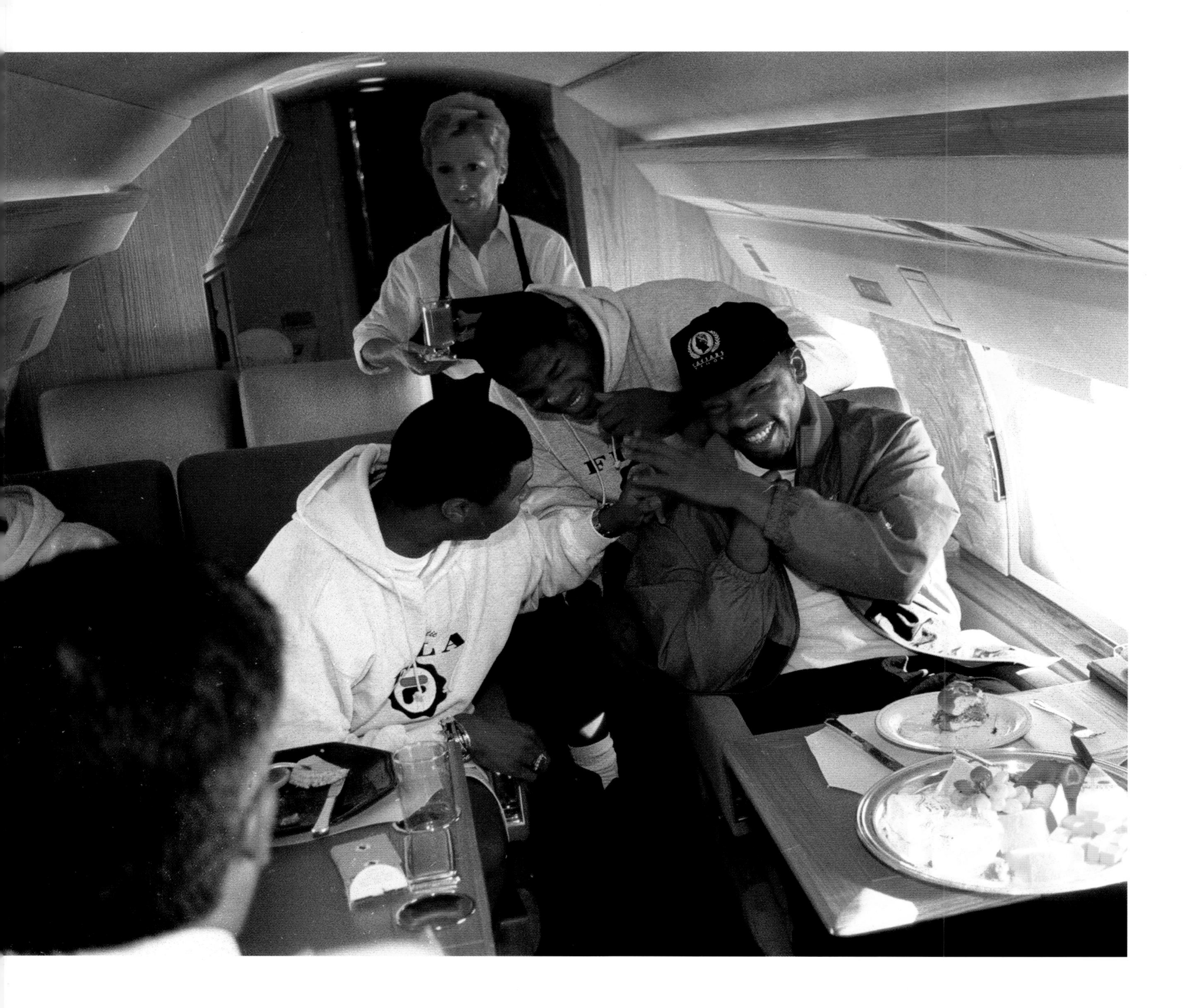

Riddick Bowe was living large after winning the heavyweight title from Evander Holyfield in 1992. Here Bowe has some fun with members of his entourage as the flight attendant looks to get past. Bowe, who was in training for his rematch with Holyfield, was being flown on the Caesars Palace jet from his training camp at Lake Tahoe to Los Angeles for a public workout and then an appearance on *The Tonight Show* with Jay Leno.

The fighter was bigger, but the right hand remained the same. George Foreman follows through with a right in his 1988 fight at the Caesars Palace pavilion against Dwight Qawi. Foreman, who stopped Qawi in the seventh round, had his first Las Vegas fight in 1969 on the undercard of the Sonny Liston-Leotis Martin heavyweight fight at the International Hotel, which later became the Las Vegas Hilton. Foreman knocked out Bob Hazelton in the first round of that fight, and 26 years later fought his last Las Vegas fight when he won a controversial decision over Axel Schulz at the MGM Grand in 1995 to keep the IBF heavyweight title.

Promoter Bob Arum could be excused for smiling. He knew he had a hit on his hands when Oscar De La Hoya and Julio Cesar Chaves met on June 7, 1996, at Caesars Palace. De La Hoya won the fight in the fourth round when it was stopped because of a bad cut on the face of Chavez. De La Hoya was leading on all three scorecards at the time.

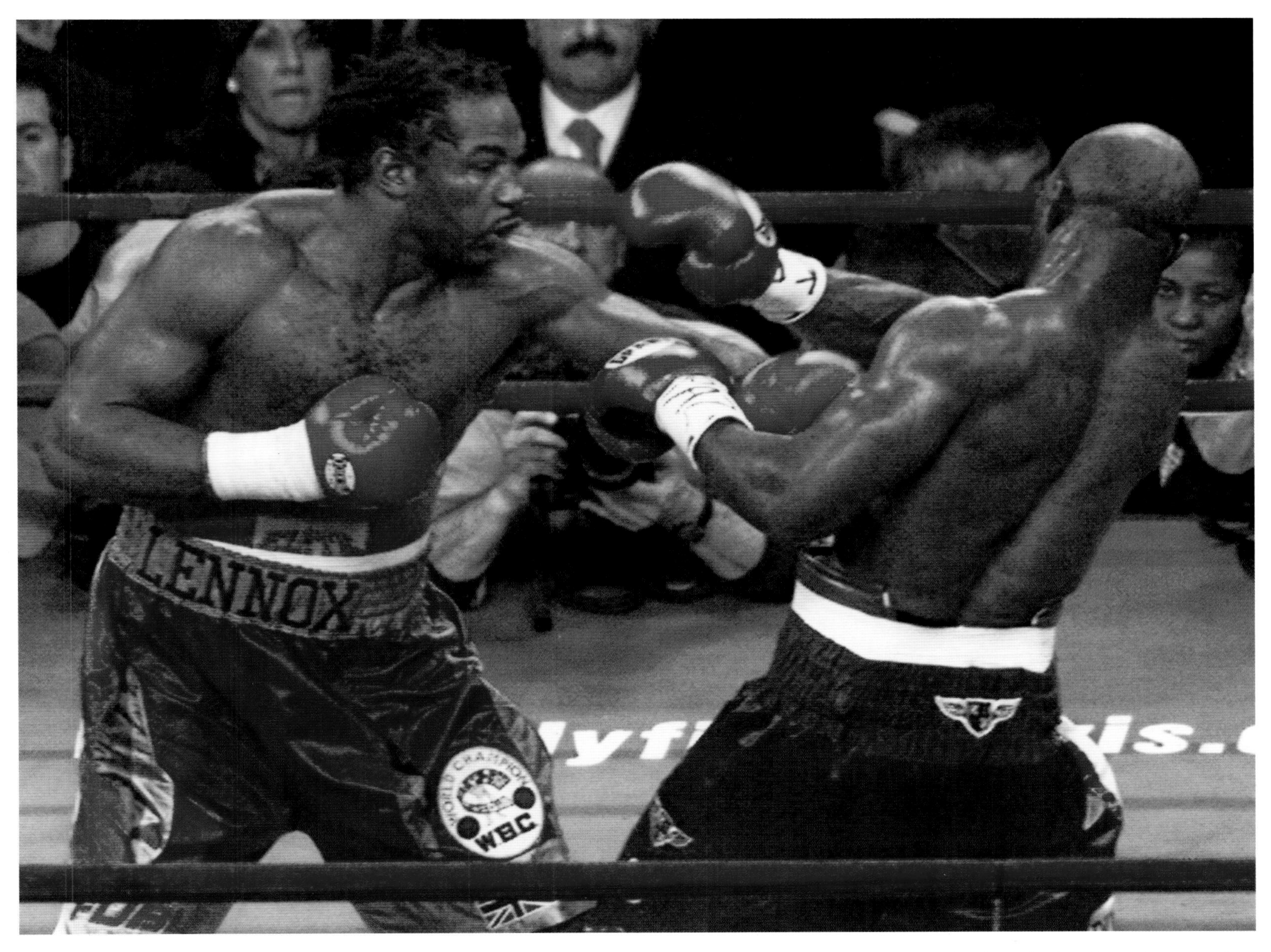

Holyfield's best efforts were behind him by the time he met Lennox Lewis in a rematch in 1999 at the Thomas and Mack Center. In a fight that lacked the drama and intensity of his wins over Riddick Bowe and Mike Tyson, Holyfield lost a decision to Lewis in the fight for the undisputed heavyweight title.

Holyfield around the ring only to take a beating himself when Holyfield came back late in the round. Bowe was the bigger man, 30 pounds heavier than Holyfield, and when he staggered the champion with a right uppercut early in the round and then followed it with an assortment of punches to the head and body, it looked like Holyfield would go. Holyfield crashed into a corner post, rolled off the ropes and draped his arms on Bowe, staying up by sheer willpower.

Suddenly, Holyfield hit Bowe with a punch and he began attacking. He stunned Bowe with a series of lefts and rights, driving him across the ring and finishing off the round with a furious flurry of his own. The crowd was on its feet, screaming itself hoarse as the two fighters went after one another. For Holyfield, though, it was a temporary reprieve, as Bowe knocked him down in the eleventh round, then went back to his corner when the round ended motioning to the crowd that he would soon be wearing the heavyweight title belts. Three minutes later, he was the new heavyweight champion of the world.

"I just about killed him and he wouldn't stop coming," Bowe said.

"It was a vicious battle," Holyfield remembered.

Later that night, Bowe celebrated then called his young son on the phone, saying, "I'm the heavyweight champion of the world, what does that make you?"

"Happy," the youngster replied.

Bowe was happy, too. Being heavyweight champion was like turning a kid loose in a candy store. He ate, ate some more, toured the world, visited the pope and threw one of his belts in a garbage can to irritate Lennox Lewis. He bloated up to 271 pounds before beginning training for his second fight with Holyfield, and his training habits weren't exactly the best. On a whirlwind fight promotion to Southern California, Bowe left a television studio interview to visit a McDonald's next door, and a few minutes later he was downing three Sausage McMuffins de-spite having a public sparring session only short time later. That afternoon, Bowe and his brother got hungry while waiting backstage for his appearance on the "Jay Leno" show and ordered six pastrami sandwiches on white bread.

De La Hoya lands a left hand (previous page) on his way to a decision win over Pernell Whitaker.

Still, Bowe was a big favorite in the November 1993 rematch—until the weigh-in revealed a 246-pound Bowe, eleven pounds heavier than he was only a year earlier.

"I remember the odds plummeting as people raced to the sports book to bet on Holyfield," said Rich Rose, the Caesars Palace executive in charge of fights and special events.

The weight did turn out to be a problem—but maybe not as big of a problem as the "Fan Man" stopping the fight for 21 minutes when he plowed into the ropes in the seventh round. Bowe had seemed to be winning that round, but Holyfield came back late and won by a majority decision so slim that if one judge who had scored the seventh round even had given it to Bowe the fight would have been a draw and Bowe would have retained his heavyweight title.

Bowe would go on to stop Holyfield two years later, but his career had already peaked. Holyfield, too, looked as if his boxing days were numbered after he lost his title to Michael Moorer in April 1994 at Caesars Palace, then mysteriously developed a heart condition and announced his retirement. Just as mysteriously, though, the condition cleared up, and Holyfield would be involved in two of the most memorable bouts in the city's history against Mike Tyson.

If Holyfield was good for boxing, Las Vegas was good for Evander. He knocked out a flabby Buster Douglas in October 1990 at the Mirage to win the title for the first time, then won pieces of the title three more times in Fight Town. Holyfield fought in heavyweight title fights 11 times during his career in Las Vegas, winning seven of them, including his big upset of Tyson and the infamous "Bite Fight" that followed. His 1999 loss to Lennox Lewis drew the biggest gate ever for a Las Vegas fight, with a crowd of 17,078 paying $16,860,300 to see Lewis win a close decision, and his two fights with Tyson ranked second and third on the list.

Like Muhammad Ali, though, Holyfield didn't know when enough was enough. He was two weeks shy of his 41st birthday and 16 years removed from his first Las Vegas fight—a cruiserweight title defense against Ricky Parkey—when he met James Toney at Mandalay Bay in October 2003 in one last bid for a win that might somehow give him another title shot.

Toney was too quick and to accurate a puncher for Holyfield, who saw his openings as many aging fighters do but could do nothing about them. He was a warrior to the end, but Toney picked him apart, hitting him with nearly every punch he threw and knocking him down in the ninth round before Holyfield's corner finally threw in the towel.

"If he was a big puncher I'd have been torn apart," Holyfield admitted.

Holyfield was an attraction to the end because of the way he fought, but Foreman became one because of the way he ate. He joked about hamburgers, buffets and eating everything in sight in an improbable comeback that peaked when he knocked out Moorer at the MGM Grand to become the heavyweight champion of the world, then got down on his knees in his corner and prayed.

Foreman's jokes weren't as good as his right hand, from which he had lost nothing in the decade he spent retired from the ring. The raw punching power was the same Foreman displayed when he and Ron Lyle opened the Caesars pavilion with a bang in a slugfest that *Ring* magazine anointed the 1976 Fight of the Year, but now Foreman was also a smarter fighter who measured his opponents and didn't let them get away with hitting him too often.

Foreman weighed a whopping 267 pounds when he began his comeback in 1987 against

Oscar De La Hoya strikes a familiar pose after stopping Yory Boy Campas in the seventh round May 3, 2003, to defend his 154-pound titles. The fight set up a rematch four months later with Shane Mosley, which De La Hoya lost in a controversial decision.

PUMA

When Oscar De La Hoya fought, it was always a big event. When he fought other big names it got even bigger. At left, he and Felix Trinidad exchange blows, while De La Hoya presses the action at right before finally stopping Fernando Vargas in the 11th round.

a fighter named Steve Zouski. Wisely, he did it in Sacramento, far away from the lights of Las Vegas where he could get a chance to see if he still had what it took. Foreman stopped Zouski in the fourth round and would have three more fights before he came to Las Vegas and fought Rocky Sekorski in December 1987 in a converted convention room at Bally's hotel-casino. By now, Foreman had his act refined and he stood in the corner between rounds staring impassively across the ring before going out and demolishing Sekorski in the third round. He was now a relatively trim 244 pounds and, if he wasn't ready for heavyweight contenders yet, he was ready enough to be fighting in boxing's mecca once again.

"You gotta be right in Vegas. You gotta be in shape," Foreman said. "No one is going to give you an easy fight there."

By the time Foreman stopped Dwight Qawi at Caesars Palace four months later, he figured his comeback was for real. He wouldn't return to Las Vegas for two more years, and he finally got a shot at the heavyweight championship against Holyfield in Atlantic City. Foreman lost, though, and after losing to Tommy Morrison at the Thomas & Mack Center in 1993, his comeback seemed to be over. Everyone still loved Big George, but it seemed he could not beat the top fighters of the era.

He needed one more chance, and he got it against Michael Moorer.

Foreman was two months shy of his 46th birthday when he met Moorer, a southpaw who beat Holyfield for the title and was in his prime. Foreman's cheeseburger jokes may have grown stale and the one-liners about middle age had spread a bit thin, and even the World Boxing Association didn't think he should be fighting for the title the 27-year-old Moorer held. But Foreman went to court and forced the WBA to sanction the fight and the two met November 5, 1994, at the MGM Grand in what everyone in attendance figured would be the jolly heavyweight's final act on boxing's big stage.

"What you see on November 5 will blow your mind," Foreman predicted before the fight.

For nine rounds, though, Foreman looked like a battered old fighter whose hopes of regaining the championship he lost when he was knocked out by Muhammad Ali in Zaire 20 years earlier would not be realized. Foreman's face was lopsided from Moorer's jabs, his left eye was closing and he was huffing and puffing. There was no way he could win the fight, and as the rounds went on those in attendance were wincing at the punishment the jolly old fighter was taking.

Then, with shocking suddenness in the tenth round, Foreman blew Moorer's house down.

Slam, came Foreman's left hook.

Crash, came his right hand.

Moorer landed flat on his back with his arms outstretched. He barely moved a muscle as referee Joe Cortez counted Foreman into boxing history. When the count was complete, the boxer-turned-preacher-turned boxer went to his corner to pray. The oldest heavyweight champion ever was also the newest.

"He never should have stepped in front of me," Foreman said.

It had taken Foreman two decades to regain a piece of the heavyweight title. More importantly, he also seemed to shed with one big right hand the years of dealing with his upset loss to Ali in the jungle.

"I exorcised the ghost of Muhammad Ali once and forever," Foreman said.

Later, Ali sent Foreman a poster, which read: "Congratulations champ, you had the courage and guts to go out and do it."

"He signed it with a big heart on the bottom," Foreman said of the man who was his nemesis. "When he says you got guts, that's something special."

Foreman would go on to defend the title only once, winning a disputed decision over Axel Schulz a year later. But no one could take away from him the improbable comeback from the jungles of Zaire to the bright lights of Sin City and another heavyweight title.

"It was great because not only did it happen but it happened in a city of dreams for boxers," Foreman said. "You say every movie star has to make it in Hollywood. Well, every boxer has to make it in Las Vegas."

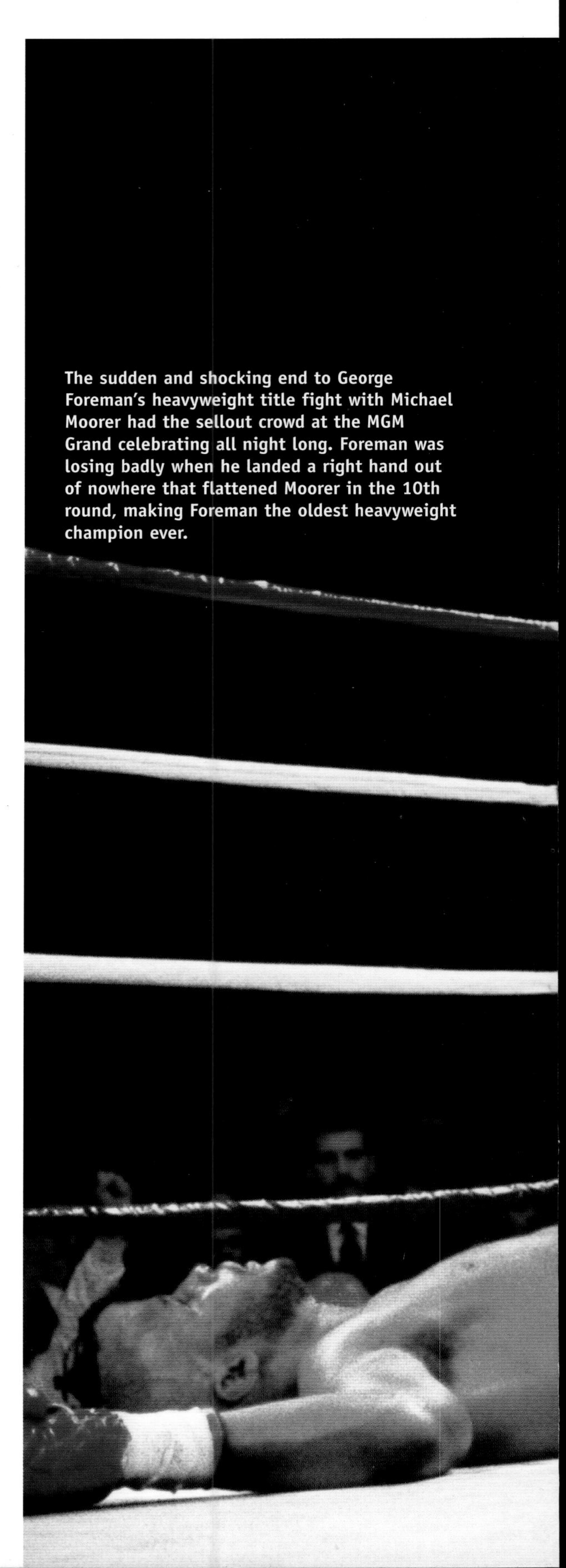

The sudden and shocking end to George Foreman's heavyweight title fight with Michael Moorer had the sellout crowd at the MGM Grand celebrating all night long. Foreman was losing badly when he landed a right hand out of nowhere that flattened Moorer in the 10th round, making Foreman the oldest heavyweight champion ever.

BUDWEISER

LENNOX
WBC
FUBU

FIGHT TOWN'S 10 BIGGEST FIGHTS

			ATTENDANCE	GROSS RECEIPTS
11/13/99	**LENNOX LEWIS VS. EVANDER HOLYFIELD**	THOMAS & MACK CENTER	17,078	**$16,860,300**
6/28/97	**EVANDER HOLYFIELD VS. MIKE TYSON II**	MGM GRAND	16,279	**14,277,200**
11/9/96	**EVANDER HOLYFIELD VS. MIKE TYSON I**	MGM GRAND	16,103	**14,150,700**
8/19/95	**MIKE TYSON VS. PETE MCNEELEY**	MGM GRAND	16,113	**13,965,600**
9/18/99	**FELIX TRINIDAD VS. OSCAR DE LA HOYA**	MANDALAY BAY	11,184	**12,949,500**
3/16/96	**MIKE TYSON VS. FRANK BRUNO**	MGM GRAND	16,143	**10,673,700**
9/13/03	**SHANE MOSLEY VS. OSCAR DE LA HOYA**	MGM GRAND	16,074	**9,840,000**
9/14/02	**OSCAR DE LA HOYA VS. FERNANDO VARGAS**	MANDALAY BAY	10,984	**8,871,300**
6/7/96	**OSCAR DE LA HOYA VS. J.C. CHAVEZ I**	CAESARS PALACE	14,738	**7,579,100**
11/17/01	**LENNOX LEWIS VS. HASIM RAHMAN**	MANDALAY BAY	9,830	**7,537,400**

SOURCE: NEVADA ATHLETIC COMMISSION

Main Event Productions, Inc. in association with Caesars Palace presents

HEARNS vs LEONARD

WORLD WELTERWEIGHT CHAMPIONSHIP

Wednesday, September 16, 1981

DIRECT FROM

LAS VEGAS

PAINTING BY DONALD MOSS

Las Vegas Hilton in association with Top Rank, Inc. proudly presents:

KNOCKOUT NITE

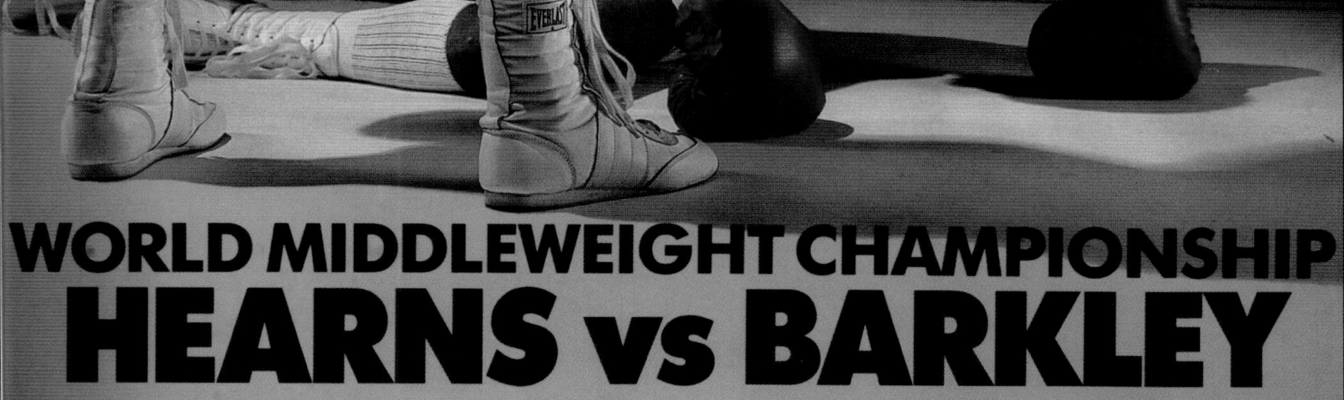

WORLD MIDDLEWEIGHT CHAMPIONSHIP

HEARNS vs BARKLEY

World Light Heavyweight Championship

VIRGIL HILL
vs
RAMZI HASSAN

World Super Lightweight Championship

ROGER MAYWEATHER
vs
HAROLD BRAZIER

Budweiser
KING OF BEERS.

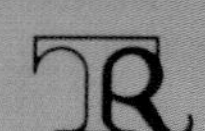

Top Rank, Inc.

Budweiser
KING OF BEERS.

LAS VEGAS HILTON JUNE 6

Holmes vs Cooney

PRESENTED BY CAESARS PALACE, IN ASSOCIATION WITH DON KING PRODUCTIONS AND TIFFANY PROMOTIONS

WBC WORLD HEAVYWEIGHT CHAMPIONSHIP

MARCH 15, 1982

There's nothing funny going on here!

MOORER
VERSUS
FOREMAN

WORLD HEAVYWEIGHT CHAMPIONSHIP

LIVE VIA HBO TELECAST

SAT. NOV. 5 10PM ET/7PM PT

ONE.

Bowe Blasts Holyfield

TWO.

THE TIMES SUNDAY, NOVEMBER 7, 1993

Holyfield Gets His Revenge

THREE.

?

BOWE 3 HOLYFIELD

THREE FIGHTS. TWO CHAMPIONS. ONE BEST.

NOVEMBER 4, 1995

CAESARS PALACE

AN ITT ENTERTAINMENT COMPANY

Champion,
Evander
Holyfield,
28-0

Challenger,
Riddick
Bowe,
31-0

WILL BOWE BE THE NEXT CHAMPION? OR JUST NEXT? ON FRIDAY, NOVEMBER 13TH, ANYTHING CAN HAPPEN.

HOLYFIELD-BOWE,
HEAVYWEIGHT CHAMPIONSHIP,
FROM THE MIRAGE, LAS VEGAS

See it live on pay-per-view.

He's Back.

The Return of

Mike Tyson.

Mike Tyson vs.
Peter McNeeley

Saturday, August 19

At the MGM Grand

Plus,

Bruce Seldon
vs. Joe Hipp,
Julian Jackson
vs. Quincy Taylor,
Miguel Angel
Gonzalez vs.
Lamar Murphy.

SET MGM GRAND

DYNAMIC DUO IN ASSOCIATION WITH THE LAS VEGAS HILTON
PRESENTS

WBC
WORLD HEAVYWEIGHT CHAMPIONSHIP

TREVOR **CHAMPION**

BERBICK

MIKE **CHALLENGER**

TYSON

Las Vegas Hilton **NOV. 22, 1986**